RESPONSIBLE PEDAGOGY

Responsible Pedagogy

Moving Beyond Authority and Mastery
in Higher Education

ERIC DETWEILER

The Pennsylvania State University Press
University Park, Pennsylvania

Library of Congress Cataloging-in-Publication Data

Names: Detweiler, Eric, 1985– author.
Title: Responsible pedagogy : moving beyond authority and mastery in
    higher education / Eric Detweiler.
Description: University Park, Pennsylvania : The Pennsylvania State
    University Press, [2022] | Includes bibliographical references and index.
Summary: "Argues for the importance of public higher education and
    the work of teaching and emphasizes the shared ethical responsibilities
    that underpin the connections between teachers and students"—
    Provided by publisher.
Identifiers: LCCN 2022020543 | ISBN 9780271093437 (hardback) | ISBN
    9780271093420 (paper)
Subjects: LCSH: Education, Higher. | Teacher-student relationships. |
    Rhetoric—Study and teaching (Higher)
Classification: LCC LB2322.2 .D48 2022 | DDC 378—dc23/eng/20220521
LC record available at https://lccn.loc.gov/2022020543

The Pennsylvania State University Press is a member of the Association
of University Presses.

It is the policy of The Pennsylvania State University Press to use acid-free
paper. Publications on uncoated stock satisfy the minimum requirements
of American National Standard for Information Sciences—Permanence
of Paper for Printed Library Material, ANSI Z39.48–1992.

To the students and teachers we have yet to welcome

CONTENTS

ACKNOWLEDGMENTS

This is a book about the many ways our relationships to writing, learning, teaching, and ourselves are inextricable from our relationships with and responsibilities to others. As such, writing this acknowledgements section is a harrowing thing, especially when it comes to the people I will inevitably leave out but without whom this book and the person who wrote it would not exist. So I will say a broad thanks to all the teachers, students, family, friends, and colleagues who have inspired the thinking and writing that overflows from this and the following pages.

I must acknowledge a few key people who shaped me before my career as a teacher and writer even began: my sister and aunts and uncles as well as my parents and grandparents, who read, told, and wove me stories about talking mice, castles in attics, and magical foxes, and who inspired an abiding interest in writing. Love and thanks are insufficient words, but love and thanks to Mom, Dad, and Nimi.

An odd note of appreciation is also due to Jake Frederick and Brandon Tullock, with whom I fostered a love for all manner of weird books, movies, stories, and turns of phrase as well as a persistent curiosity about the words and worlds around us.

Thanks to Bonnie Smith Whitehouse, Bronwyn Williams, and Samantha Morgan-Curtis, a trio without whom my commitment to the craft of teaching as an ethical, rhetorical, and intellectual responsibility and joy would not be what it is.

As for the more direct influences on this book itself, I am infinitely grateful to Diane Davis, who helped shape early drafts and whose responses—equally insightful and incisive, and always offered generously—made it what it is. Thanks also to Jeffrey Walker, Marjorie Curry Woods, Patricia Roberts-Miller, and Cynthia Haynes for their wisdom and guidance as I drafted, revised, and beat my head against various parts of the manuscript.

I also need to take a moment to praise Kendall Gerdes and Steven LeMieux, as well as Will Burdette, Noble Frank, and Beck Wise, all of whom responded to various drafts and documents and were indispensable sounding boards as I talked and wrote and wrangled with this book's arguments and points. Kendall and Steven, this book would not exist without the unsubstitutable combination of generosity, care, good humor, and intellectual acumen you provided. You encouraged me to take risks, and in so doing you contributed to this book's legacy.

Thanks to Rosa Eberly and Paul Lynch for sharp, timely, and engaged feedback on the full manuscript and to Ryan Korstange for his advice as I revised the early parts of the book to speak to readers beyond rhetoric and writing studies. I'm also grateful to Ryan Peterson at Penn State University Press for his initial interest in the project and his patient, helpful guidance as I developed and revised it, not to mention the rest of the team who helped prepare the manuscript for publication: Brian Beer, Josie DiNovo, Jennifer Norton, Laura Reed-Morrisson, Carl Zebrowski, and Regina Starace.

And thanks to my colleagues at Middle Tennessee State University, particularly Kate Pantelides, Julie Myatt, Erica Cirillo-McCarthy, and Erica Stone, who have supported this work both directly and indirectly through conversation, mutual care, and all the underappreciated work they do to support writing pedagogy and research in our shared institutional environment.

Gus and Stella, thanks for hopping in my lap and demanding a scratch behind the ears when I probably needed to take a break anyway.

And thanks most of all to Megan Moss, a partner and friend who has taught me more than I can express about what it means to be responsible to and for others. Megan, your never-ending, immeasurable care for those you come into contact with, from me to friends to family to unexpected acquaintances, is a constant source of wonder and inspiration. I would not be the teacher, the writer, the person I am without your love and your example.

Introduction

Indeed, to take responsibility for oneself is to avow the limits of any self-understanding, and to establish these limits not only as a condition for the subject but as the predicament of the human community.

—JUDITH BUTLER

In 2017, the for-profit University of Phoenix released a commercial entitled "We Can Do IT." Reminiscent of a short Pixar film, the computer-animated ad gives viewers a series of glimpses into the life of an unnamed woman.

She is at home, using a stuffed bunny to cheer up her son after he has a small fall in the kitchen. Her daughter watches from the table. She appears to be a single mother.

She is at work, doing her job on a factory floor. In the background, a group of men observes a robot doing the same job. Time accelerates and the surrounding human-staffed workstations are replaced by similar robots until our heroine is the last person standing—but soon a faceless suit looms behind her. She and the viewer both know what's coming.

She sits alone in her darkened kitchen, all of her possessions from work gathered in a box on the table. Among those possessions is a poster emblazoned with the iconic image of Rosie the Riveter and the line "We Can Do It!" Her son runs up to her with his stuffed bunny, attempting to lift her spirits as she once lifted his. Mom can barely muster a smile, but she pulls her son close and glances at Rosie. So far, the commercial has lasted about forty seconds.

Now she is looking at a University of Phoenix web page promoting a degree in information technology. She clicks a button at the bottom of the page: "Get Started." In a montage laden with multitasking, she works on her degree while cooking dinner, sitting alone in the kitchen late at night, lying in bed while her children sleep beside her. Approximately seven seconds after we see her enroll, we see that she's graduated. Standing in the kitchen wearing a graduation gown, she celebrates with the kids.

Finally, we see her at a new IT job. The Rosie poster now hangs in her cubicle, and she uses a marker to turn "We Can Do It!" into "We Can Do IT!" As she examines a bank of computer servers, the University of Phoenix's tagline fades in: "We rise."

Call me sentimental, but the first time I saw that commercial, I had a hard time not getting pulled in by the promises of its narrative. Despite the fact that I am a staunch supporter of public universities, know the University of Phoenix's history of settlements related to questionable admissions practices and its students' inordinate loan debt,[1] and have a PhD in rhetoric and writing that you think would have prepared me to resist the ad's persuasive tactics, I wanted to root for its protagonist. But why? Part of it is probably my idealistic desire for higher education to be accessible to a wide range of people—including working-class single mothers—and for it to be a means of class mobility. I know the predatory practices of many for-profit universities have warped and exploited such ideals, and I know the improbability of the ad's fantastical story given a host of real-world factors. But what am I supposed to do? Hope that the woman fails? I want to see her exercise agency and end up with something to show for it.

In the weeks after I first saw the commercial, I saw it again. And again. And again. A streaming service I used decided I was among the target audience for "We Can Do IT" and started playing it ad nauseam. The sheer number of times I was exposed to it wrecked the commercial's initial appeal, but my inclination to make sense of that appeal meant that even after copious viewings, I was still paying attention.

I became pretty familiar with everything in the ad—the characters, the soundtrack, the narrative beats—before I started to notice everything that wasn't. One notable omission in what is ostensibly an advertisement for higher education: educators. At no point in the commercial do we see any indication of interaction with a teacher (or another student, for that matter). It's not just that we don't see any sign of a teacher's physical presence; the teachers are also digitally absent. We see no emails exchanged, no assignment prompts, no comments on homework or a test. The seven-second sequence during which the woman successfully begins, pursues, and receives her degree suggests her diligence and exhaustion, but she's the only actor involved. The University of Phoenix seems no more dependent on human employees or interactions than the ad's automated factory. Thank goodness our protagonist majored in IT and not education.

As someone who makes a living teaching at a public university, my subsequent realizations about the commercial's omissions evoked a lot of professional anxieties. Over the last few decades, much has been made of new digital technologies that could potentially disrupt, take over, or redistribute work traditionally done by teachers. At the same time, the humans who continue to teach in higher education have become more disposable as states have axed funding and institutions have become increasingly reliant on undercompensated contingent faculty.[2] In this environment, what role remains for the teacher? And at what point do an educator's working conditions render such a question moot? That is, even if a human teacher can do things that the inventions of innovators and investors in the educational technology sector can't, are those things worth the effort for a few thousand dollars per class with no benefits?

This book explores the relentlessly precarious figure of the teacher in relation to students as well as a wide range of educational technologies, social structures, classroom materials, and rhetorical devices that have helped define that figure. I spend time on the aforementioned factors shaping teachers' roles in twenty-first-century college classrooms but also argue that these factors echo back through much of the history of education, particularly the history of rhetorical education.

For readers unfamiliar with the broad contours of rhetoric and rhetorical education, a brief overview: Rhetoric's roots are often traced back to ancient Athens, where people like Aspasia, Isocrates, Gorgias, and Aristotle instructed students in the theory and practice of effective communication and argumentation. Those figures were *rhetoricians*: theorists and teachers of the art of rhetoric. They were not necessarily *rhetors*, a term more nearly synonymous with "orator," though many rhetoricians were also known for their oratorical prowess. That's a reductive version of the story, of course. Rhetorical activity was happening far beyond the bounds of one Greek city.[3] Even within Athens, there were all kinds of internecine squabbles over the merits and meanings of rhetoric and rhetorical education, which I address in chapter 1. I offer a simplified story here not only to provide those without backgrounds in rhetoric with a sense of what I mean when I refer to "rhetoric" and "rhetoricians" but also to foreground rhetoric's unique influence on the shape of Western education. For example, in addition to creating one of the earliest recorded schools of rhetoric, Isocrates arguably established the concept of liberal arts education. Moreover, in ancient Greek and Roman education, rhetoric was often not just part of a student's education but its culmination, and it remained a core component of Western education for centuries afterward (for example, as one of the three parts of the medieval trivium).[4] While rhetorical education's fortunes have waxed and waned dramatically over the past millennium, rhetorically inclined courses in speech and writing remain curricular staples at colleges and universities across the United States, and many facets of Western higher education would not be what they are without rhetoric's pedagogical and theoretical legacies.

Thus, while the cases and illustrations in this book are often drawn specifically from the history of rhetoric, I present the figure of the rhetorician as a meaningful metonymic stand-in for the figure of the teacher. My scholarly training and teaching experience are in rhetoric and writing studies, a field that developed in tandem with the modern first-year composition course. This book was inspired by what I see as key challenges for those committed to making the case for rhetoric as a scholarly pursuit and educational endeavor—challenges I've experienced in the course of teaching first-year composition and other rhetoric and writing courses at an array of institutions. Increasingly, I have come to see those challenges as inseparable from how we conceptualize the role of the teacher and as a microcosmic version of the complexities involved in making the case for public education more generally. In short, this book is about rhetorical education, but its arguments unfold in ways that I hope will be relevant to educators who don't think of themselves as rhetoricians.[5]

Specifically, I argue that we need to find alternatives to the concept of agency—often positioned as the *sine qua non* of educational theory and practice—in which to ground our approaches to and cases for higher education. Scholars within and beyond rhetoric have critiqued, extended, and enriched that concept in diverse and compelling ways, taking it far beyond simplistic notions of unqualified individual autonomy. To offer just one example, rhetoric and writing scholar Marilyn M. Cooper has defined agency as "the process through which organisms create meanings through acting into the world and changing their structure in response to the perceived consequences of their actions."[6] Yoking agency to responsibility, Cooper argues that "rhetorical agency is a big responsibility. It means being responsible for oneself, for others, and for the common world we construct together."[7] However, even the most thoroughgoing critiques of traditional conceptions of agency tend to end by presenting new conceptions of agency. In these contexts, agency can take on an inviolable power all its own, an essential foundation for human action and rhetorical education's efficacy that must be maintained at all costs. While I'm not interested in dismissing agency from the scene, I aim to reframe the work of teaching in terms of a conception of responsibility that is not grounded in agency. I do so for two intertwined reasons.

The first is what you might call a theoretical concern. Drawing on scholarship at the intersection of rhetoric and ethics, I argue that anything we might call agency is the product of responsibility. Instead of agency allowing a person to take responsibility for others and for their own actions, I argue that agency is premised on our inescapable exposure to others, the fact that we cannot help *responding* to others. In making this argument, I hope to show that, despite what many scholars have claimed, questioning agency does not necessarily undermine the case for education. Instead, I present responsibility as a key term that allows us to rethink the ethics of student-teacher relationships and the theoretical significance of teachers' work.

The second is what you might call a practical concern. The complex ways in which most scholars theorize agency are far from the common senses in which agency gets thrown around in everyday usage. For these scholars, agency means anything but the simplistic notion that individuals can, like the woman in the University of Phoenix commercial, pull themselves up by their bootstraps, exerting uninhibited control over themselves and their circumstances regardless of external influences. However, given the ongoing prominence of individualistic conceptions of agency and responsibility in American culture, it's all too easy for even the most nuanced account of agency to be reduced to or heard as basic bootstrap logic. As I'll argue, even folks who should know better often equate human agency with something like a student's self-guided seven-second journey from unemployment to an IT gig, as if it's only a matter of giving an agentive individual the right educational tools and opportunities to succeed, never mind all manner of social, economic, political, material, and professional inequities and barriers. From a practical perspective, I argue that agency's rhetorical power is constrained by this ready-made recuperation into the fantastical all-American dream that "I" (not "we," not really) "can do it." While scholars have done significant work conceptualizing agency as a powerful force for social action—a force that is rarely if ever exercised by a single person, even as its consequences and benefits often accrue to individuals—*agency* is easily gobbled up by dubious discourses of *mastery* over self, skills, and content knowledge. Describing the work of education in terms of responsibility lets us make a significantly different case for what's lost when entities like the University of Phoenix eliminate the teacher from the equation.

To return to the advertisement with which I began, this is a book about how and to what extent teachers are or should be included in the "we" of higher ed's "We Can Do It." If so, what is our role in this "we," and does it involve creating something better for students and teachers than the isolated vision of education forwarded by the University of Phoenix, and even the somewhat less chimerical visions that have shaped the United States' public higher education system as we know it? What does it mean to be a teacher in relation to students? Are teachers authoritative masters of certain skills necessary to private, professional, or public life? Are we adjuncts who are ideally left behind once our students master such skills? Do we lead students along paths of knowledge or trail behind them? Are we curators? Scholars? Theorists? Instructors? Collaborators? Grading machines? Humanists? Essential workers? Disposable adjuncts? I begin with no certain answers to these questions. In many ways, I end having only managed to proliferate some more questions. But the asking of them and the attempt to respond is, I'd wager, part and parcel of the rhetorical, ethical, relational work of teaching.

In the rest of this introduction, I offer an initial historical and theoretical overview of and justification for this book's key terms: authority, agency, and responsibility. Specifically, I set up how teachers' authority and students' agency, despite supplying two very different rationales for education, share a similar reliance on the logic of individual mastery. I then take my first steps toward a theory of pedagogical responsibility that seeks to unsettle that logic, which I continue pursuing throughout the rest of this book.

WHAT IS PEDAGOGICAL AUTHORITY?

Through radical shifts in economic and political systems, material conditions, and family ties, the student-teacher relationship has remained a remarkably stable characterization of a particular kind of connection between people, especially between the young and the old, between adults and those who are for one reason or another seen as not yet fully formed. In the present, the work of the teacher is often described as empowering students, granting them agency so that they can act more effectively and efficiently in their future lives. But for much of educational history, the emphasis was on the power and authority of the teacher. This emphasis has waned significantly over the past century, though defenses of teacherly authority are by no means a thing of the past. As Raffaella Cribiore notes, "After the attacks on teachers' rule in post-1960s educational politics, today there are attempts to revive a traditional image of the Teacher and to restore pedagogical authority, together with a heightened emphasis on teacher accountability and control of teachers' work."[8] While I am not an advocate of reinstating traditional notions of teacherly authority, that authority has been a distinctly influential force in the history of student-teacher relationships and thus provides an important backdrop for matters of pedagogical agency and responsibility. Over the next few pages, I dig into the history of teacherly authority, including cases in which it was far from the stable force its present-day defenders often make it out to be.

Speaking historically, the student-teacher relationship has frequently been positioned as bridging the gap between, on one side, parent-child relationships and, on the other, relations between citizens and the various political, social, and professional authorities to and for which they are responsible. This is the view taken by political theorist Hannah Arendt, one of the twentieth century's most influential thinkers on authority. In "The Crisis in Education" (1958), Arendt writes, "Now school is by no means the world and must not pretend to be; it is rather the institution that we interpose between the private domain of home and the world in order to make the transition from the family to the world possible at all. . . . [S]chool in a sense represents the world, although it is not yet actually the world."[9]

Within this "institution," Arendt argues, teachers' authority over students should be a given.[10] But, she claims, "modern society" has made a hash of the proper authority relationship between teachers and students. She describes this society—the United States in particular—as undergoing a "process of emancipation" that has rightly liberated groups such as "workers and women" by shifting the value of their members' lives from a private to a public concern.[11] But when it is extended to schoolchildren, this process goes off the rails: "Children cannot throw off educational authority as though they were in a position of oppression by an adult majority—though even this absurdity of treating children as an oppressed minority in need of liberation has actually been tried out in modern educational practice. Authority has been discarded by the adults, and this can mean only one thing: that the adults refuse to assume responsibility for the world into which they have brought the children."[12]

Arendt presents this crisis of educational authority, which is also a crisis of educational responsibility, as part of a broader authority crisis. As she puts it in another essay, "It is my contention that ... authority has vanished from the modern world."[13] She continues, "The most significant symptom of this crisis ... is that it has spread to such prepolitical areas as ... education, where authority in the widest sense has always been accepted as a natural necessity. ... [T]he fact that even this prepolitical authority which ruled the relations between adults and children, teachers and pupils, is no longer secure signifies that all the old time-honored metaphors and models for authoritarian relations have lost their plausibility. Practically as well as theoretically, we are no longer in a position to know what authority really *is*."[14]

At the political level, Arendt takes authority's newfound insecurity as a reason to think rather than a reason to panic—a crisis that leaves us "confronted anew . . . by the elementary problems of human living-together."[15] But she posits a disconnect between the realms of politics and education that explains her consternation about this crisis's consequences for schools and their wards. For Arendt, "nothing is more questionable than the political relevance of examples drawn from the field of education" and vice versa,[16] so, unlike the relation between a political leader and citizens, a teacher's authority over students is distinctly *un*questionable, an indispensable check on "the tyranny of the majority" that would otherwise take hold among students.[17] In other words, in being "emancipated" from the authority of adults in general and teachers in particular, "the child has not been freed but has been subjected to a much more terrifying and truly tyrannical authority."[18]

But however much Arendt's dire descriptions make the modern class-room sound like *Lord of the Flies*, examining the history of Western education makes one question how much better things actually were under the watch of teachers whose authority was, at least at first glance, more established.

Consider the violent practices that went hand in hand with medieval rhetoric pedagogy. According to Jody Enders, the memory techniques taught and theorized about by medieval rhetoricians are particularly emblematic of such practices.[19] From a mnemonic device for the zodiac that involves a ram kicking a bull in the testicles to the whip marks teachers inscribed on student bodies—which were meant to teach students a differ-ent kind of commemorative lesson—Enders traces a grisly genealogy born of rhetoric, pedagogy, and memory. Countering those who claim rhetoric and rhetorical education offer alternatives to violence, Enders argues, "Inas-much as the ostensibly mediatory powers of a rhetoric grounded in the memory must originate in violence, rhetoric itself must remain at odds with itself and civilization must be paired with cruelty."[20] Venturing beyond the Middle Ages, she further warns against assuming a clean break between the violence of medieval rhetoric pedagogy and "the myth of a non-violent [modern] pedagogy."[21]

In Enders's examples, the pedagogical scene's predominant violence is enacted on students. From "unjust floggings" to the epistemic discipline that bent students' linguistic and rhetorical habits to match those of the schoolmaster, Enders makes readers feel for medieval students.[22] But her argument is literally wrapped in a different story. The book jacket for the collection in which Enders's essay appears depicts the death of Cassian of Imola, a schoolteacher and canonized Catholic martyr. As his story has been handed down, Cassian was fatally attacked by his students, who broke their writing tablets over his body, gouged him with their styluses, and scrawled their assigned grammar lessons on his corpse.[23] The tale of Cassian's death underscores the varied forces that haunt the relationship between teachers and students, a relationship that is historically entan-gled with various forms of corporeal, religious, sexual, political, and rhetorical authority.

Moreover, it underscores that, contra Enders, these forms of authority were (and are) not just imposed by teachers on students. And contra Arendt, it suggests that the authority of Western teachers has been decidedly unstable for a long time. It's worth remembering that in ancient Greece and Rome, many of those charged with tutoring students at home and leading them to school were enslaved. In fact, the very word "pedagogy" has etymological ties to slavery.[24] From enslaved pedagogues to the precariously positioned rhetoricians of the Roman Empire, from the dead lettered of the Middle Ages to the contingent and adjunct instructors who teach first-year writing and speech courses in contemporary universities, those who teach rhetoric have frequently occupied marginal positions in the very structures of authority that they've helped—willingly or unwillingly—to perpetuate and challenge. While rhetoricians often received a slightly greater degree of social and cultural prestige than other teachers, their professional and political lives were nevertheless unsteady.[25]

To put it bluntly, students are not the only ones punished by educational systems. Again, I don't say this to insist teachers' authority must be shored up. I'm not interested in simply inverting the matter and arguing that teachers need to be protected from students—an argumentative tack taken by an array of professors and commentators flipping out over alarmist conceptions of trigger warnings, "cancel culture," and the threat to free speech purportedly posed by student activists protesting the conditions faced by marginalized students—for example, activists pursuing racial justice on the campuses of US colleges and universities.[26]

Which brings me back to Hannah Arendt, whose own writings on race and education met with serious, justifiable resistance. While Arendt's claims about the waning authority of teachers might overstate that authority's historical clout, her defense of educational authority possesses a certain appeal. After all, how many teachers—myself included—sometimes assert a sort of pedagogical authority in the pursuit of more equitable pedagogical spaces? Even in higher education, where teachers are no longer simply adults instructing children, and even in college-level rhetoric and writing courses, whose practitioners and proponents have spent decades advocating for student-centered pedagogies, how many teachers exercise authority in order to, say, prevent a small handful of students from monopolizing class discussions or keep the rhetorical preconceptions of the most self-assured students from going unchallenged? How many of us assert our pedagogical authority as a way of resisting "the tyranny of the majority"?[27]

But to see the limits of Arendt's ideas about educational authority, one need only turn to Little Rock, Arkansas, which, in 1957, became a flashpoint in the civil rights movement and the struggle for racial justice in the United States. In the fall of that year, three years after the US Supreme Court declared all laws establishing segregated schools unconstitutional, nine Black students enrolled in the newly desegregated Little Rock Central High School. Two years after that, Arendt published an infamous essay entitled "Reflections on Little Rock."[28] She argued that, in the case of school desegregation, adults were abdicating their proper authority by putting children on the front lines of political upheaval. She writes, "I think no one will find it easy to forget the photograph reproduced in newspapers and magazines throughout the country, showing a . . . girl [Elizabeth Eckford], accompanied by a white friend of her father, walking away from school, persecuted . . . by a jeering and grimacing mob of youngsters."[29] Arendt goes on to argue, "The girl, obviously, was asked to be a hero . . . something neither her absent father nor the equally absent representatives of the NAACP felt called upon to be. . . . The picture looked to me like a fantastic caricature of progressive education which, by abolishing the authority of adults, implicitly denies their responsibility for the world into which they have borne their children and refuses the duty of guiding them into it. Have we now come to the point where . . . we intend to have our political battles fought out in the school yards?"[30]

In the ensuing decades, critics disputed and defended various parts of Arendt's argument. I want to focus briefly on the response of novelist and essayist Ralph Ellison. In short, Ellison didn't think Arendt understood the particular situation faced by Black people, including Black students, in the South. He describes that situation as "the basic, implicit heroism of people who must live in a society without recognition. . . . Such a position raises a people above a simple position of social and political inferiority and it imposes upon them the necessity of understanding" others and "themselves too . . . in relationship to other Americans. Men in our situation simply cannot afford to ignore the nuances of human relationships."[31] For Ellison,

one of the important clues to the meaning of that experience lies in the idea, the *ideal* of sacrifice. Hannah Arendt's failure to grasp the importance of this ideal . . . caused her to fly way off into left field in her "Reflections on Little Rock." . . . [S]he has absolutely no conception of what goes on in the minds of Negro parents when they send their kids through those lines of hostile people. . . . [I]n the outlook of many of these parents (who wish that the problem didn't exist), the child is expected to face the terror and contain his fear and anger *precisely* because he is a Negro American.[32]

Ellison positions the social situation faced by Black schoolchildren and their parents as radically contingent, with their lives unfolding in a network of hostility and terror that requires relentless attunement to relationships, racial inequalities, and social and political structures. As he puts it, "There are no abstract rules. . . . Each group must play the cards as history deals them."[33] Ellison's points are elaborated by political theorist Danielle Allen, who notes that white Southerners' history of "maintaining key public spaces as their exclusive possession" forced Black Southerners to become "accustomed to acquiescing to such norms and to the acts of violence that enforced them."[34] The desegregation of Little Rock Central thus played out in the context of "two etiquettes of citizenship—the one of dominance, the other of acquiescence"—rooted in historical, political, and racial dealings "meant to police the boundaries of the public sphere," including public schools attended by white students, "as a 'whites-only' space."[35] Arendt minimizes this context insofar as she explicitly generalizes her concern with the cause of Black people in the South by aligning it with the struggles of "all oppressed or under-privileged peoples."[36]

I highlight Ellison's response to Arendt not to suggest that her thoughts on educational authority are entirely bankrupt. Even in "Reflections on Little Rock," one can see flashes of good intention, even if they are quickly snuffed out by Arendt's jab at Eckford's "absent father" or her lack of attention to the everyday circumstances faced by Black parents, children, and students.[37] Rather, I do so to point out the ways in which a theory of educational authority collapses when it does not or cannot account for and *respond* to the particular situations inhabited by those populating the classrooms and sidewalks on which that theory is brought to bear. As Hanna Fenichel Pitkin points out, Arendt herself was frequently troubled by the relationship between abstraction and particularity.[38] At times, Arendt would swear off "dangerous abstraction," aware that "no general category can fully capture or do justice to who a particular individual is."[39] And yet in many of her works, Arendt nevertheless abstracts from particulars.[40] Arendt was far from unaware of the risks involved in applying theoretical generalities to specific situations, even as "Reflections on Little Rock" dramatically disregards the specifics highlighted by Ellison and Allen.

In fact, in some ways I'd suggest Arendt's writings on educational authority have more to offer the situations of the present moment than they did those of 1959. In the early twenty-first century, we have faced a different set of political tensions when it comes to the relation between race and educational institutions, especially institutions of higher education. While Arendt was concerned that Black students were being granted insufficient safety and protection in what she thought should be the relatively authoritarian confines of schools, many recent observers are concerned that marginalized college students are demanding an *excess* of safety. Writing about students who, in 2015, spoke out against the conditions faced by Black students at the University of Missouri and at Yale University, *Atlantic* columnist Conor Friedersdorf claimed, "It is as if they've weaponized the concept of 'safe spaces.'"[41] Friedersdorf's argument reflects a broader trend in discourse around college students, especially feminist students, queer students, and students of color: that they've become too protected, too desirous of safety, too "coddled."[42] The notion that college students have grown dangerously sensitive has become a powerful and abstract commonplace, in many ways laying the groundwork for more recent conservative moral panics over "cancel culture." Given its power in contemporary political discourse and relevance to some of this book's key terms, it's worth dwelling on this notion at length.

By way of illustration, consider Friedersdorf's account of a series of events that took place at Yale University in late 2015.[43] He begins by quickly noting that, in advance of Halloween, "Yale administrators" sent an email containing "heavy-handed advice" about costumes students should avoid. (The email, which was sent by the university's Intercultural Affairs Committee and about which Friedersdorf provides minimal detail, strikes me as a rather benign bit of institutional boilerplate. It notes past cases of Yale students wearing Halloween costumes involving blackface and redface, and the writers state that while students "definitely have a right to express themselves, we would hope" they avoid costumes that disrespect "segments of our population." It goes on to "encourage" students to consider such questions as "Does this costume reduce cultural differences to jokes or stereotypes?"[44]) Friedersdorf then jumps to a subsequent email critiquing that advice, which he treats in much more detail. The critique was written by Erika Christakis, a lecturer at Yale and wife of Nicholas Christakis, a professor who at the time served as residential "master" of Yale's Silliman College. In her email, Christakis worries about "the consequences of an institutional (bureaucratic and administrative) exercise of implied control over college students."[45] After citing her background as an "educator concerned with the developmental stages of childhood and young adulthood" and "a former preschool teacher," she ventures several hypotheticals, including the statute of limitations "on dreaming of dressing as [Disney character] Tiana the Frog Princess if you aren't a black girl from New Orleans."[46] Friedersdorf lauds Christakis's email, which was sent to all Silliman students, as "a model of relevant, thoughtful, civil engagement."[47] (In Friedersdorf's telling, the immaculately civil Christakises sound not so distant from the martyred Cassian of Imola.) However, the letter prompted "a faction of students" to launch what Friedersdorf calls "a campaign of public shaming" against Christakis and her husband, which included calling for the couple to be "removed from their residential positions." After characterizing Nicholas Christakis's engagement with members of this student "faction" as "restrained," "civil," and magnanimous, Friedersdorf criticizes the students' claims from a number of angles. I want to highlight just one of his critiques—one that draws inspiration from Greg Lukianoff and Jonathan Haidt's "The Coddling of the American Mind," a 2015 *Atlantic* piece subsequently expanded into a book of the same name. Lukianoff and Haidt's arguments about "coddling" have frequently been cited by pundits and writers concerned that student activists' sensitivity and overzealousness for social justice makes them a threat to free speech and to themselves.

Borrowing the language of cognitive behavioral therapy, Friedersdorf paraphrases Lukianoff and Haidt's claim that "too many college students engage in 'catastrophizing,' which is to say, turning common events into nightmarish trials." He goes on to quote an open letter responding to Christakis's email signed by hundreds of "Concerned Yale Students, Alumni, Family, Friends, and Staff." While the letter explicitly states that the writers "are not asking to be coddled,"[48] Friedersdorf makes it pretty clear he thinks they are. But as he sees it, to ask to be coddled is a self-defeating proposition. That's because in claiming to be victims, the students are in fact victimizing themselves: "These students . . . need someone to teach them how empowered they are by virtue of their mere enrollment [at Yale]; . . . that their worth is inherent, not contingent; . . . that they are capable of

tremendous resilience; and that most possess it now despite the disempow-
ering ideology foisted on them by well-intentioned, wrongheaded
ideologues encouraging them to imagine that they are not privileged."[49]

Note here that Friedersdorf falls into a bit of abstraction akin to
Arendt's: specifically, he emphasizes that students' worth "is inherent, not
contingent." When it comes to moral values and democratic ideals, I—and
I would bet many of the students he criticizes—share his conviction. However, even though his objections to *how* some of the student activists argued
and behaved may merit consideration, his rejection of the contingency of
students' empowerment and worth falls into the same trap as Arendt's
"Reflections on Little Rock": he writes from an idealized, abstracted position that cannot or will not account for the particulars that have made
students of color at Yale feel the tenuousness of their own position, including the fact of white Yale students wearing blackface as recently as 2007.[50]
In other words, by displacing arguments about institutional politics and
patterns of behavior toward students of color into the realm of abstract
moral arguments about the inherent worth of individuals, Friedersdorf
loses the trees for the forest.

A few years later, a variation of Friedersdorf's argument was forwarded
by powerful ideological companions. In 2020, the Trump administration
issued a directive that federal agencies should identify and divert funds
away from any training programs on "'critical race theory,' 'white privilege,'
or any other training or propaganda effort that teaches or suggests either
(1) that the United States is an inherently racist or evil country or (2) that
any race or ethnicity is inherently racist or evil."[51] Following Trump's loss in
the 2020 presidential election, a number of conservative state governments
pursued legislation that echoed that directive.[52] For example, the Tennessee
state legislature passed a bill preventing "teachers or other employees" of
local education agencies from using "supplemental instructional materials
that include or promote the following concepts: (1) One race or sex is inherently superior to another race or sex; (2) Any individual, by virtue of the
individual's race or sex, is inherently privileged, racist, sexist, or oppressive,
whether consciously or subconsciously."[53] Many of these bills make an
abstraction similar to Friedersdorf's: whether in response to such publications as *The 1619 Project*, actions by the Biden administration, or critical race
theory, they displace arguments about historical contingencies and present
realities into the realm of moral and political abstractions about the *inherent*

equality of individuals.[54] In these cases, critical race theory—a legal and academic framework whose practitioners have carefully traced the diverse, particular historical and current inequities faced by people of color in the United States—is misconstrued as claiming just the opposite: that racial inequities are inherent rather than contingent.[55] Ironically, then, critical race theorists would likely concur with many of the abstract principles these bills advocate (i.e., that no race is inherently superior to or worthier than another) even as the bills themselves make it less likely that the particular injustices that have granted white Americans an aggregate position of material, political, and social superiority will be addressed in US classrooms.

I dwell on Friedersdorf's argument to demonstrate how it inverts Arendt's abstractions in "Reflections on Little Rock," leveraging abstraction to position US students as too protected, too sensitive, too coddled rather than insufficiently protected. This case is often made by extracting marginalized students from their particular context and the patterns of aggression and dismissal that they face, expecting them to behave as transcendently rational and moral beings in the face of peers' immanently offensive behaviors—the kinds of "regressive, or even transgressive" behaviors for which Erika Christakis and Friedersdorf seem to think college campuses *should* provide a safe space.[56] Cussing out cool and collected authority figures, on the other hand, would seem to be a bridge too far, marking an excess of sensitivity that, unlike the historically acceptable offenses and transgressions of white students, cannot be tolerated.

However, scholars have offered compelling rejoinders to the alleged crisis of campus sensitivity. For example, Sara Ahmed writes, "We need to be too sensitive if we are to challenge what is not being addressed": "issues of racism, power, and sexism on campus."[57] Drawing on Ahmed, Kendall Gerdes argues, "Understanding that the safe house is a precondition for the contact zone—and that sensitivity is the precondition for rhetorical affection—should change the way we think and argue about trigger warnings and other issues of academic freedom and free speech on campus where figures of 'sensitive students' are likely to appear."[58]

In summation, I trace the contours of Arendt's response to Little Rock and Friedersdorf's critique of students at Yale with an eye toward responsibility. In both pieces, the writers' abstractions serve to shore up conventional notions of authority. While that is less obvious in Friedersdorf's case, note that he almost always presents individual campus authority figures (though not the faceless "Yale administrators" he barely defines) as rational, civil actors holding the coddled mob at bay. And yet he also holds up an abstract notion of agency of which I am highly skeptical: the individual student who, despite the repeated offensive behaviors of those in more secure positions, should remain ever the rational, self-controlled, idealized citizen-in-training. My case for responsibility as an alternate relational trope to authority and agency resonates with Gerdes's reframing of dismissive claims about "sensitive students." The kind of responsibility I'm calling attention to is, like sensitivity, a "precondition for rhetorical affection," an exposure to others that may pave the way to authoritative or agentive action but is itself a key ethical component of pedagogical relations that cannot be contained within the abstracted parameters of authority and/or agency. In short, responsibility is a sensitive thing, and how I'm using the term merits careful explication.

RESPONSIBILITY AND AGENCY IN THEORY AND PRACTICE

Recent scholarship in rhetorical theory has called fresh attention to the intersections of rhetoric and ethics.[59] A well-established area of rhetorical studies, rhetorical theory is generally concerned with how symbols structure and mediate relations between beings. The scope and definition of rhetorical theory is subject to much debate,[60] but Ira Allen provides a helpful gloss: *"the self-consciously ethical study of how symbolic animals negotiate constraint."*[61] In other words, rhetorical theory entails the study of the symbols (sometimes linguistic, sometimes not) that shape and are shaped by beings (sometimes humans, sometimes others) as well as the use of those symbols to articulate new theories and practices of symbolic engagement with and between others. Scholars have framed rhetorical theory as an "ethical study" to the significant, and arguably inherent, extent that ethics and rhetoric are intertwined because of the symbolic dimensions of how we emerge and exist with others.

While rhetorical theorists have drawn on and sketched out a variety of ethical frameworks, the writings of Emmanuel Levinas have provided a key source of inspiration, with Levinas's conception of responsibility attracting particular attention. Ethics, in the Levinasian sense, is not a matter of building categorical or conditional systems of moral precepts to guide human behavior and relations. Instead, it is about considering the conditions that make such relations possible. In this context, responsibility is not something an agentive individual simply possesses or intentionally enacts but a condition that precedes agency and is bound up with our inherent exposedness—one might also say "sensitivity"—to others. Rhetorical theorists have demonstrated how Levinasian ethics and responsibility can illuminate the conditions that make rhetorical activity possible.[62] In short, both Levinas and rhetorical theorists emphasize the ethical complexities at work in the ways relations between beings unfold through, in, and beyond language. However, most rhetorical work on Levinas focuses on extracurricular activities, addressing pedagogical matters implicitly or incidentally. One of this book's primary arguments is that the ethical questions raised by Levinas-inspired rhetorical theory have important implications for teaching and vice versa. That said, Levinasian ethics is difficult to gloss, and I save my primary explication for chapter 4. Here, I take just a few pages to distinguish Levinasian responsibility from rhetorical theories and everyday notions that ground responsibility in agency. I then suggest important ways in which it allows us to reframe the significance of teacher-student relationships.

To frame this introductory account, let's revisit Jody Enders's characterization of such relationships, which is explicitly indebted to an account of subject formation laid out by Friedrich Nietzsche. In Nietzsche's account, human subjectivity emerges in response to aggressive punishment, which, as Judith Butler glosses it, "compels an originally aggressive human to turn that aggression 'inward,' to craft an inner world composed of a guilty conscience and to vent that aggression against oneself in the name of morality."[63] In other words, a subject becomes self-conscious because someone else finds that subject wanting, issuing a punishment or judgment that causes the subject to internalize the other's aggression. For Enders, the medieval rhetoric teacher serves as an emblematic dispenser of punishment and fabricator of self-loathing student-subjects.

But, drawing on Levinas, Butler argues Nietzsche's account "does not fully take into account the scene of address through which *responsibility* is queried and then either accepted or denied."[64] Butler positions the scene of address as "the rhetorical condition for responsibility," a condition upon which Nietzsche's "scene of punishment" depends, and describes responsibility as "an unwilled susceptibility" rather than something a person consciously cultivates.[65] Butler thus suggests that "to take responsibility for oneself is to avow the limits of any self-understanding, and to establish these limits not only as a condition for the subject but as the predicament of the human community."[66] Responding to theorists who assert that responsibility requires a decisively self-aware agent who is in control of and can be held accountable for their actions, Butler suggests that responsibility establishes and is established by the *limits* of "self-understanding."

For the sake of my argument, Butler's Levinasian scene of address opens the possibility for a scene of *pedagogical* address that stands as an indispensable supplement to Enders's Nietzschean scene of pedagogical punishment. But while the kinds of "limits" Butler describes are not ignored in the field of rhetoric, they are often positioned as at odds with or ancillary to the field's pedagogical and practical pursuits. Responsibility, whether seen as an unwilled susceptibility or a capacity taken on by a willful subject, tends to play second fiddle to agency.[67] As one quick example, the 2011 *Framework for Success in Postsecondary Writing* includes responsibility as one of the "eight habits of mind essential for success in college writing" but defines it as "the ability to take ownership of one's actions and understand the consequences of those actions for oneself and others."[68] Even though responsibility gets a nod, it is positioned as the agentive ability of a self-aware individual rather than a susceptibility or vulnerability to others. In other words, responsibility becomes a way of exercising agency rather than a condition for agency. I argue that careful thinking about responsibility can enrich—and, yes, limit—the ways we write about and take up agency. In doing so, I seek to offer an alternative to the argument that theorists "can pursue an unrestrained deconstruction of the agency of speakers and writers only at the risk of theorizing themselves out of their jobs," and to suggest that the unrestrained valorization of agency comes with its own professional risks.[69]

As a more extensive illustration of the relative positions of agency and responsibility in rhetorical scholarship, consider Arabella Lyon's engagement with Butler's work. In *Deliberative Acts*, Lyon draws on Butler to develop "a theory of performative deliberation, where deliberation is an action or a practice."[70] As a part of her theory, Lyon conceptualizes agency as shared and intersubjective, intertwined with matters of "recognition, responsibility, and reciprocity."[71] However, Lyon defines those terms quite differently than Butler. "Recognition," for instance, is "a self-willed engagement with another," a far cry from unwilled susceptibility.[72] Ultimately, Lyon concludes, "Theorizing recognition is difficult in the best of times, but Butler's site of accusation and accounting seems more fraught with desire, distrust, and disengagement, more difficult and demanding than recognition theorized through a pragmatics of sanction and narratable lives. To account for oneself and one's acts toward another, I argue, one must go beyond performative and constative acts of basic recognition. . . . Butler will not help us here. . . . Butler's sense of accounting escapes . . . [the] operational difficulties of difference and the other through its solipsism."[73]

There are potential challenges to Lyon's reading of Butler.[74] But setting those aside, Lyon makes a persuasive case that Butler's theory of recognition is a bad fit for her theory of performative deliberation. Lyon engages Butler's work in a chapter focused on Libyan lawyer Eman al-Obeidi, who drew international media attention in 2011 when she reported her captivity and assault by a group of Muammar Gaddafi's soldiers. Lyon analyzes the strategies by which al-Obeidi "redefined the normative discourse for her own story" and "succeeded in . . . making her narratable self no longer the sexualized woman but the hurt citizen."[75] For Lyon, one of the many factors that makes al-Obeidi's story noteworthy is "the force of her agency in extending rights norms to all Libyans."[76] Despite the intractability of Western media frameworks, al-Obeidi was able to "claim and manipulate human rights discourse and norms in the service of performative deliberation."[77] This is a case where it is completely understandable to emphasize and respect al-Obeidi's agency—intersubjective and constrained by norms though it may be—over her unwilled susceptibility.

I would extend this point to many projects in rhetoric. Rhetoricians have published a wide array of articles and books focused on the laudable, remarkable practices of marginalized rhetors. It will come as no surprise to those familiar with such scholarship that these rhetors were vulnerable to material, political, and discursive powers beyond their immediate control. What is striking is their ability to exert agency in the context of such constraining power structures, and downplaying that agency can be, to say the very least, profoundly disrespectful. For that reason and others, while this book advocates for and draws on theories that decenter agency, I want to proceed cautiously and carefully. To argue for more attention to responsibility in the context of rhetorical education is, again, not to dismiss agency, nor to argue for responsibility as the new preeminent term for all rhetorical projects. After all, no theory is a fit for every situation.

Rather, theorizing teacher-student relationships requires constant attendance to the rhetorical, cultural, and contextual variables that shape those relationships in any given situation. For example, to the extent that contemporary universities are seen as transitional sites that mediate between private and public life, the teachers they employ do not fit neatly into culturally constructed gender binaries that such thinkers as Arendt often, even if unintentionally, rely on to analyze different types of authority.[78] That is, because such institutions are "protopublic" rather than simply private *or* public,[79] populated by students who might range in age from seventeen to seventy and beyond, higher educators do not necessarily possess either the authority over public matters conventionally (and problematically) associated with masculinity or the authority over children's private upbringing conventionally (and problematically) associated with femininity. A rhetorical theory must respond to such situational complexities. In the case of rhetoricians, matters are further complicated by such factors as the precarious employment situations of most of those who teach rhetoric and writing at the college level as well as the feminization of rhetoric in Western intellectual traditions.[80] So while I am interested in asking when teachers and students alike might embrace, or at least acknowledge, responsibility as an alternative to agency, readers and I should bear in mind that who is imbued with more or less agency, granted the authority of abstraction, or situated as vulnerable or responsible is a moving target. As a significant body of intersectional scholarship has pointed out, critiquing power dynamics is not a simple matter of identifying the empowered and disempowered parties in simplistic, isolated, exclusionary binaries (e.g., teacher/student, male/female).[81] Even in the relatively delimited context of first-year composition courses, everything from gender to race to employment situation to age to professional title can affect the delicate dynamics of teacher-student relationships.[82] And even in relationships *between* students, "claims to authority" are "interactionally contingent," which raises further complications for teachers attempting to navigate questions of relative authority, agency, and responsibility.[83]

In the end, it is because neither teachers nor students are absolutely marginalized figures that I resist dismissing alternatives or challenges to agency from the pedagogical scene. I put the radically responsible subject described by Levinas-inspired work in rhetorical theory in conversation with pedagogy because pedagogical practices involve teachers *and* students interrupting and being interrupted. They involve, in a word, responding. My approach emphasizes the ways in which teachers and students are unwillingly susceptible to each other, never wholly sealed off by either authority or agency. I do not deny that teacherly authority and student agency exist, but I position them as contingent states, relentlessly fragile rather than steadily accumulated and strengthened over time. Ethics, as articulated by Levinas, lets us dwell in the moments in which these contingent states crystallize or shatter, calling attention to the responsibility on which they are premised. It thus offers a way to counteract the seemingly diminishing profile of the teacher-student relationship by refusing to frame it purely or primarily in service of other authoritative or agentive ends. As advocates of critical pedagogy have long challenged the notion that education is the process of teachers depositing information in students, my engagement with Levinasian ethics challenges the notion that education is primarily or solely the process of teachers fomenting agency in students. It highlights the unwilled responsibilities of teachers and students, not just their mutual capacities, as an indispensable (though not always laudatory) part of pedagogical relationships. And in doing so, it can call attention to what is lost when those relationships dissipate, replaced by presumably authoritative educational technologies or fantastically agentive students who can do it themselves, no teachers required.

STRUCTURE AND METHODOLOGY

Over the course of this book, I move back and forth between theoretical matters and pedagogical ones. For readers used to books that start with the elaboration of a theory and then offer a pedagogical or practical application of that theory, this may seem surprising or idiosyncratic. The same goes for readers who have grown accustomed to clean distinctions between theoretical work and scholarship of teaching and learning. But as I have tried to demonstrate in this introduction, it is my conviction that the theoretical and pedagogical matters at stake are inextricable from one another. To my mind, it is more productive to let theory and pedagogy respond to one another than to grant one priority over the other.

In pursuing this goal, I again echo Levinas: in the preface to his book *Totality and Infinity*, he points out that he runs the risk of "appearing to confuse theory and practice."[84] As he argues, "Hitherto the relation between theory and practice was not conceivable other than as a solidarity or a hierarchy: activity rests on cognitions that illuminate it." In other words, practical activity rests on theoretical knowledge. Levinas, however, resists the hierarchical notion that "knowledge requires from acts the mastery of matter, minds, and societies"; thus the "apparent confusion [of theory and practice] . . . constitutes one of the theses of" his book.[85] The same goes here.[86]

Similarly, I do not focus on a single historical era or move through the history of education in strictly chronological fashion. Instead, I adopt something akin to what rhetoricians Debra Hawhee and Christa J. Olson call "pan-historiography," approaching "documents and materials, however incongruous, with an eye toward making those materials move, reanimating them in a way that renders visible, audible, and lively a variety of historical figures, voices, and viewpoints."[87] Just as I argue that seemingly disparate corners of theory and pedagogy have significant things to say to one another, I argue that different moments in the history of education—modern, medieval, ancient, today, last year, tomorrow—can speak to, without subsuming, one another. In doing so, I make the implicit and explicit argument that we can better understand the place of authority, agency, and responsibility in the past, present, and future of education by looking at a variety of historical and rhetorical contexts without assuming that history moves in a teleological manner. Like theory and practice, history can be an interruptive force, and its interruptions tell us something.

CHAPTER OUTLINES

As I've attempted to demonstrate, teacher-student relationships and the ways we theorize and enact them do not occur in a vacuum. They are mediated, constrained, and supported by a range of material, political, economic, social, cultural, and technological systems and assumptions. And in turn, how those relationships unfold affects those systems and assumptions. For that reason, while teachers and students are central to this book, its chapters focus on key rhetorical structures that have mediated and continue to mediate relationships between them. By "structures," I mean everything from ancient tropes to digital platforms—the multifarious devices and technologies that have helped set the parameters within and beyond which rhetorical education has unfolded. While these structures span the history of Western education, I argue that they meaningfully illustrate diverse attempts to define education in terms of teacherly authority and/or student agency; juxtaposing them with one another thus allows us to see the particularity and persistence of authority and agency within and across eras. Moreover, I argue that reframing these structures in terms of responsibility—which is already lurking around their edges, waiting to be recognized—allows us to sketch out a different rhetorical and ethical paradigm for higher education. En route to responsibility, I begin with a pair of chapters on teacherly authority, examining and challenging the ways it has served as a primary conceptual justification and framework for teacher-student relationships at certain moments in the history of education. I then turn to more contemporary contexts in which student agency has taken over much of the conceptual terrain once held by teacherly authority. Despite the apparent shift in emphasis from teacherly authority to student agency, I argue that both depend on a logic of individual mastery that can and should be called into question by pedagogies premised on responsibility.

In chapter 1, I focus on Socratic irony. One of the most tenacious ways of conceptualizing the teacher-student relation, Socratic irony is often figured as a way for a canny, masterful teacher to demonstrate and propagate intellectual authority. I reposition such irony as an uncontrollable force that can humble and humiliate teacher and student alike. Focusing on Plato's *Gorgias* and Aristophanes's *Clouds*, I demonstrate how rethinking Socratic irony might unsettle the teacher's position of authoritative mastery with regard to both students and systematized bodies of knowledge. I end by connecting this line of argument to the ways in which pedagogy's infrastructural contexts have influenced student-teacher relationships in the wake of ancient Athens's rhetorical upheavals.

Extending chapter 1's critique of teacherly authority, chapter 2 turns to *prosopopoeiae*, imitation exercises that have been a pedagogical staple throughout much of the history of rhetorical education. These exercises, which asked students to write and deliver speeches in the voices of well-known literary and historical figures, were often seen as a way of instilling the rhetorical authority of the schoolmaster in the students, turning them into rhetorical masters in training. I begin by presenting a reworked version of one such exercise from a contemporary classroom—a version that attempts to move away from tropes of mastery and authority. However, I then call attention to the limitations of that exercise, showing how even the most presumably nonauthoritative pedagogical practices carry the residue of mastery. In all, I use the history of imitation exercises to demonstrate how attempts to move from teacherly authority to student agency can reinscribe notions of mastery and how attention to responsibility might help us recognize and question that process of reinscription.

In the second half of the book, I shift the emphasis to more recent pedagogical contexts and notions of student agency. In chapters 3 and 4, I analyze and present alternatives to commonplace arguments around online education. My goal is not to dismiss online education as a whole but to critique the overblown utopianism that often accompanies new educational technologies and that, through appeals to student agency, can serve as an excuse for slashing public investment in education. In chapter 3, I focus specifically on the ways for-profit massive open online courses, or xMOOCs, purported to refigure the relationship between teachers and students, arguing that xMOOC advocates in fact relied on hypertrophied and questionable notions of student agency that educators have long deployed. I offer a history of the arguments for and against xMOOCs, emphasizing the ways in which those arguments diverge from and reiterate the clichés of historical and ongoing debates about education's ability to empower students and the potential of new technologies to democratize access to education. While some may see xMOOCs as a relic of the 2010s, I demonstrate that the tropes and clichés on which their advocates relied have been a staple of alleged innovations throughout the history of educational technology and are all but certain to keep recurring in education's not-so-distant future. Understanding and being prepared to rebut such commonplace arguments are far from bygone concerns.

In chapter 4, I challenge xMOOC advocates' agency-based assumptions about how students learn by explicating Levinas's concept of responsibility. Expanding on this introduction's engagement with that concept, I argue that Levinasian responsibility offers a significant alternative to theories of education grounded in agency-centered notions of freedom and autonomy. Challenging xMOOCs' valorization of individual student agency, I forward what I call pedagogies of responsibility. I then compare and contrast two different agency-based visions of peer engagement: (1) the way xMOOC advocates describe the role of such courses' "peer networks" and (2) the forms of peer response that have long been a staple of rhetoric and writing classrooms. After examining points of similarity and difference between these two approaches to peer engagement, I present an alternative conception of peer response grounded in responsibility.

Finally, in chapter 5, I offer an open-ended illustration of the possibilities of responsibility and the limitations of authoritative, agentive mastery by questioning the power of the thesis statement. One of contemporary rhetoric and writing instruction's most ubiquitous devices, the thesis statement is a rhetorical move that places students in a position of progressive mastery relative to the act of writing and the topics they research. Linking confident, unqualified thesis statements with a lack of nuance in contemporary public argument, I argue for a greater emphasis on uncertainty, hypothesizing, and hesitation in both writing pedagogy and rhetorical theory. I use the conceit of a hedge maze to structure the chapter, with its arguments recursively returning and responding to each other rather than moving in a straight line toward increasingly masterful conclusions. In so doing, I aim to perform the antithetical approach to educational theory and practice for which my final chapter—if not the entirety of this book—argues.

In all, what follows constitutes a series of attempts to work humbly and haltingly toward new models of teacher-student relationships. In making those attempts, I am responsible to teachers, students, and systems past and present as I posit that rhetorical claims to agency and authority are dependent upon responsibility. I want to be clear that this book does not offer an unqualified defense of the US higher education system as it currently operates, nor of the Western rhetorical and pedagogical traditions that inform much of that system. The arguments I make are in many ways critical of both. What I offer, rather, is a case for a more generous, caring, and sensitive approach to public higher education than US universities—historically entangled with broader national inequities, from slavery to the violent expropriation of Indigenous land to segregation to current forms of economic inequality—have ever managed to cultivate.[88] I offer implicit and explicit critiques of the historical tendency to defund public education at the very moments when teachers and students stop representing the interests of the already well-heeled, and I'm not just posturing in asking when and whether the work teachers and students do is actually worth it given the material and rhetorical conditions in which they're learning and working. But I also offer a hesitant defense of what higher education *could be*, and occasionally manages to be, bearing in mind that many of the institutions most eager and prepared to replace public colleges and universities are predatory or parasitic for-profit entities that feed on and perpetuate the most utopian versions of student agency and teacherly authority laid out in this introduction—which, not coincidentally, also tend to be the most hollow and exploitative versions of such concepts, ultimately unburdened by the *responsibility* without which we wouldn't have much of anything to learn from one another. It is to that responsibility that I, in conversation with you, hope to attend.

CHAPTER 1

Interrupting Socrates

Let us count, rather, on disarray.

—MAURICE BLANCHOT

Insofar as the heterogenous Western "pedagogical tradition" has its roots in ancient Greek rhetoric, the figure of the teacher has, from that tradition's very inception, had a remarkably fraught relationship with cultural and political authority.[1] Just consider the double legacy of Socrates as both (on the one hand) the original wise man, a revered and beloved teacher, *and* (on the other) a bothersome wise guy and disruptive corrupter of youth.[2] In Aristophanes's *Clouds*, which positions Socrates as a sophist rather than a philosopher, he even comes across as a bit of a huckster. The word "sophist," often affiliated with rhetoric's practitioners, itself suggests similar tensions: it is used as a label for teachers of wisdom and virtue as well as an insult.[3] Take *Against the Sophists*, in which Isocrates distances himself from so-called sophists by arguing that they are driven by a "desire for . . . profit" and have "a [deservedly] bad reputation among the general public" even as he advertises his own educational program.[4] Later in his career, Isocrates positions himself as a man of humble means, an adjunct of the "leisured class" whose students left his care "with regret and tears."[5]

These tensions between humility and authority, between masterful wisdom and pretentious chicanery, were also commonplace during Rome's Second Sophistic. Even as rhetorical education received a degree of imperial recognition and sanction, "the rhetorician's school" remained "a small, and in many cases precarious, business."[6] Libanius, a sophist who held the municipal chair of rhetoric in Antioch during the fourth century CE, conceives of the rhetorician as a second father to his students, with "a student's dependence on and closeness to his teacher . . . produc[ing] mutual feelings of affection."[7] At the same time, however, he complains of inadequate funding as well as disrespectful students who despise their instructors and threaten to take their parents' money elsewhere at the first hint of disciplinary action.[8]

In short, teachers were never far from both reverence and revulsion, positioned as authoritative yet humble masters as well as effete deceivers with their heads in the clouds and hands in their students' purses. Their authority as surrogate father figures was transient and constantly destabilized by parents, parodists, pupils—even by fellow teachers with whom they competed for students and funds. Raffaella Cribiore notes that "accusing someone of being a schoolteacher, or of having a schoolteacher as a father, was a common insult."[9] For ancient teachers, stabilizing their authority frequently involved situating themselves as affiliates but not members of the "leisured class," leveling invective at their competitors, and winning the devotion of students and support of political and cultural authorities.

In subtly similar ways, contemporary teachers also experience these tensions. For every movie about an adept writing teacher who inspires a class of students to change themselves and the world, there's a comedy featuring an absent-minded professor who can barely manage a piece of chalk. And while colleges and universities afford some teachers a much greater degree of professional stability than the precarious enterprises of their ancient forerunners, the adjunctification of higher education in general and of rhetoric and writing in particular leaves many teachers in distinctly marginal positions.[10]

But while the outrageous financial situations faced by contingent faculty may be surprisingly similar to those faced by Libanius's contemporaries, the antinomies of pedagogical authority resonate quite differently for many present-day teachers of rhetoric than they did for their premodern predecessors. That is, while many teachers' economic problems remain, commonplace ethical concerns about authority relations between teachers, students, and broader institutions and structures have shifted dramatically. Consider Sharon Crowley's warning that "classical rhetorical theory was devised a long time ago in cultures that were rigidly classbound . . . [and] invented for the use of privileged men."[11] If the struggle for ancient rhetoricians was stabilizing an ethos of pedagogical authority reliant on and defined by rigidly patriarchal and class-bound (if occasionally democratic) systems—systems in which the goal was often to turn out students prepared to inhabit and/or protect similarly rigid systems—then what are teachers suspicious of such systems to do? How are we to negotiate our *own* authority if we wish to resist a model of education designed to "produce a professional managerial class schooled in the art of obedience to authority and accepting of dominator-based hierarchy"?[12] Put otherwise, how might we teach our student bodies—no longer just male, no longer constituting a homogeneous cultural, ideological, or socioeconomic milieu—to question structural authority without abdicating our own pedagogical authority or participating in the broad denigration of teachers as ethically and intellectually suspect (a denigration that persists in overwrought attacks on radical college professors and much of the discourse surrounding the "reform" and privatization of higher education)?

In this chapter, I explore the questions above by going back to the start, taking up a tricky trope (or perhaps not a trope) that's haunted the Western pedagogical tradition since its inception: Socratic irony. I argue that this trope, which troubles the borders of authority and humility, wisdom and foolishness, contains a multitude of ethically and intellectually responsible approaches to rethinking pedagogical and rhetorical "authority." Rather than going right to Socratic irony, however, let me spend a moment dwelling with irony more generally, a trope that has—historically, practically, and conceptually—troubled quite a few borders of its own. I'll recall this stopover with irony as I go on to examine iterations of Socrates in the works of various rhetoricians, philosophers, and theorists. From there, I'll consider Plato's *Gorgias*, questioning the rhetorical stability of that text's Socrates. I'll then turn to Bruno Latour's reading of the *Gorgias*, juxtaposing it with Aristophanes's *Clouds* to argue that *Gorgias* and *Clouds* alike serve to befog further both Socrates's fractured figurations and the irony that those figurations so frequently claim does *not* characterize Socratic discourse. I end with some inconclusive conclusions that hitch these conceptual and figural concerns to the pedagogical situations faced by contemporary teachers.

DON'T YOU THINK?

What is irony? A dense question if ever there was one, but perhaps my inescapable starting point. It is, after all, what one might call a Platonic question, and Socratic irony obviously owes Plato much of its historical legacy.[13] I position "What is irony?" as Platonic insofar as the question presumes "irony" has some essence and that that essence has fixed, generalizable qualities toward which one could gesture. But tying irony to constative meanings and fixed qualities entails certain difficulties.[14] In many ways, it's easier to describe what irony *does* than it is to say what irony *is*. It's easier, in other words, to speak about it in performative terms, which leads to an odd paradox: if irony *is* anything, it is what it does (i.e., it "is" performative) and so maybe doesn't have any substantial, substantive identity at all. Some of these difficulties are present—if less obviously—in all speech acts, but "irony" seems particularly peculiar.[15] Paul de Man gestures toward this in a 1977 lecture entitled "The Concept of Irony." Despite the best efforts of German Romanticism, American literary criticism, and de Man himself, "it seems to be uncannily difficult to give a definition of irony. . . . [T]here seems to be something inherently difficult in the definition of the term, because it seems to encompass all tropes, on the one hand, but it is, on the other hand, very difficult to define it as a trope. Is irony a trope? Traditionally, of course, it is, but: is it a trope?"[16]

De Man notes a persistent trend in writings about irony: writers are adept at complaining that their forerunners didn't "really seem to know what irony is," but they tend to reenact rather than overcome this lack of knowledge.[17] He fleshes out the difficulty of grasping irony by turning to a pair of terms from Greek comedy:

> It helps a little to think of it [irony] in terms of the ironic man, in terms of the traditional opposition between *eiron* and *alazon*, as they appear in Greek or Hellenic comedy, the smart guy and the dumb guy. Most discourses about irony are set up that way, and this one will also be set up that way. You must then keep in mind that the smart guy, who is by necessity the speaker, always turns out to be the dumb guy, and that he's always being set up by the person he thinks of as being the dumb guy, the *alazon*.[18]

Whether pursued by an *eiron* or an *alazon*, a Platonic approach to defining irony would require the sort of interminable subdividing showcased in Plato's *Sophist*, in which the interlocutors slowly try to reach a set definition of "the sophist," that slippery fish. In other words, even if we could agree that irony is a trope, we still might question whether this trope is a "literary device," a "rhetorical device," and/or both; we might break up its "verbal," "dramatic," and "situational" variations.[19] Moreover, as any good sophist knows (though perhaps not Plato and Socrates, delinquent sophists that they were), the rhetorical openings any given situation affords—what rhetoricians have long called *kairos*—are highly unstable, so what counts as "situational" irony might fluctuate based not only on such traditional rhetorical variables as "speaker" and "audience," "intention" and "interpretation," but also on the complex workings of language itself and the network of historical, material, and cultural contexts in which a potentially ironic utterance attempts to coalesce.[20]

"What is irony?" seems an insufficient question, then, even if I might have to return to it throughout this chapter. Bearing that in mind, let's proliferate a few alternate questions to help us approach, if never quite meet, "irony" otherwise.

Take, for instance, one of the late twentieth century's most popular questions about irony: "Isn't it ironic?" This question sets up the chorus of 1995's "Ironic," a tune by singer-songwriter Alanis Morissette. The Morissettean question might seem cannier than its Platonic relative, focusing on a descriptive judgment of a single instance of irony (i.e., "it," the irony of which is rendered at least rhetorically questionable by the preceding "isn't"). Instead of having to discover or invent universal qualities prescriptively applicable to all instances of irony, the question humbly limits itself to a tentative decision about a single example. Unfortunately for Generation X, the relative irony of Morissette's lyrics became a contentious issue. The song launched endless arguments about what counts as ironic. Nearly a decade after the song's release, *New York Times* music critic Jon Pareles found an excuse to reference "the unironic 'Ironic'" while reviewing one of Morissette's subsequent albums.[21] Let's consider the song's first verse:

> An old man turned ninety-eight
> He won the lottery and died the next day
> It's a black fly in your Chardonnay
> It's a death row pardon two minutes too late
> Isn't it ironic, don't you think?[22]

The song's examples are obviously unfortunate, but if we want to attribute a degree of "the unexpected" to irony—the *Oxford English Dictionary* does, offering a "state of affairs or an event that seems deliberately contrary to what was or might be expected" as one of irony's meanings—it is questionable whether Morissette's examples are "ironic."[23] Various tropes and turns of phrase in English, from the emblematic "fly in the ointment" to jokes about finding a fly in your soup, suggest that while "a black fly in your Chardonnay" might be unfortunate, it's far from uncommon or unexpected. In some ways, that pesky fly might even be paradigmatic: an insect that's been spoiling the finer things in life since the days of ancient symposia. In other words, whether or not that fly is ironic depends on millennia of accreted tropes, turns of events, and linguistic tics. And even if a fly in the wine *is* a surprise, one would also have to consider whether or not misfortune itself is to be expected—whether the surprising quality of a single misfortune is rendered unsurprising within a broader web of commonplaces. That is, while an optimist might see Morissette's fly as ironically defying expectations (maybe even helping the glass be half full), a pessimist might see it as eminently predictable: further proof that Murphy's Law truly does guide the universe.

So far, though, all I've managed is to set up Plato and Alanis Morissette as two *alazons*, a pair who both came at irony wrong. And nothing puts one at risk of ironic effacement like trying to exert ironic authority or pronounce authoritatively on irony. After all, if the efforts of Plato and Morissette didn't quite pan out, I have yet to do anything but rehearse their efforts and a handful of well-worn responses.

I might instead, then, follow in the footsteps of those who've approached irony more haltingly, more attentive to its predilection to make you play the fool. Though aware of irony's resistance to definition and unsure whether it's (just) a trope, de Man riffs on Friedrich Schlegel to offer this heavily hedged antidefinition: "If Schlegel said irony is permanent parabasis, we would say that irony is the permanent parabasis of the allegory of tropes."[24] It takes another two years and the entirety of *Allegories of Reading* for de Man to offer another, related take on irony. In that book's final two sentences, he writes, "Irony is no longer a trope but the undoing of the deconstructive allegory of all tropological cognitions, *the systematic undoing, in other words, of understanding.* As such, far from closing off the tropological system, irony enforces the repetition of its aberration."[25] Irony functions here like a child who either doesn't know or refuses to follow the rules of a knock-knock joke: "Knock, knock," says the joker.

"Knock, knock!" replies the child, who—perhaps seeing the joker's exasperation, perhaps just amused by the game—giggles and, regardless of the joker's attempts to break the cycle, demands, "Again! Again!"

In "The Rhetoric of Testing," Avital Ronell writes, "Often the decisive interventions on the part of irony bear effects of physicality; they give a sound beating to a language that closes in on itself. . . . Like Socrates, it functions as gadfly, as an internal allergen that appears to come from a place of exteriority, undoing all transcendental systems, constantly rewriting the text that it submits to endless retests, retaking acknowledged premises on a permanent basis. This is why irony is no joke."[26]

Of course, not everyone is down with this approach to irony. Take Wayne Booth's A Rhetoric of Irony, a book de Man considers at length in "The Concept of Irony."[27] Booth, trying to contain irony, begins by recounting a conversation he had with a "very sophisticated" but misguided graduate student who believed all of Pride and Prejudice to be ironic.[28] Booth offers the "embarrass[ed]" student a more persuasive and limited view of the novel's irony, but remains unsure long enough to ask, "In what sense do I 'know' Jane Austen's intentions? How is such a peculiar kind of knowledge possible, if it is? . . . How do we talk about the precise and peculiar relationship between authors and readers of those passages which are unquestionably ironic?"[29] Concerned that "a spate of uninterpretable ironies has the same effect as providing no experience in irony at all," Booth decides to be a practical joker, focusing on irony's "stable" manifestations and placing "uninterpretable" ironies in the peripheral realms of footnotes and momentary concessions, at times subsuming them within broader schemes of intelligibility and stability.[30] He expresses particular skepticism about Romantic accounts of figures of speech—accounts in which irony, like metaphor, has "ranged from a minute oratorical device, one among many, to an imperialistic world conqueror."[31]

But irony's extensive and troubling range stretches back much further than German Romanticism. Going back to the Greeks, Claire Colebrook argues that Plato's Socrates used irony as both "a complex figure of speech and [in] the creation of an enigmatic personality."[32] It thus remains possible to ask whether Socrates was espousing a "true" philosophical program or just playing the role of a "superior sophist."[33] Though Colebrook begins with Socratic irony, she moves on to irony's role in literary theory. In so doing, her book resembles many other accountings of irony: Søren Kierkegaard's

The Concept of Irony may make continual reference to Socrates, but it ends by attempting to critique the writings of German Romantics and Idealists. Even the pragmatic Booth, who begins with a pedagogical anecdote, "center[s] his argument . . . on the practice of eighteenth-century English fiction" and the "relationship between authors and readers."[34] In short, texts on irony often spend more time situating it as a literary or theoretical phenomenon—one that marks and mars the relation between author and reader—than as a pedagogical phenomenon at work in the rhetorical relation between student and teacher.

The pedagogical dimensions of irony are precisely what concern me here. In concert with the issues of authority considered in this book's introduction, that concern leads me to stick close to Socrates, whom various scholars continue to position as *the* preeminent figure in the Western pedagogical tradition. Shoshana Felman, for instance, describes him as "that extraordinary teacher who taught humanity what pedagogy is, and whose name personifies the birth of pedagogics as a science" but who "inaugurates his teaching practice, paradoxically enough, by asserting not just his own ignorance, but the radical impossibility of teaching."[35] Socrates holds a double position as the paradoxically dislocated and unfounded "founder" of Western conceptions of both pedagogy and irony, one who establishes his authority as a teacher by giving up his authority and ability to teach and to know.

While hermeneutic approaches to Socratic pedagogy and irony might aim for comprehensive interpretations grounded in stabilized meanings and authorial intention, I position my approach as antihermeneutic in that I set out expecting the unexpected: that the borders of concepts, theories, practices, and disciplines will blur in curious ways—not that my expectations will guarantee any meaningful transcendence or ironic refixing of such borders.[36] Contrast this project, if you will, with Iakovos Vasiliou's "Socrates' Reverse Irony." Via sharp readings of Plato's *Apology* and *Gorgias*, Vasiliou pinpoints a "trope" he calls "reverse irony" and concludes, "Recognizing reverse irony is important for understanding Socrates' method. . . . [It] is . . . an expedient and efficient means of generating perplexity."[37] Meanwhile, I, via a dull reading of the *Gorgias* and a handful of other texts, am stuck on what happens when neither the interlocutor *nor* the Socratic figure "walk[s] away . . . from a Socratic discussion believing that he has the sort of expert knowledge of a virtue that would reliably enable him to pick out instances of that virtue."[38] I set out expecting to get buffeted and buffaloed by irony "constructed as the rhetorical test site par excellence,"[39] poised to fall into yet another trope that Vasiliou names early on: "that most Socratic of all results: *aporia*."[40]

FIGURES OF SOCRATES

I try to hold open the preceding questions about "irony" as I consider this: What is *Socratic* irony, and can one approach it while avoiding precisely that Platonic question? To whatever extent Western notions of irony and education are traceable to Socrates, does the Socratic teacher use or get used by irony? To the extent that irony bears "effects of physicality," is a Socratic irony that doesn't do violence to students, teachers, and their languages desirable and/or possible? And, all told, might such questions lead us to rethink the authority relations between students, teachers, language systems, and knowledge? I don't think any of these are yes-or-no questions.

Nevertheless, in contemporary parlance, what is often glossed as "Socratic irony" or "Socratic method" largely depends on yes-or-no questions, or at least on questions enclosed within systems meant to delineate what counts as a "right" or "wrong" answer: Platonic idealism, the American legal code—even standardized tests might fit the bill here.[41] Whether the goal is capital-T Truth, a law degree, or a high SAT score, the deep unpleasantness of such systems is unmistakable, from the unenviable rhetorical position of the yes men spurred by Plato's Socrates to modern students tossing and turning the night before a big multiple-choice test. Within these systems' more traditional iterations, the author (e.g., Plato) or other authority figure (e.g., the College Board) has presumably mastered the system's contents and method, and any apparent lack of knowledge on the part of that masterful, authoritative figure is pure dissemblance. This is a further limiting of the conception of "the Socratic" offered by Yun Lee Too, who writes, "The erotic teacher [for Too, Socrates is one such teacher] is . . . one who *temporarily* stages the scene of intellectual resourcelessness, whether actual or feigned of her own part, such that lack of knowledge remains specific to the pedagogical scenario and stands apart from any actual inadequacy that the student may feel."[42] Contra Too, the conceptions and deployments of "Socratic irony" described above position the master's staging of "intellectual resourcelessness" as *always* "feigned" and—whether purpose-fully or accidentally—seem to excel at feeding students' feelings of anxious "inadequacy."

Such systems may claim to proceed in a "Socratic" manner, but a number of critics have positioned Plato, not Socrates himself, as their pro-genitor. Michel Foucault puts it like this: "In every society the production of discourse is at once controlled, selected, organized, and redistributed according to a certain number of procedures, whose role is to avert its powers and its dangers, to cope with chance events, to evade its ponderous, awesome materiality."[43] Foucault then elaborates on three such "proce-dures": prohibited speech, the division of reason and folly (which I bracket here, though folly and irony often run in the same circles), and the opposi-tion between "true" and "false" discourse.[44] He is particularly interested in the last of the three, which he blames on Plato. Foucault claims that Plato's "rout[ing]" of the sophists instantiated the "true"/"false" opposition by relegating discourse to its "said" form and attempting to sunder all links to the allure of its "saying."[45] Foucault's powerful, desirous "saying" resonates with the iconic sophist Gorgias's "Encomium of Helen." In the enco-mium—which Gorgias describes as a *"paignion"* (amusement or plaything) that aims to absolve Helen of Troy from the blame and accusations regularly leveled at her—he describes "speech" as "a powerful lord that with the smallest and most invisible body accomplishes most godlike works."[46]

Foucault might thus point to Plato's *Gorgias* as a key moment in the incarceration of the sophists and sophistic sayings. Near its start, Plato's Socrates requests that Gorgias, who is his first major counterpart in the dialogue, stick to "the short style of speech, and leave the long style for some other time."[47] Plato's Gorgias obliges, at least initially, replying with the abrupt yes-or-no answers so typical of the interlocutors of Plato's Socrates.

But given that I'm on the trail of Socratic irony, let me note two com-plications before playing around with the *Gorgias* in the "long style." First, despite Plato's singular influence on contemporary perceptions of Socrates, we have at least two other accounts that complicate his portrait: those of Xenophon and Aristophanes. Kierkegaard elaborates on and compares these views at the start of *The Concept of Irony*. Despite confessing a "per-haps somewhat youthful infatuation with Plato," Kierkegaard is not entirely dismissive of Xenophon, "a second-rate fellow were it not for the chinks in his presentation."[48] These presentational gaps have to do with Plato's and Xenophon's respective approaches to irony, which Kierkegaard touches on in a footnote: "The ironic in Xenophon is never the floating of irony blissfully resting in itself but is a means of education, therefore at times encouraging to those from whom Socrates is actually expecting something."[49] For Kierkegaard, the "education" provided by the Socrates of Xenophon's dialogues is a "utilitarian" reinscription of Greek cultural commonplaces. Meanwhile Plato, Kierkegaard's dreamy crush, uses Socratic irony to transcend such commonness.

But even the infatuated Kierkegaard doesn't give Plato the last word on irony, turning from Xenophon to Plato to the comic playwright Aristophanes. He positions the Socrates of Aristophanes's *Clouds* as "just the necessary contrast to Plato's. . . . Indeed, it would be a great lack if we did not have the Aristophanic appraisal of Socrates; for just as every parody is an assurance that this process has outlived its day, so the comic view is an element, in many ways a perpetually corrective element, in making a personality or an enterprise completely intelligible."[50]

The notion of rendering something "completely intelligible" might seem inimical to my proclaimed antihermeneutic approach to irony. As noted above, irony is often associated with *un*intelligibility.[51] That Kierkegaard positions the "comic view" as a *perpetually* corrective element, however, suggests that for him, "complete" intelligibility is always a work in progress. *The Concept of Irony*'s next sentence frustrates intelligibility even further: "Even though we lack direct evidence about Socrates, even though *we lack an altogether reliable view* of him, we do have in recompense all the various nuances of *misunderstanding*, and in my opinion this is our best asset with a personality such as Socrates."[52] If Kierkegaard is claiming Aristophanes makes Socrates "completely intelligible," then, it is only insofar as the playwright rounds out a gallery of misunderstandings, adding another shady character to a lineup of unusual subjects. For Kierkegaard, laying Plato's, Xenophon's, and Aristophanes's characterizations beside or on top of one another reveals not a full picture of Socrates but "the cryptic nothing that actually constitutes the point in Socrates' life," a lack that constitutes Socrates's core.[53]

This view challenges those who would either (a) valorize Socrates as the progenitor or mouthpiece of earnest Platonic doctrines or (b) critique Socrates as a figure who uses irony as a mode of straightforward dissemblance, a duplicitous trap deployed to flip the script on relativistic wise guys.[54] This brings me back to the second complication I promised a few paragraphs ago: even if we isolate Plato from Xenophon and Aristophanes, Plato's Socrates is already fragmented. This is well established in the traditional subdividing of Plato's dialogues into early, middle, and late. As Donald J. Zeyl notes, "The *Gorgias* is generally considered to be one of the last of Plato's early dialogues and so is often thought to represent the views, methods, and personality of the historical Socrates."[55] In what follows, I give this screw one more turn, claiming that even within the discrete text called the *Gorgias*, interlocutors and readers encounter a patchwork Socrates written by a multivalent Plato who shifts views and methods in a manner that troubles not only a unified conception of "the Socratic" but also the border between "Socratic" and "sophistic." Although many scholars in rhetoric and philosophy have positioned "the quarrel between Gorgias and Plato" as "highlight[ing] how lingering issues for establishing rhetoric's intellectual stance is modernism's permutation of philosophy's ancient dispute with rhetoric,"[56] I explore this "quarrel" as a way to—perhaps ironically—question the lines not only between Socratic/sophistic but also between such other pairs as philosophy/rhetoric, student/teacher, and *eiron/alazon*. So let's fall into the "cryptic nothing" of the *Gorgias*, probing some potentially unintelligible moments in the text.

SOME VIEWS MADE POSSIBLE: INTERRUPTING THE *GORGIAS*

In the *Gorgias*, Socrates debates the nature, qualities, and political merits of rhetoric with three main interlocutors. First up is the sophist, teacher, and orator Gorgias, who has just finished giving "an admirable, varied presentation."[57] Gorgias is followed by two of his admirers: Polus and Callicles. Some readers of the dialogue—Bruno Latour, for instance—describe Socrates as "defeat[ing]" these interlocutors "one after the other: Gorgias, a bit tired from the lecture he has just given; Polus, a bit slow; and finally the harshest of the three, the famous and infamous Callicles."[58] I will return to Latour's reading later on—for now, I pause only to note that "defeat" may be too strong a word. Zeyl, for instance, claims that "Polus is reduced to silence (but not to consent) and *retires* from the discussion."[59] It's also worth noting that Polus seems to enter the dialogue by interrupting, jumping in before Gorgias can reply to one of Socrates's rejoinders and doing so with a frustrated, flustered, fractured utterance that begins, "Really, Socrates?" (461b). It thus seems questionable whether Gorgias is overcome by an antagonist or pushed aside by a would-be ally.

Until Polus's interjection, in fact, Gorgias seems comfortable playing along with Socrates, the only one of the interlocutors who takes any pleasure in the proceedings.⁶⁰ Though Socrates later enjoins Callicles not to "jest [*paizein*]" (500b), Gorgias seems to approach the affair with significantly less exasperation than his followers—not surprising given that, as we've seen in the "Encomium of Helen," he has a fondness for playthings.⁶¹ Again, then: that Gorgias is "defeated" seems questionable.

Callicles, like Polus and unlike Gorgias, enters the conversation with an expression of disbelief. After Socrates claims that suffering injustice is better than doing it, Callicles turns to Socrates's friend Chaerephon and asks, "Is Socrates in earnest about this or is he joking [*paizei*]?" (481b). Callicles repeats the question to Socrates himself, who doesn't offer a direct answer. It isn't until a bit later in their conversation that Socrates directly denies that he's dissembling. After he asks Callicles to "go easier on me in your teaching, so that I won't quit your school," Callicles replies, "You're being ironic [*eirōneuēi*], Socrates" (489d–e).⁶² Socrates dismisses the charge and turns it back on Callicles: "No I'm not, Callicles, by Zethus—the character you were invoking in being ironic with me so often just now!" (489e).

Whether Socrates's inversion of Callicles's accusation is itself ironic, however, remains unclear. After all, despite his claim to earnestness, Socrates seems subtly playful if not utterly obtuse when it comes to following the rhetorical rules he himself establishes for the dialogue. Take his request that Gorgias stick to "the short style of speech [*braxulogias*], and leave the long style [*makrologias*] for some other time" (449c). Gorgias, adaptable sophist that he is, consents and delivers. Socrates, however, violates his own precepts and speaks at greater length than any of his interlocutors. He's not entirely unaware of this twist, offering Polus the following justification: "Perhaps I've done an absurd thing: I wouldn't let you make long speeches, and here I've just composed a lengthy one myself. I deserve to be forgiven, though, for when I made my statements short you didn't understand and didn't know how to deal with the answers I gave you, but you needed a narration. So if I don't know how to deal with your answers either, you must spin out a speech, too. But if I do, just let me deal with them. That's only fair" (465e–466a).

In addition to troubling the limits of his self-imposed stylistic restrictions, Socrates is also slippery about what constitutes an admissible proof. Still speaking with Polus, Socrates says, "Whereas everyone but me agrees with you, you are all I need, although you're just a party of one, for your agreement and testimony. It's you alone whom I call on for a vote; *the others I disregard*" (475e–476a; emphasis added). Just a few lines earlier, however, Socrates pursues a line of argument by asking, "Now didn't the majority [*pollós*] of mankind [*anthropos*], and you earlier, agree with us that doing what's unjust is more shameful than suffering it?" (475d). Polus concurs, giving Socrates the assent of the only one that the gadfly claims to care about. But Socrates's subsequent claim that he "disregard[s]" the "others [*alius*]" is already undercut by this apparent appeal to a great deal of "others" ("the majority") that precedes his rejection of such appeals' legitimacy. Perhaps this is a playful demonstration that he can, by appealing to the *pollós*, beat Polus at his own game—that the "philosopher" is in fact better than the sophist at winning over both the one and the many. But if it is such a demonstration, it only contributes to the ironic undecidability of the dialogue, opening the question of whether we can trust Socrates's claims to earnestness in a dialogue in which he is ironically granted the very persuasive powers he projects onto the sophist.[63] Perhaps we could work around this problem by reading the appeal to the *pollós* of *anthropos* as an appeal to human *nature* (rather than majority *opinion*) that Plato's Socrates doesn't see as conflicting with the suspicion he expresses toward the "*demos* [people]" during his exchange with Callicles (481d). But at the very least, that would seem to validate Callicles's claim that Socrates is "slyly" manipulating the distinction between "terms of nature [*physis*]" and "terms of law [*nomos*]" for his own benefit, again throwing into question Socrates's status as *eiron* and/or *alazon* (483a). Who knows?

I'm posing the question "Who knows?" not as a rhetorical question—at least not in the usual sense of "rhetorical question." I ask it not to foreclose response but to explore some mutually inclusive possible responses. More specifically, the question is this: in the case of the *Gorgias*, who knows if or when Socrates is dissembling, ironically breaking his own rhetorical rules, and how do the fuzzy boundaries of that "who" bind or unbind the dialogue's rhetorical and pedagogical significance? Furthermore, how might this question complicate our sense of who's reading and who's getting read, who's teaching and who's learning, who's the sophist and who's the philosopher, who's the *eiron* and who's the *alazon*, over the course of the dialogue? Some possibilities:

(1) One could take the fairly traditional view that Plato knows and that he means for his Socrates to know as well. In other words, the author and his speaker are unified in understanding when and whether they're being ironic. We could take this to mean that a wise and wily Plato is deploying a similarly clever Socrates to outfox the sophists and thus prove philosophy's essential superiority. This would mean Callicles doesn't get it—that he's asking after Socrates's irony due to a sincere lack of understanding. In this case, it could even be Socrates's very sincerity that renders him the ironic master and Callicles the unwitting student: having "abandoned any hope of educating his listeners," he utilizes a "reverse irony," speaking sincerely in the understanding that those hapless listeners will be unable to hear his earnest views as anything other than ironic.[64] In such a reading, Socrates becomes either the *eiron* whose mastery never slips or the *alazon* whose simple wisdom topples Callicles, the pretentious *eiron*.

(2) Perhaps Plato, Socrates, *and* the interlocutors are in on it: Plato and his Socrates are playing a game *with* rather than *at* the expense of Callicles, Polus, and Gorgias. In this case, we can perhaps take the dialogue as one of the written "amusements" Plato's Socrates describes in the *Phaedrus*.[65] Socrates is jesting with Callicles when he asks him not to jest, Callicles is just jesting back, Gorgias is having a good time in the margins rather than growing incensed at the philosopher's insults, and so on.[66] In addition to the later *Phaedrus*, such a reading could resonate with George Kennedy's claim that in the "early dialogues" both Plato and his Socrates were, like Gorgias, "probably content to encourage debate and suspend final judgment."[67] It would also mesh with Plato's *Seventh Letter*, in which the writer claims that, of the "truth" of the matters with which he concerns himself, "No treatise by me concerning it exists or ever will exist."[68] We could shuffle the deck here a bit, presuming Gorgias is amused while Callicles and Polus are bemused or that Polus alone is left out in the cold.[69]

(3) Perhaps Plato gets it but means to situate everyone on the "inside" of the dialogue, Socrates included, as *alazons*. Imagine that Plato, like the writer of a sitcom episode, sets his characters off into a web of scrambled messages and miscommunications, with the supernatural "account [*logos*]" at the dialogue's end intended not as metaphysical Truth but as a means of rebuilding camaraderie in the wake of so many flared tempers.[70] In this case,

the dialogue's "lesson" might be similar to one that concludes another of Plato's early dialogues: at the end of the *Lysis*, the characters' failed attempt to find a stable and coherent philosophy of friendship is precisely what turns them all into bosom buddies.[71]

(4) Or one could switch pop-culture idioms: "Like the survivor of so many police films, Plato was set off by the murder of his partner."[72] Imagine Plato, after so many years on the beat, retired from his job policing the borders of the pedagogical, rhetorical, and philosophical. Finally understanding that—in the end—there's nothing to understand, he turns to writing dialogues that prefigure film noir scripts. In this case, perhaps it's Plato's *Callicles* who gets it, with his ominous, pragmatic warnings to Socrates—that clueless idealist—foreshadowing the philosopher's fate.[73] Plato's posthumous lesson: give up trying to track down transcendent truth. Look where that got my partner. No *eirons* or *alazons* here—just us nihilists.

(5) Additionally, one could invert the previous option, questioning intentionality by positioning Socrates as the *eiron* and Plato as the clueless *alazon* who never gets it. In other words, imagine Socrates shouting some lesson from the pages that the writer is somehow missing. Plato, following Socrates around and frantically marking down the teacher's words, misses the point or lack thereof. He is, like one of Franz Kafka's renditions of Abraham, "the class dummkopf . . . too dumb to know that he cannot be the smart one beckoned forth on this day."[74] Perhaps the "smart one" is Aristophanes, about whom more in a bit, and perhaps he's the smart one because (option 5b) he realizes that Plato and Socrates are *both* full of hot air.

(6) Finally, though not exhaustively, we could even question whether there's anything for the *reader* to get, whether the dialogue has any didactic or dialectical end. Reiterating Socrates's comments about writing in the *Phaedrus*, we could question whether Plato intends—though here we would again hit the limits of intentionality—for his writings to communicate *anything* to anyone else, or whether he is just "storing up reminders for himself 'when he reaches forgetful old age.'"[75] Is there any intended lesson for the *Gorgias*'s recipients, or is it just a cryptic entry in Plato's diary?

Who knows? Who ironizes and who's ironized? Who's learned and who learns? These myriad troubled interpretations also trouble such categorizations: every party involved "could swing on either side of the boundary," not only via oscillations over time but also via simultaneous doublings—a laughing at oneself that could be clever and/or stupid.[76]

AN ADDITIONAL IMPOSSIBILITY

The possibilities I've inscribed above—their proliferation gesturing toward the relative impossibility of ascribing one fixed meaning to the *Gorgias*—may seem too playful. Not only might I have ignored or misunderstood Socrates's request that his interlocutors refrain from jesting,[77] but maybe I need to remind myself that "irony is no joke."[78] Or perhaps playfulness is a way to resist slipping into flippancy. Perhaps I might otherwise end up like the "family of theoreticians" Jacques Derrida takes and sends up in *Limited Inc*: "The more they seek to produce serious utterances, the less they can be taken seriously. It is up to them whether they will take advantage of this opportunity to transform infelicity into delight [*jouissance*]. For example, by proclaiming: everything that we have said-written-done up to now wasn't really serious or strict; it was all a joke: sarcastic, even a bit ironic, parasitical, metaphorical, citational, cryptic, fictional, literary, insincere, etc."[79]

To expand on and test the limits of this playfulness, let's bounce it off the serious concerns Bruno Latour raises in his reading of the *Gorgias*: "Socrates' and Callicles' Settlement—or, The Invention of the Impossible Body Politic." For Latour, all the figures in and around the *Gorgias* are in on this "settlement," the consequences of which are no laughing matter for the *demos*. In his reading, the differences between Socrates and "the *straw* Callicles"—whom Latour opposes to "the *positive*, or the *historical*, or the *anthropological* Callicles"—only disguise a broader agreement: "the simple fact that they all wish to stand alone against the people."[80] Socrates and Callicles's shadowboxing diverts attention from "a *second* fight going on silently, off-stage, pitting the people of Athens, the ten thousand fools, against Socrates and Callicles, allied buddies, *agreeing on everything* and differing *only* about the swiftest means to silence the crowd."[81] Rather than displacing straw Callicles's claim that it's only natural for "the better man and the more capable man to have a greater share than the worse man and the less capable man,"[82] Latour sees the dialogue's proceedings as recruiting "Force," "Reason," "Morality," "Knowledge," and "Power" in the service of Plato's united Socrates and Callicles, and thus against the *demos*: "Professor Socrates writes on the blackboard his triumphant equation: Politics *plus* absolute morality *minus* practical means *equals* the Impossible Body Politic."[83] In Latour's reading, this equation of Plato's Socrates is a "political weapon" and "war cry" deployed to issue the command, "Keep your mouth shut!"[84] Latour forwards an alternative model of deliberation that, though he is primarily focused on scientific argument, he positions as relevant to the sorts of social and political controversies addressed in the *Gorgias*. It's a discussion-dependent model he aligns with extending access, "through experiments and calculations, to entities that do not at first have the same characters as humans."[85]

Latour sees this alternative as "the best and fastest way to free science from politics" and ironically argues that it finds its "clearest" definition in the *Gorgias*. Who offers this definition? According to Latour, "Socrates— and here I want to . . . make amends for having ironized so much at the expense of this master of irony" (an epithet that I hope has, by this point in this chapter, been rendered highly questionable).[86] Latour quotes the following lines from the Socrates of Plato's *Gorgias*: "In fact, Callicles, the experts' opinion is that co-operation, love, order, discipline, and justice *bind heaven and earth, gods and men*. That's why they call the universe an ordered whole, my friend, rather than a disorderly mess or an unruly shambles [*kai to olon touto dia tauta kosmon kalousin, ô etaire, ouk akosmian oude akolasian*]."[87]

Latour uses this quote to spin out a valorous agenda for scientific and social deliberation, "the task being to turn this collective [of humans and nonhuman 'entities'] into a 'cosmos' instead of an 'unruly shambles.'"[88] This task refuses the pernicious "acceleration" of scientific dogmatism and anti-democratic Platonism, with Latour arguing that "it has now been shown that instead of simply adding order," such acceleration "adds disorder as well."[89] He draws a link between his decelerated style of deliberation and "the conditions of felicity for the slow creation of a consensus in the harsh conditions of the agora," conditions that he hopes would allow controversies to be repositioned as "between 'unruly shambles' and 'cosmos'" rather than "descendants of Socrates against descendants of Callicles."[90]

But, as someone who's constantly undone by the "tropologically insecure nature of irony,"[91] let me offer a messy defense of what Latour calls "unruly shambles." The agora may be preferable to the exclusive violence of a politics powered by tyrannical capitals: Force, Reason, Knowledge, etc. Nevertheless, the agora was quite adept at instituting exclusions of its own: women, enslaved peoples, noncitizens, and gadflies all fared pretty poorly in its "harsh conditions." Though I find much to admire about the expansion of access that Latour advances, I hesitate when he links it to an "ordered whole." In pursuit of such a totality, Latour claims, "no shortcuts are possible, no short-circuits, and no acceleration." His pursuit of "order" proceeds slowly and carefully, then, but remains tied to a certain set of ends that seem too readily resonant with—were we to read the *Gorgias* in/as earnest—Socrates's obsession with all things "orderly."[92] I wonder whether one might instead linger and wander among the shambles, perhaps accounting for the inevitability of a different class of "short-circuits" (of understanding, of reason, of order itself) that so often lead to reactionary violence against those slapped with the label of "disorder"—those shambling along too slowly to keep up with even the decelerated pace of the agora. I'd ask, in short, how we might resist simply replacing Platonic tyranny with yet another (albeit slower) pursuit of order, how we might skid along behind the agora and its related institutions, perhaps picking up and dwelling with those others who've been deemed witless *alazons*, unwitting *eirons*, imprudent students, or cretinous teachers—those who can't, or prefer not to, or don't know how to keep up. It is in the detritus of orderly systems that we might catch up with the victims and followers of irony's disorderly conduct.

BURNING DOWN THE HOUSE

Let me follow Kierkegaard in letting Aristophanes come after and complicate Plato. Specifically, let's approach a loose ending by sticking our heads into Aristophanes's *Clouds*. The play opens with the laments of Strepsiades, an "old bumpkin" whose son, Phidippides, has a passion for horse racing.[93] That passion, Strepsiades gripes, has "infected [his] estate with the galloping trots," leaving him "eaten alive by . . . bills and stable fees and debts" (70, 13). Desperate, Strepsiades seeks to enroll his son in the "Thinkery" of Socrates. Socrates is here depicted as an inveterate "arch-sophist"[94] whose school is watched over by a chorus of apparently irreverent muses: the clouds (331–34). At the Thinkery, Strepsiades expects his son will receive a newfangled education allowing him to, in the spirit of the sophist Protagoras, make the weaker argument the stronger, and thus to talk his father's creditors out of collecting (94–99). When Phidippides refuses, dad enrolls instead. Socrates, who's gluing shoes on the feet of a flea when Strepsiades arrives, attempts to teach his new student all manner of abstruse knowledge (149–52). Strepsiades seems an inept pupil, though: he's forgetful and distracted, has a significant tendency toward non sequiturs, and forces Socrates's esoteric teachings into economic contexts. For instance, when Socrates asks whether he'd prefer to learn "measures, or rhythms, or words," Strepsiades replies, "I'll take the measures: the other day a corn dealer shorted me two quarts" (636–40). After using sophistic logic to take his student's cloak and turn him into an atheist, Socrates eventually expels the hopelessly exasperating Strepsiades, who can't seem to retain what he's supposed to have learned about grammar and declension—though he does display a momentary knack for dodging lawsuits (769–90).

But Strepsiades subsequently manages to convince Phidippides and Socrates to let the son enroll in the Thinkery instead (866–87). A contest between personified versions of conservative Stronger Argument and fashionable Weaker Argument ends with Stronger defeated, and so Strepsiades leaves his son in Weaker's pedagogical care (1105–10). When Phidippides returns from his studies, he provides his father with some newly strengthened weaker arguments against the family's creditors (1170–213). Strepsiades manages to run off two creditors—whether he "persuades" them seems doubtful—by deploying wildly incoherent and wayward reiterations of Socrates's and his son's arguments. He drives the first away, for instance, by returning to Socrates's lessons on the declension of nouns, claiming he "wouldn't repay a single penny to anyone who calls a morté a mortar" (1249–51). But then the scheme backfires, with Phidippides making and acting on arguments in favor of children beating their parents (1332–475). A scarified Strepsiades heads to the Thinkery and, in an act of destruction that ends the play, sets it on fire. As Socrates and his pupils suffocate and burn, Strepsiades justifies his actions, claiming, "They've got it coming many times over, but most of all for wronging the gods" (1504–9).

As Ian C. Storey points out, *Clouds* is something of an oddity among Aristophanes's works. Its "'down' ending" stands in contrast to his other plays, which usually wrap up with "general rejoicing."[95] Strepsiades himself is also an outlier: in some ways, he does fit the mold of Aristophanes's typical "comic hero, the old countryman who achieves his great idea and comes out on top."[96] But, pointing to the scene in which Socrates attempts and apparently fails to teach Strepsiades, Storey notes that "the scene depends on stretching the spectator's reactions in two opposite directions: he wants to be a *sophos* like Socrates, for (unlike Strepsiades) he knows about measures and rhythms, and at the same time wants to see the *sophos* taken down a rung or two. We admire Strepsiades' low cunning and desire not to pay his debts, but at the same time we wince at his essential dishonesty and insistence at learning . . . [Weaker] Argument. It can be observed that the 'great idea' is undone at the end, that . . . the play ends with destruction rather than jubilation and reconciliation."[97]

Storey chalks this up to the fact that *Clouds* itself was a loser: after it was ranked last at a theatrical festival, Aristophanes revised it, mocking his tasteless spectators in an updated parabasis and, Storey speculates, giving the play a darker ending.[98] In other words, Strepsiades is not necessarily, unlike some of Aristophanes's other "comic hero[es]," a common-sense *alazon* who gets the goat of a highfalutin *eiron*. He has his revenge on Socrates but doesn't seem to have learned anything. Is his credibility, not to mention the credibility of the gods and Stronger Argument, purified in the flames of the burning Thinkery? An open question.

Given the account of irony offered above, perhaps Strepsiades is neither *alazon* nor *eiron*. Perhaps his role is—if I may say so—irony itself: He gets the first word in the play, interrupting all the other characters before they can begin to speak. He learns Socrates's lessons, but only to fragment them in wildly irrational ways that shatter the teacher's educational and rhetorical protocols—ways that "give a sound beating to a language that closes in on itself."[99] And in the end, the beaten and broken rube suddenly manifests the play's final act of destruction, burning the house of thought and its questionable inhabitants to the ground. Irony proves uncontrollable, abusing its Socratic master rather than getting used in that master's service. And so the unfigurable student gets the last word, which might be serious and might be a laugh, as well.

If, as teachers, we were to imagine ourselves in the place of an Aristophanic Socrates, laid low by a hapless pupil previously dismissed as stupid, what (if anything) might we learn from irony's violence? Perhaps we should have attuned ourselves to it earlier. Perhaps Socrates would have succeeded with Strepsiades if he'd been more considerate of the latter's speechifying rather than proclaiming, "To hell and be damned with you, you oblivious, moronic old coot!"—if he'd accepted the purported fool's responses as inventive interruptions, as openings for further response, rather than aberrations in need of foreclosure.[100] (After all, in other iterations of Socrates's story, it is precisely his unwillingness or inability to respond in the proper register that gets him killed.) Perhaps he could have even made room for this intractable dunce alongside the Thinkery's more facile pupils, opened a space for disorder—a place for an out-of-place student—and thus saved the rest from going up in smoke along with the teacher. At the very least, listening for Strepsiades might have allowed a cannier Socrates to hear his destruction coming, leaving time to clear everyone out before the Thinkery burned down.

Or perhaps we always expect the unexpected too late, only recognizing irony's unmasterable disaster after the fact, and the most Socrates could have done would have been to take action in the wake of a disaster that "is . . . always already past."[101] Following the lead of the historical Socrates's accusers, he could have organized his surviving students and marched to Strepsiades's door, demanding recompense and declaring himself Strepsiades's new creditor or roasting Strepsiades to even the score.

In short, it may be that irony's arrival never gives us the chance to be a good host and extend hospitality. It renders us, rather, a pedagogical hostage, stuck following after it rather than leading it or using it to lead—thus interrupting one etymological sense of "pedagogue," the one who leads (*agogos*) the child (*pais*). In terms of pedagogical authority, then, what I'm after is a "Socratic irony" that isn't used by a masterful Socratic figure to lead students into orderly anamnesis and a deferral of deliberative authority to the teacher, but that disorders and deauthorizes teacher and student alike. It is a linguistic violence to be weathered by us all even as it leads us to question the limits of such categories as "us" and "all."

All this may seem to have come entirely unglued from the pedagogical exigencies faced by teachers today, so let me tie it to something more apparently concrete. In *Teaching Community*, writer and educator bell hooks recounts the following:

> When the tragic events of 9/11 occurred it was as though, in just a few moments in time, all our work to end domination in all its forms, all our pedagogies of hope, were rendered meaningless as much of the American public . . . responded with an outpouring of . . . patriarchal rage against terrorists defined as dark-skinned others. . . . Even though I could walk to the sites of the 9/11 tragedy, I was not able to speak about these events for some time because I had come face-to-face with the limits of what I know. . . . What I knew, the limits of my knowing, was defined by information in

alternative mass media and by the boundaries of what I experienced, of all that I witnessed. That's all I could account for. Anything more would have been interpretations of interpretations offered me by a media whose agenda I hold suspect.[102]

Though hooks is specifically critiquing the rush to craft a comprehensible, reactionary narrative in the wake of 9/11, I would like to trace out some broader implications from her reflections. The drive to fight fire with fire, whether in the interpretations hooks describes or in hypothetical extensions of the *Clouds*, is a powerful one. It is in many ways an understandable response to events that shatter the limits of understanding: a refusal to admit and dwell with the fact that one has "come face-to-face with the limits" of knowledge, with a disaster we cannot simply experience or coherently account for. And it is here that I wonder about the interruptive, humbling, humiliating possibilities of a Socratic irony that would not seek to dissemble, to play on "unknown knowns" and "unknown unknowns" in order to preemptively justify the authority of patriarchal figures and render students and the rest of the *demos* ignorant of or unable to take responsibility for deliberative response in the wake of irony's disasters. And this is not just about such obviously horrifying events as 9/11, or the more recent mass shootings, pandemics, climate disasters, and other devastating events that defy attempts to teach and think through, around, and about them. It is also, I would argue, about the hundreds of moments that test the limits of us, of students, and of our discourses every day, even when, mercifully, the day doesn't involve literal fire. Irony might arrive as a grammar "error" in a student paper that, if responded to and not simply struck out, reveals rhetorical possibilities we had yet to consider;[103] or as an interruptive comment in a class discussion that might disfigure our conceptions of students, ourselves, and educational decorum but, if left to unfold rather than being ejected from the realm of what's allowed, could generate a moment of pedagogical hospitality—a welcoming of the Other's expression that "means: to be taught."[104]

But let me be clear: this does not mean irony is readily recuperated in the form of constructive, satisfying pedagogical moments. These interruptive moments can bear the mark of cruelty, of disorientation; they do not simply regrant teachers an ironically mediated authority or teach the ironic lesson that students are better, more thoughtful teachers than us if only we'll free them from the constraints of traditional classroom structures (though such possibilities might occasionally be the case). Consider an anecdote Sharon Crowley recalls near the end of her book *Composition in the University*: After receiving "the worst teaching evaluations of [her] career," she was informed by a female student that a number of white male students in her class had "felt silenced" by what they perceived as their teacher's feminism. Writes Crowley,

> I was angry . . . that this matter was not brought to my attention while class was in progress. . . . I would have liked the opportunity to discuss their feeling of being silenced, with the men themselves and with the class as a whole. . . . [T]heir commentary after the fact elided discussion of the entire issue of gender relations and teacherly authority. . . . These young men did not like being in a class where an old woman had opinions, expressed them with force, and was, to boot, their professor. There is absolutely nothing I can do about this particular ideological construction—except to challenge it.[105]

Both Crowley and the male students experienced at least one interruption here. For the students, it was the experience of feeling silenced by one they did not think should have the authority to do so—an aberration in the patriarchal pedagogical structures they expected and were perhaps used to inhabiting. For Crowley, it was the after-the-fact interruption in her perception of the class, which she was forced to reevaluate in the wake of these students' evaluations. But whereas Crowley expresses a willingness to respond in the wake of this rhetorical volley—to converse about "gender relations and teacherly authority,"[106] to, in Levinasian terms, "approach the Other in conversation"[107] in the wake of interruption—the students chose a rhetorical mode that rendered them unresponsive and irresponsible. They chose to respond to feeling as though they'd been rendered passive by taking an action that rebounded passivity upon their professor *without* the chance of further conversation, choosing the freedom of "remaining the same in the midst of the other" rather than leaving space for further conversation.[108]

Some readers might interpret this situation otherwise: it's not that the students were being irresponsible; it's that, in a situation in which they possessed relatively less power by virtue of their position as students, they were responding via an anonymized procedure that protects them from a teacher's retribution. However, several factors complicate the professor's relative power in such a situation: the well-documented gender biases of student evaluations, the dubious quality of such evaluations in even the most ideal and purportedly unbiased conditions, and the role that evaluations—despite these biases and other demonstrable flaws—continue to play when it comes to hiring, retention, and promotion decisions in higher education.[109] While Crowley's authority might have been palpable enough to make these students feel silenced, that authority was far from unqualified, as indicated by the Strepsiadian burn of the evaluations themselves.

Given the frequency with which such events unfold, I am glad that there were protections in place—tenure, for example—that shielded Crowley from evaluators to whom she could not respond. This is not only because of the aforementioned problems with student evaluations but also because of the disproportionate rate at which teachers who bear the brunt of those problems, including women and faculty of color, lack such institutional protections.[110] In other situations, I am glad there are structures—for instance, Title IX—that afford students protections of their own. The sort of irony I'm tracking here doesn't call for the reactionary demolition of such things, which could amount to an inhumane call for precarity for all. Rather, it reminds us that such protections are never as authoritative as we might assume. That is not to say they shouldn't be questioned, with institutional policies and procedures shored up until they are impervious to the vagaries of teachers and students alike. But it offers a caution in light of a widespread tendency in the other direction: the weakening of protections on the assumption that teacherly authority and student agency tend toward order rather than, as the history of education has frequently shown, teetering on the brink of shambles. One person's stultifying educational bureaucracy is another person's life-sustaining infrastructure, so navigating the tension between imperfect institutions and idealized alternatives requires careful work, not simple disruption or destruction.[111]

For that and other reasons, I don't share the conviction that "[educational] bureaucracy . . . is the enemy of liberation," even when the point is made in good-faith defenses of student agency and critical pedagogy to which I am in other respects sympathetic.[112] A kneejerk fear of bureaucracy too readily slides into a totalizing opposition to infrastructure. As I will argue in subsequent chapters, such opposition can feed and resonate with hasty arguments for destroying institutions that support students and teachers in meaningful though imperfect ways rather than careful critiques that point to the ways institutions can better support those to and for whom they are responsible. To give just one example, I am grateful that universities have Americans with Disabilities Act compliance offices, even if some faculty may see such offices as evidence of administrative bloat and even though the work of such offices is too meager in both practice and theory.[113] Replacing protections that do not or cannot sufficiently respond to the needs of those they serve with more responsible ones is complex work, even at the level of a single university.

At their best, the kinds of educational safeguards for which I'm advocating do not simply protect the irresponsible, the coddled, or the already over-protected, as various advocates of defunding, deregulating, or otherwise "disrupting" public education argue—though institutions might occasionally err in the direction of excessive care. They hold open space for response, for extending some small assurance in anticipation and the wake of irony's attacks, not imposing order but pursuing pedagogical hospitality in the face of the shambles. And they will, inevitably, break down and break up at some moment or other. At their best, they foster perhaps nothing more and nothing less than room for one to be stupefied, to admit without recuperation the limits of one's ability to understand and offer an account. In resisting authoritarian attempts to institute supposedly unquestionable structures, they might allow a teacher to aver without certainty the limits of their understanding, to dwell with disorder and otherness and engage students in conversation so that they might do the same, perhaps with the humble, unmasterable realization that the teacher's position *as* authoritative master is eminently undoable. What would it mean to safeguard educational institutions not as places where teachers and students grow more certain, more orderly, more authoritative and agentive, but as places of protection among and for the incessantly uncertain? Within such places, the teacher's authority could be, in the wake of violence, nothing more than a relentlessly responsible resistance, a hesitance, in the face of unqualified agency or authority. We might find ourselves, ironically, systemically unmastered together. Perhaps.

CHAPTER 2

An Exercise in Rhetorical Unmastery

In Dido's place. But I am not Dido.

—HÉLÈNE CIXOUS

Let me begin this chapter with a brief discussion of its structure. In terms of content, this chapter continues chapter 1's treatment of pedagogical authority and sets up the arguments about student agency that occupy the book's second half. Bearing that in mind, readers acclimated to the conventions of academic writing might expect this chapter to spend a little more time on theoretical and historical arguments about teachers' authority before concluding with a few practical pedagogical applications based on those arguments. From there, I could make a clean pivot to agency in the second half of the book. Or, some might expect, this will be yet another theoretically focused chapter that will ultimately lead to practical pedagogical takeaways in the book's second half. Either move would serve as an organizational performance of the widespread assumption that scholarship moves from theory to practice—in other words, that scholarly work begins with theoretical and experimental pursuits that lead the way to practical knowledge and application. This sense of linear movement informs popular attitudes about the purpose of university research and teaching (just consider the public skepticism often directed at academic disciplines that aren't seen as generating practical payoffs) as well as the structure of academic writing.

In the particular case of rhetoric and writing studies, this linearity manifests itself in a well-documented feature of the field's scholarship: the pedagogical turn.[1] Rhetoric and writing studies scholars often spend the earlier sections of a published work explicating a theory, then conclude by turning toward pedagogy (i.e., offering a pedagogical application of that theory). The implications of the move, I would argue, are at least twofold: (1) practical application is the appropriate end goal of theoretical work; (2) practical application should be based on theory. In other words, theory and practice are inseparable partners. Theory is the journey without which the destination couldn't be reached, and practice is the destination without which the journey would be inconsequential. I don't think those implications are without merit. In fact, rhetoric and writing studies' emphasis on pedagogy was one of the things that drew me to the field in the first place. I appreciated and continue to appreciate that, unlike disciplines that position teaching as ancillary to research, rhetoric and writing studies has an established history of treating teaching as a meaningful scholarly pursuit in its own right. For that reason, I am not interested in simply renouncing the pedagogical turn or denigrating research that offers pedagogical applications. However, I do want to highlight and challenge a structural implication of the pedagogical turn I think *is* worth questioning: that research is a process of increasing certainty. That is, the structure of published scholarly work that deploys a pedagogical turn suggests that early theoretical questions and hypotheses, even if attended by caveats and hesitations, give way to relatively certain pedagogical and practical outcomes.

For readers used to the pedagogical turn, or the broader assumption that practice is theory's ultimate end, this chapter's structure may seem idiosyncratic—hence this careful introduction. Instead of starting with theoretical and historical investigations that build toward pedagogical application, I lead with a pedagogical anecdote and spend the rest of the chapter alternating between theory, history, and pedagogy. I do so as a way of illustrating the responsive relation between theory and pedagogy that characterizes the everyday experiences of teachers.[2] That is, while those of us who teach rhetoric and writing may do so in ways that are informed by particular theories, principles, and convictions, these are not unshakable foundations upon which our pedagogical practices are built. For my part, I find that my experiences in the classroom unsettle my theories at least as often as encountering theoretical work leads me to rethink my pedagogy.

It is a decidedly nonlinear process that persistently unsettles my sense of teacherly authority, one that does not necessarily lead to greater certainty so much as a relentless questioning within which moments of crystallization are fleeting and contingent.

In short, this is an extension of chapter 1's attempts to rethink teacherly authority en route to a related rethinking of student agency. But rather than drawing certain conclusions that follow from chapter 1, I perform the fractured account of pedagogical authority laid out in my consideration of Socratic irony. I twist and turn as a way of showing how theory and pedagogy, student and teacher, authority and agency *respond* to each other—nonlinearly and often interruptively—and in doing so call attention to the limits of pedagogical mastery and the indispensable role of responsibility in our attempts to theorize and enact authority in educational spaces.

In the following section, I describe a pedagogical exercise I assigned in a past class. This chapter thus exists in the realm of autocritique, calling my own inscriptions into question under the assumption that, as a Levinas-inspired Jacques Derrida puts it, "one is never responsible enough"—not even when one bears this fact in mind.[3] Derrida's work frequently recalls Maurice Blanchot's description of writing as a "double movement": "To write is to be absolutely distrustful of writing, while entrusting oneself to it entirely."[4] Both Derrida and the figure of the "double bind" are referenced in the first lines of Gayatri Chakravorty Spivak's essay "Translation as Culture." Spivak opens the body of that essay as follows: "In every possible sense, translation is necessary but impossible."[5] She later reiterates the point by writing, "Translation is . . . not only necessary but unavoidable. . . . The ethical task is never quite performed."[6] Spivak is primarily focused on the ways that standard, officially sanctioned languages run roughshod over marginalized idioms, and she ends by calling for a dictionary that "translat[es] from idiom to standard even as it resists the necessary impossibility of translation."[7] According to Spivak, such a dictionary would, for instance, enable speakers of "subaltern" varieties of Bengali to learn standard Bengali. It would also, however, require its writer(s) to listen painstakingly to the "irreducible importance of idiom," not presuming the existence of ready-made reciprocal terms that would facilitate the lossless translation of idiom into standard and vice versa.[8] In a subsequent essay, Spivak elaborates further on the ethical task of the translator: "The translator should make an attempt to grasp the writer's presuppositions. . . . Grasping the writer's presuppositions ... is what Jacques Derrida ... calls entering the protocols of a text—not the general laws of the language, but the laws specific to *this* text. And this is why it is my sense that translation is the most intimate act of reading, a prayer to be haunted."[9]

In a few senses, the nonlinear pursuits of this chapter resonate with Spivak's approach to "translation." First, it is an attempt to translate back and forth between the idioms of pedagogy and theory, and while it is true that those two discourses share intertwined histories and are not purely discrete, neither one can be entirely reduced to the other's terms. Second, the exercise I'm about to introduce is an exercise in something akin to translation—specifically, an exercise in imitation that asks student writers to attend to "the laws specific to *this* [i.e., a particular] text," to practice a certain sort of translation while bearing in mind the "necessary impossibility of translation." A rhetorical and ethical conundrum I dwell on throughout this chapter: be they teacher or student, the writer-translator, who is never *not* translating, citing, imitating, is never responsible enough.[10]

A PEDAGOGICAL TURN

In Fall 2013, I taught a section of Banned Books and Novel Ideas, an undergraduate course offered by the Department of English at The University of Texas at Austin. At the time, the course was typically taught by PhD students and served two audiences and purposes. For the general student body, the course was one way to fulfill a university-wide "Writing Flag" requirement. For English majors, it served as an introduction to the major. The course was intended to teach both audiences to read, write, and revise formal, historical, and cultural literary criticism.[11]

As the course's title indicates, Banned Books and Novel Ideas focused on controversial texts. My iteration of the course put particular emphasis on the rhetorical dimensions of book bans and challenges. After a preliminary unit on debates around both contemporary textbooks and a 2010 Arizona bill that banned schools from teaching "ethnic studies," students read Aristophanes's *Clouds*, a selection from Plato's *Republic*, J. K. Rowling's *Harry Potter and the Sorcerer's Stone,* selections from Gloria Anzaldúa's *Borderlands / La Frontera*, Alison Bechdel's graphic narrative *Fun Home*, Ralph Ellison's *Invisible Man*, and secondary sources detailing controversies around those texts.[12] In concert with *Fun Home*, for instance, students read coverage of ongoing disputes surrounding the book's assignment in under-graduate courses at both the College of Charleston and the University of South Carolina Upstate—disputes that eventually led the South Carolina legislature to threaten to cut both institutions' funding.[13]

Fun Home was one of the texts with which students and I engaged most extensively in the course. As Bechdel herself describes it, the book is "about my childhood growing up with my closeted gay (or possibly bisexual) dad [Bruce Bechdel]. He was a high-school English teacher who was obsessed with interior design and spent all his free time restoring and redecorating our Gothic Revival house. He also worked as a funeral director at the family funeral home in the small Pennsylvania town where we lived."[14]

Combining meticulously illustrated panels with dialogue and retrospec-tive narrative commentary, *Fun Home* is an intricate text: Bechdel modeled the book's structure on the labyrinthine and ornate arrangement of the house in which she grew up. She interlaces copious and often subtle refer-ences to Greek mythology, lesbian literature, the novels of James Joyce, and contemporary political events in a text that blurs lines between a number of genres. In a 2011 interview, Bechdel claimed that "removing one word [from *Fun Home*] would be like pulling on a thread that unravels the whole sweater."[15]

Given the intricacy of *Fun Home*'s weave, I developed writing assign-ments that required students to engage slowly and carefully with Bechdel's book and its myriad media, voices, and temporal layers. In addition to an annotated bibliography and a conventional piece of literary criticism, I gave students the following writing assignment, which was one of six four-hundred-word "mini-papers" they wrote for the course:

> This mini-paper asks you to take on the voices of Bruce and Alison Bechdel—to try to engage and imitate *Fun Home*'s language care-fully. Your assignment is to imagine the conversation that Alison and her father might have had if they weren't turned away from the bar on page 223.[16] Don't speculate in your voice—write the dialogue that Alison Bechdel speculates "might have been [their] Circe chap-ter" (223).[17] You have evidence of both characters' writing and language habits from the book (Alison's diaries, her father's letter on page 224, etc.), so do your research and try to imitate the tone and voice of the characters. Keep in mind, however, that Alison the

narrator is not identical to Alison the drawn character, that the style in which her father speaks to her is not identical to the style in which he writes, and so on. Your primary task here is to try to be faithful to Bechdel's characterization of their personalities and relationship.

When class began the day the mini-papers were due, I gave students a supplemental task: add three footnotes to your mini-paper, pinpointing specific evidence from *Fun Home* that you used to make three particular rhetorical decisions in the exercise.

From my perspective, those mini-papers constituted some of the most creatively and critically engaged writing the students did all semester. Impersonating Bechdel and her father gave students a sense of responsibility to and for both *Fun Home* and the exercise that, in a class discussion about the exercise, one student described as simultaneously pleasurable and challenging. This combination of pleasure and difficulty, as evinced by students' footnotes, made for four-hundred-word exercises that were arguably more engaged and thoughtful than the standard two-thousand-word critical papers students turned in at the end of the semester. That's not to deride those final papers. Rather, it is to emphasize that the imitation exercise generated a sense of responsibility that in many ways exceeded the sense of responsibility generated by a more traditional critical assignment. I believe I witnessed students' attempts at "entering the protocols of a text . . . the laws specific to *this* text."[18] In short, the experience made me understand why imitation exercises were a mainstay of rhetorical education for centuries.

But a narrative of pedagogical success is not the end of the story, nor was success the end of the exercise. In truth, it was one of the assignments from that course with which I was most uncomfortable, of which I remain most uncertain. To explain my uncertainty, let me turn now to the complicated history of imitation exercises and some of the rhetorical and ethical baggage they bring to the contemporary pedagogical scene.

LEFT TO HISTORY

In recent decades, numerous scholars have argued for ancient rhetoric's relevance to contemporary writing instruction.[19] Many such scholars have concentrated on the *progymnasmata*, a sequence of exercises that was long a prevalent component of rhetorical education.[20] Specifically, the *progymnasmata* were preliminary exercises designed to prepare students for declamation, a fully realized oration that was a sort of capstone project in many schools of rhetoric.[21] Young students began with simpler tasks (e.g., explicating a proverb), then moved on to more complicated exercises (e.g., proposing a law) that incorporated skills developed in earlier ones. In proposing a law, for instance, a student might deploy commonly accepted proverbs to strengthen their case by aligning it with conventional bits of cultural wisdom. On the whole, *progymnasmata* exercises were structured and sequenced to help students gradually develop a rhetorical dexterity that would make them masterful declaimers, orators, and writers, both in the classroom and in their subsequent public and professional lives.

Among the *progymnasmata*, an exercise called *ethopoeia* or *prosopopoeia* has attracted particular attention from present-day rhetoricians, and it is this exercise on which I modeled the mini-paper described above.[22] Aphthonius the Sophist's treatise on the *progymnasmata*, which was written around the fourth century CE and resurfaced as an influential pedagogical text in early modern Europe, breaks *ethopoeia* down as follows: "Ethopoeia (*êthopoiia*) is imitation of the character of a proposed speaker. There are three different forms of it: apparition-making (*eidôlopoiia*), personification (*prosôpooiia*), and characterization (*êthopoiia*)."[23] Within Aphthonius's framework, the *Fun Home* exercise would fall in the subcategory of *ethopoeia*. However, in an earlier progymnasmatic treatise attributed to the rhetorician Aelius Theon, the term *prosopopoeia* is used as a comprehensive term for all imitation exercises.[24] Because it resonates with other modern meanings of *prosopopoeia* (i.e., a rhetorical device by which a writer or character speaks in the voice of someone or something else), I use *prosopopoeia* and the plural *prosopopoeiae* throughout this chapter.

Libanius's *Progymnasmata*—a collection of sample exercises from the fourth, fifth, and sixth centuries CE—includes a number of *prosopopoeiae*. The samples include speeches written in the voices of both specific mythological and historical figures (e.g., "What words would Chiron say when he hears that Achilles is living in the girls' quarters?," "What words would Odysseus say to the Cyclops when he sees him eating his comrades?") and more generic stock characters (e.g., "What words would a money-loving coward say upon finding a golden sword?," "What words would a eunuch say when he falls in love?").

Though the *progymnasmata* emerged in the centuries during which Aelius Theon, Libanius, and Aphthonius wrote, the sequence remained a staple of rhetorical education in the English Renaissance. As Lynn Enterline argues in *Shakespeare's Schoolroom, prosopopoeia* fit especially well with the emphasis Renaissance humanist educators placed on "*imitatio*—the demand that boys imitate the schoolmaster's facial movements, vocal modulation, and bodily gestures as much as his Latin words and texts."[25] *Prosopopoeiae* were a key part of this "new pedagogical method of constant imitation," which humanist schoolmasters claimed "would benefit the English commonwealth and grant Latin initiates a certain degree of upward mobility."[26]

As Enterline tells it, *imitatio* was intended to make students love and identify with their schoolmasters, turning boys into little masters who would uphold the principles of Renaissance humanism. Training students in the norms and prejudices of English masculinity was of particular concern: "A cruel misogyny . . . inform[s] many school textbooks, which often distinguish a boy's coddling mother from the bracing discipline of his Latin schoolmaster. . . . [I]t does not take exhaustive research to show how profoundly the linguistic and rhetorical basis of the school's curriculum influenced commonplace, dismissive views about female inferiority."[27]

In short, the pedagogical practices of *imitatio* in general and *prosopopoeia* in particular were meant not only to shape a student's "grammatical abilities" and rhetorical aptitude but to have a strong influence on "the formation of his character."[28] Students imitated exemplary figures—from Cicero to Achilles to the birch-wielding man at the front of the class—as a means of developing their own masterfully masculine, classically inflected humanist character.

But as Enterline goes on to argue, the pedagogical program of "humanist rhetorical master[s]" was not as rigid and unbending as those masters hoped: "literary and school texts . . . reveal a deep, unstable conflict at the heart of the very regime of identity and difference (between girls and boys, mother and father tongues, vulgar and learned) that its avatars worked so hard to install."[29] As evidence, she notes both "the widespread practice of cross-dressing" in Renaissance schools and the commonality of "female personifications"—*prosopopoeiae* that required students to imitate not male exemplars but "Lady Peace, Lady Quietness, Dame Tranquility, Ecclesia, Veritas, and Heresy."[30]

Marjorie Curry Woods makes a similar claim regarding the Middle Ages: women, particularly women who had just suffered some sort of emotional and physical trauma, were common subjects for medieval *prosopopoeiae*. Woods notes that the *Aeneid*'s Dido, who stabs herself atop a funeral pyre after being abandoned by her husband Aeneas, "was the most famous of these, but equally indicative of schoolboy experiences were Niobe, Juno, and Hecuba."[31] Like Enterline, Woods points to the prevalence of cross-dressing in pedagogical environments. In both the Middle Ages and the Renaissance, it was common for schoolboys to put on plays that required some pupils to play female characters. In these contexts, in fact, boys portraying women was not seen as a noteworthy dramatic accomplishment. The challenge, as Linda Phyllis Austern observes, was boys playing *men*: "At the most basic levels of psychology and physiology, a large number of Renaissance thinkers noted the specific similarities between boys' and women's underdeveloped masculinity, for the true distinction in this patriarchal society was not between the sexes but between fathers and children."[32] In this tradition, Woods explains, "shared powerlessness at the hands of adult men created the possibility of imagined empathy between women and boys."[33]

Woods and Enterline acknowledge both empathy *and* misogyny, conformity *and* nonconformity to conventional gender roles, as possible outcomes of schoolboys' imitation of women, whether such imitation was performed on the stage in the context of a play or in the classroom in the context of *prosopopoeia*. Woods follows her point about the "possibility of imagined empathy between women and boys" with a troubling alternative: noting that the imitation of women generally occurred in male-only spaces, she writes, "I suspect that, rather than encouraging an understanding of empathy with 'real' women, such nostalgic feelings may have furthered male bonding and gender differentiation among adults."[34] Following a close examination of Geoffrey Chaucer's *Legend of Good Women*, she observes that "all-male environments were often famously hostile to women; responding to fictional women who had been mistreated by adult men did not translate into sympathy with adult women outside the classroom."[35] However, in another piece, Woods ends on a less pessimistic note. After acknowledging that the *prosopopoeiae* assigned to and written by premodern students "reinforce[d] traditional, conventional types of characters and appropriate behavior and expression," Woods argues,

For the modern student, such an exercise can function very differently. During the Middle Ages, students were usually of one age, gender, and cultural background. Today they are not. Exercises in which students rewrite or refocus canonical texts are especially important in today's diverse, multicultural, and postcolonial classrooms. When students are allowed to choose the character in whose voice they will speak, the assignment offers them a chance to change, or at least to challenge, the political and social implications of canonical texts produced in eras with values very different from our own. For example, a student may express [themself] as a woman not to reinforce traditional ways of thinking about women, but in order to challenge those very traditions.[36]

She concludes by noting that while historical classrooms are often analyzed in terms of "the weight of dominant ideology" in the power relations between teachers and students, "the tradition of such exercises reminds us that the classroom always has been a place, not just of repression, but also of possible escape and transformation."[37]

Enterline's line of argument in *Shakespeare's Schoolroom* shares points of commonality with Woods's claim, likewise emphasizing "possible escape and transformation" over "the weight of dominant ideology." Though she foregrounds the "cruel misogyny" of humanist pedagogy, Enterline dwells at greater length on the supplementary possibility that "the distinction between genders central to humanist claims for their curriculum's social efficacy did not always survive a boy's experience of that institution's material practices."[38] In psychoanalytic readings of the plays of Shakespeare and the compositions of Renaissance schoolboys, Enterline repeatedly emphasizes that "school training in Latin rhetoric," which she notes operated hand in hand with corporal punishment, "inculcated something one could call a *habit of alterity*, even though its teachers probably did not anticipate some of the directions in which a talent for impersonating other voices would lead."[39] In other words, the schoolmaster's masculine mastery and authority, which school training was meant to extend to young "master[s] in the making," did not always or only result in the "seamless production of rhetorically capable 'gentlemen' with a univocally 'male' *ego*."[40] Rather, Enterline argues, this training installed in the student "a circuitous route to experiencing one's own feelings," rerouting the student's affect through a series of rhetorical and ethical detours.[41] Enterline thus argues that humanist rhetorical education produced divided subjects—"gentlemen" whose self-mastery, no matter how vigorously and repeatedly proclaimed, was always unsettled by the "habit of alterity" that rhetorical training in *imitatio* and *prosopopoeia* also inscribed in and on students.

A RETURN TO PEDAGOGY

Let me begin this return by restating a pair of tensions considered so far in this chapter. Scattered across the preceding sections, I draw them together here to illustrate the intertwined theoretical, historical, pedagogical, and ethical issues at play in the *Fun Home* imitation exercise I described earlier.

First, there are Spivak's claims that "in every possible sense, translation is necessary but impossible" and that, moreover, "translation is . . . not only necessary but unavoidable."[42] While Spivak's primary focus is on the ethical and linguistic complications that attend attempts to translate "idiomatic" varieties of Bengali into the established "standard," I'm echoing her claims as a way of thinking about the issues of "translating" back and forth between rhetoric's idioms—pedagogical, historical, theoretical—in addition to the work involved in *prosopopoeia*. Already, then, there is slippage between Spivak's points and the context in which I'm taking those points up. Yes, the discourses of rhetorical theory and rhetorical education might be said to exist in a sort of ideological imbalance. In some contexts, theoretical work is prioritized over the pedagogical by virtue of its affiliation with more traditional notions of scholarly production and intellectual rigor. In others, it is devalued for its supposed density and wanton complexity, with pedagogical discourses prioritized by virtue of their more immediate applicability. As someone with affinity for both theoretical and pedagogical research and practices, I know that, depending on my audience, discussing either might get me knowing nods or furrowed brows. But while theoretical and pedagogical discourses are far from identical, the distinction and the challenges involved in translating between them is more ambivalent than the historically hierarchical relations between "standard" and "subaltern" dialects, including the varieties of Bengali to which Spivak attends.[43] And yet, because I think Spivak's observations about the necessary impossibility of translation speak, if indirectly, to rhetoric's Western manifestations, I am working to translate them while acknowledging that "the ethical task is never quite performed."[44]

Second, there is the tension between what Enterline calls a "habit of alterity" and the tropes and habits of mastery that drove humanist education in Renaissance England—a tension that resonates with the tensions between empathy and misogyny, identification and exclusion, articulated in both Enterline's and Woods's historical research. According to Enterline, a habit of alterity was an unmasterable excess produced in students by humanist schoolmasters' methods. That is, while this habit ran counter to the intended outcomes of the imitative pedagogical practices her book describes, it was also *produced* by these practices—an unavoidable interruption in the programs of authoritative mastery that humanist schoolmasters sought both to embody and to inculcate.

As mentioned above, I am interested in imitation exercises as a way of having students engage with what Spivak calls the protocols or "laws specific to *this* [i.e., a particular] text"—in the case of the exercise I'm discussing here, the protocols specific to *Fun Home*—without thinking those protocols can be reinscribed with perfect responsibility, mastered and repeated without loss or slippage. One could say that I'm interested in swapping an emphasis on mastery for Enterline's "habit of alterity," foregrounding an unmasterable rhetorical excess rather than a graspable rhetorical dexterity.

As Woods points out, however, contemporary rhetoricians working in college and university settings are dealing with very different institutional contexts, social surroundings, and student bodies than those with which medieval rhetoricians dealt—thus her argument for imitation exercises that offer contemporary students a chance to "change, or at least to challenge, the political and social implications of canonical texts produced in eras with values very different from our own."[45] The *Fun Home* exercise engages these contextual changes from a different angle. While it is arguably becoming something like a canonical text in some arenas, the challenges *Fun Home* has received from the likes of the South Carolina legislature illustrate that its story is far from "dominant ideology."[46] As Ann Cvetkovich argues, *Fun Home* occupies the fringes even of the dominant threads of "LGBTQ politics," offering an "alternative to public discourses about LGBTQ politics that are increasingly homonormative and dedicated to family values."[47]

In asking students to imitate *Fun Home*, then, my motivation was not to have them "change" or "challenge" the dominant values of a canonical text but to dwell with the voices and relationships portrayed in a text that receives frequent challenges because of its perceived "values"—a memoir, moreover, that is ambivalent about the values of even its own "characters." To return again to Spivak, I was asking students to "be haunted" by "the protocols of a text," to "attempt to grasp the writer's presuppositions."[48] And yet the very notion of "grasping" is also something I was asking students to resist. On one hand, I wanted them to be as careful in composing their *prosopopoeiae* as Bechdel was in composing *Fun Home*, and in so doing to attempt to understand the book, its composer, and those who populate its pages. On the other, I didn't want to suggest that a meticulous approach to imitating *Fun Home* would mean they'd mastered it, gotten to its essential core. I had at least two motives for doing so.

The first motive was largely a matter of feeling: I felt obligated to protect *Fun Home* because of its social and historical context as well as the protocols Bechdel herself followed in composing and editing it. In an interview published in *The Comics Journal*, Lynn Emmert asks Bechdel if she edited *Fun Home* based on feedback from her surviving family members. Bechdel responds, "Yes. I changed a few little things. There wasn't much that they really asked me to change, but most of their requests I implemented. Some of them I didn't, we sort of argued about those. I wanted them to know what I was doing all along, so I showed it to my brothers, I showed it to my mom." In other words, Bechdel worked to be responsible to those whose stories she was telling and whose lives she would be affecting by publishing the book. In designing and presenting my assignment prompt, then, I wanted to encourage students to pursue a similar responsibility. Though it's of course doubtful that Bechdel will ever hear about this assignment or read one of the *prosopopoeiae* it produced, I presented Bechdel as a working artist and writer as well as a person with feelings and a relationship with her subject matter. While it is easy to approach, say, Virgil or Dido as abstract figures encased in history and myth, representatives of crystallized values whose legacies and lives are not particularly threatened by an odd *prosopopoeia* or two, I wanted to position *Fun Home* and those involved in it as vulnerable and open to affection. The historical *prosopopoeiae* I've been describing are, after all, often exercises centered on affect, feeling, emotion. In short, I wanted students to feel responsible to and for *Fun Home*, and I wanted to make them aware of the wide range of responses their mini-papers might in turn provoke, even if only in theory. They were engaging with and listening to someone else's voice and story—not exercising mastery over it.

My second motive had to do with the protocols of *Fun Home*. In the article "Drawing the Archive in Alison Bechdel's *Fun Home*," which students read in concert with the book itself, Ann Cvetkovich argues that, as a genre, graphic narrative "reminds us that we are not gaining access to an unmediated form of vision."[49] In the case of *Fun Home*, Cvetkovich claims that Bechdel's text acknowledges the "unassimilability" of her father's story, assiduously "map[ping] a history that she can't comprehend as a direct witness."[50] That is, though Bechdel notes that "removing one word would be like pulling on a thread that unravels the whole sweater," *Fun Home* is also a necessarily incomplete text—one that can't not encounter the limits of an unassimilable story that even its author doesn't claim to grasp completely.[51]

In composing the *prosopopoeia* prompt, then, I tried to write in a manner that would encourage students to encounter *Fun Home* in a way that resonated with Bechdel's simultaneously painstaking and incomplete retelling of her own and her father's stories. Along with reading Cvetkovich's article, a class discussion on aporia (one of a few rhetorical devices explicitly addressed in the course), and the recursive quality of the assignment's unannounced footnote component, I hoped that both the prompt and my initial presentation of it would slow students down, make them second-guess their ability to represent Bechdel and her book.

However, my attempts at hesitation and hedging for the sake of control over the assignment's outcomes led me and continue to lead me back to one of my earlier claims—one I'd now like to trouble: that I was trying to swap classical *prosopopoeia*'s emphasis on tropes of mastery, including self-mastery, for tropes and habits of alterity. This swap, in short, is too easy. Given Enterline's extensive argument that the mastery-driven pedagogical method of Renaissance schoolmasters produced a habit of alterity (perhaps inadvertently, perhaps unavoidably) as a supplement, what of the risk that my focus on alterity would produce (perhaps inadvertently, perhaps unavoidably) a habit of mastery as a supplement? All the pains I took in composing and reflecting on the assignment, all the pains I asked students to take in composing and reflecting on their *prosopopoeiae*, can begin to sound like a sort of hypertrophied mastery—as if attending relentlessly to the seams can produce a seamlessly masterful text or pedagogy, a mastery that is all the more masterful for trying to attend to alterity. As if one could be infinitely responsible by simply bearing in mind that one's attempts to be responsible are always finite, never responsible enough. This, of course, is not the case. Students could still abdicate responsibility to and for me, *Fun Home*, and/or the assignment: they could troll me, feign earnestness, slap something together before class. I could always fail to communicate or live up to the pedagogical trajectory I tried to lay out, could always have done more or prepared and presented things a little more carefully. This is one of the risks of translating theory into pedagogy: there is always the chance that one did so too hastily, too thoughtlessly. It is perhaps also related to one of the misgivings those who privilege practice have with theory: that the latter is too slow to take risks, irresponsible for trying to be too responsible. Nevertheless, because of the vagaries of practice, and having entrusted myself and my students to writing and to a certain writing pedagogy while remaining distrustful of writing, I found and continue to find myself turning toward theory again.

RIGHT TO THEORY

In 2002, Stanford University Press published the first volume of an English translation of Jacques Derrida's *Du droit à la philosophie*, which translator Jan Plug renders as *Right to Philosophy*. The volume is entitled *Who's Afraid of Philosophy? Right to Philosophy 1*. In his translator's note, Plug describes *Right to Philosophy* as "consist[ing] of essays, interviews, and talks given by Jacques Derrida between 1974 and 1990 concerning philosophical research, the teaching of philosophy, and the relation between philosophy and institutions, in particular, the university."[32] In other words, the collection—though its titular focus is on philosophy rather than rhetoric—focuses on relations between pedagogy, research, and educational institutions that overlap significantly with the rhetorical relations explored in this book. In the collection's opening piece, Derrida considers the hierarchies and traditions that privilege certain disciplines, practices, and speech acts—that let various entities take precedence over others. He begins with the phenomenon of the title: "Title, chapter, chapter heading, heading, capital, capital letter: questions of title will always be questions of authority, of reserve and right, of *rights reserved*, of hierarchy or hegemony. The title 'Right to Philosophy,' for example, keeps in reserve a multiplicity of possible meanings."[53]

After exploring a few such possible meanings, Derrida considers what happens when one reads the title's "right" as an adverb: "right to philosophy," in this case, would suggest a philosophizing that would proceed "*straight-forwardly, directly*, immediately, without the mediation of training, teaching, or philosophical institutions, without even the mediation of the other or of language, this or that language."[54] Derrida questions both the possibility and the ethics of such philosophizing:

> Certain people are always impatient to *access-the-things-themselves-directly-and-reach-right-away-without-waiting-the-true-content-of-the-urgent-and-serious-problems-that-face-us-all-etc.* Thus, they will no doubt judge an analysis that deploys [a] range of meanings and possible sentences playful, precious, and formal, indeed futile: "Why be so slow and self-indulgent? Why these linguistic stages? Why don't we just speak directly about the true questions? Why not go right to the things themselves?" Of course, one can share this impatience and nonetheless think, as I do, that not only do we gain nothing by immediately giving into it, but that this lure has a history, interest, and a sort of *hypocritical* structure, and that one would always be better off to begin by acknowledging it by giving oneself the time for a detour and analysis.[55]

I return to the ethical and rhetorical questions raised by this quote in chapter 5. For the moment, I want to consider it alongside the structure of the current one. In this chapter, I tried to go, introductory remarks notably excepted, right to pedagogy. At the level of a single chapter, I suggested that such an approach inverts a commonplace structure deployed in a lot of rhetoric and writing scholarship: going right to theory before turning to practice—in many cases, pedagogical practice. That said, within the overall structure of this book, this chapter's beginning can also be read as part and parcel of such a turn, taking place as it does after a more theoretically oriented chapter and thus still constituting a traditionally deferred pedagogical turn. Bearing that in mind, I am seeking to question an institutional and disciplinary structure, but without pretending to escape from or step outside it. Tracing the pedagogical turn from the inside and the outside, I've tried to consider its limitations and possibilities. In so doing, I've perhaps been self-indulgent and also acted on the "impatience" Derrida describes, going right to pedagogy without taking "the time for detour and analysis."[56] Instead, I'm trying to detour intermittently, speeding into the realm of pedagogy only to backtrack to the city limits as soon as I arrive. Traveling the path of a Mobius strip folded into the shape of the symbol for infinity (∞), I'm cycling in and out, always returning to the pedagogical terrain where I spend so much of my time, but doing so from different angles and trying not to stick around so long that I take its topography for granted. But before returning to more explicitly pedagogical concerns in the coming chapters, I want to loop back into the "desert" of theory, though without leaving behind what's been covered so far.[57]

Near the beginning of "Sorties: Out and Out: Attacks / Ways Out / Forays," feminist writer and theorist Hélène Cixous elaborates on how women have been taught to internalize an "antinarcissism": "They have committed the greatest crime against women: insidiously and violently, they have led them to hate women, to be their own enemies, to mobilize their immense power against themselves, to do the male's dirty work."[58] Throughout much of the remaining essay, Cixous identifies a number of figures that she's inhabited in an attempt to escape the "antinarcissism" heaped upon women. On the way to Cleopatra, she dwells with Achilles, Theseus, and Ariadne before reaching one of the most common subjects of historical *prosopopoeiae*: Dido. Writes Cixous, "I could not have been Ariadne: it's all right that she gives herself out of love. But to whom? Theseus doesn't tremble, doesn't adore, doesn't desire; following his own destiny, he goes over bodies that are never even idealized. Every woman is a means. I see that clearly. But I would have dared to be Dido."[59] This identification only lasts a page, however. After noting the number of women, Dido included, that Aeneas abandons—and the fact that the gods are always there to justify his abandonments—Cixous positions herself "in Dido's place. But I am not Dido. I cannot inhabit a victim, no matter how noble. I resist: detest a certain passivity, it promises death for me. So who shall I be?"[60] Many of Cixous's inhabitations are written in this paradoxical manner. Writing about Joan of Arc, for instance, Cixous notes that she finds her "totally uninhabitable. But otherwise I am with her."[61] Much of Cixous's argument, both autobiographical and theoretical, unfolds through a series of imperfect identifications—identifications that are moved past but never simply left behind, informing as they do the "ways out" she subsequently pursues: "I was Antony for Cleopatra and she for him; I was also Juliet. . . . I was Saint Teresa of Avila. . . . I have always been a bird."[62] Through all these lives, Cixous recounts a continuous struggling "against false ideas, codes, 'values,' mastery's ignoble and murderous stupidity."[63] In a manner resonant with Woods's suggestions for present-day students, Cixous's imitations serve to challenge "the political and social implications of canonical texts."[64]

Though my circuitous path is different from the one traveled by Cixous, it overlaps with "Sorties" insofar as I'm trying to approach a *prosopopoeia* that struggles against "mastery's ignoble and murderous stupidity." In the preceding section, I noted my motives for reframing *prosopopoeia* as an exercise focused on something like alterity or *un*mastery, as well as some of the ways in which I tried to resist tropes of mastery in the assignment's presentation and structure. I also noted, however, that these motives and ways of fostering unmastery were and are never airtight, never in fact masterful in the struggle against mastery.

But Cixous's meditations on inhabitation and identification in "Sorties" point to another problematic of mastery. So far, I've mostly discussed mastery in terms of a relation between entities—between student and text, text and teacher, teacher and student. While I've drawn on Enterline's observations about the "habit of alterity" that interrupted and rerouted the self-mastery that Renaissance masters tried to instill in students, the pedagogical turns I've so far taken have not dwelt with self-mastery at great length. I would argue, however, that "Sorties" describes and performs a key point about self-mastery—one that resonates with this chapter's emphasis on imitation and *prosopopoeia* while also setting the stage for questions of agency that will drive this book's remaining chapters.

In resisting mastery, Cixous has to be relentlessly careful not to fall into tropes of self-mastery. Take, for instance, her disdain for the hero of the *Odyssey*: "I was afraid of being Ulysses, and wasn't I sometimes? . . . But I didn't like to catch myself being Ulysses, the artist of flight. The Winner: the one who was saved, the homecoming man! Always returning to himself—in spite of the most fantastic detours."[65] Cixous describes Ulysses as self-identical, a traveler who always "return[s] to himself." As she reads his story, he always ends up remaining in control of himself and his destiny, and this is what makes Cixous so incredulous.

Cixous articulates her own identity—in contrast with that of Ulysses—as constantly shifting and never completely returning. She is not identical to herself and, though she occupies and sheds identification after identification over the course of "Sorties," never becomes "herself." Rather, the figures she inhabits (Ariadne, Achilles, Dido, a bird, and—as much as she doesn't like to admit it—Ulysses) affect the selves she has been and will be. She is not moving toward her true self by sloughing off identifications with others. Rather, these fluctuating identifications *are* her non-self-identical "self."

In "Autozoography: Notes Toward a Rhetoricity of the Living," Diane Davis makes an argument that resonates with Cixous's, though it's written in a different register. She notes that, both in philosophy and in the sciences, the ability to recognize oneself has long been positioned as the ability dividing humans from the rest of the animal kingdom. For example, both René Descartes and the zoologist Carl Linnaeus "propose that the irruption of the specifically human being takes place in a scene of self-recognition."[66] Just as Ulysses travels away from home, learns something about the world, and returns to take charge of both his kingdom and his fate, so the purportedly human "scene of self-recognition" involves a departure and reflexive return to oneself—a gesture that travels down the length of the arm only to, via a crooked finger, point back to its origin and declare: "I am." Davis traces a different trajectory. She argues that this pointing back at oneself always misses the mark. In order to refer to myself, I have to pin myself down like a taxidermied bird in a museum exhibit, fixed in a static imitation of flight. The "self" to which "I" refer in, say, autobiography is thus always dead and gone, already moved past by a "self" that, in the very attempt to point to its "self," leaves that self behind. As Davis puts it, "The self to which 'I' refers . . . 'only appears to itself in this bereaved allegory, in this hallucinatory prosopopoeia.'"[67] Riffing on the imperative that Carl Linnaeus issued to human beings—"Know yourself"—Davis writes, "The autobiographical animal conjures itself but never finally gets to itself or becomes itself, which is maybe why 'know yourself' had to be inscribed as an eternal imperative."[68] Like Cixous, Davis's autobiographical animal never quite reaches a self-identical destination. Instead, autobiography is a sort of *prosopopoeia* in which the human, thinking it is speaking for and of itself, is in fact using "a language that is always on the scene" prior to the arrival of the "I" in order to imitate an artificially configured "self": "There can be no saying 'I' or doing *I* that is not already a citation, an imitation."[69]

Davis's point is dramatically demonstrated in Cixous's "Sorties." Rather than becoming or mastering her essential self, Cixous's "I" emerges through an interminable series of incomplete imitations and identifications. *Prosopopoeia*, in this case, is not a figure by which a self engages with an other in order to better understand both the other and itself, but a process by which a being *becomes* itself only through a sort of imitation—a citational process that calls into question what is usually meant by "self."

The sort of "autobiography" described by Davis and practiced by Cixous gestures toward "ways out" of self-mastery that are very different than the ones pursued by contemporary rhetoricians, many of whom are also interested in ways out of tropes and hierarchies premised on mastery or other manifestations of dominant, domineering ideologies. As I've argued, these ways out are often premised on tropes of agency and empowerment—tropes that are not so far from the promise of self-mastery. A major way that rhetoric and writing teachers have sought to challenge dominant ideologies about language and identity in the context of writing classrooms has been the Conference on College Composition and Communication's "Students' Right to Their Own Language" resolution. An explanation of the resolution appeared in a 1974 issue of the journal *College Composition and Communication*, and that explanation reproduces the resolution as follows:

> We affirm the students' right to their own patterns and varieties of language—the dialects of their nurture or whatever dialects in which they find their own identity and style. Language scholars long ago denied that the myth of a standard American dialect has any validity. The claim that any one dialect is unacceptable amounts to an attempt of one social group to exert its dominance over another. Such a claim leads to false advice for speakers and writers, and immoral advice for humans. A nation proud of its diverse heritage and its cultural and racial variety will preserve its heritage of dialects. We affirm strongly that teachers must have the experiences and training that will enable them to respect diversity and uphold the right of students to their own language.[70]

In one sense, the resolution acknowledges that students' language is not in fact their "own." The phrase "dialects of their nurture" serves as a reminder that people do not simply choose their language but are, to a significant extent, given it. Yet the resolution, in both its title and its legacy, has been used to emphasize the notion that one's language *is* one's "own."[71]

To be clear, I'm not arguing that this is a universally bad thing. As the resolution points out, it is well documented that which dialects get dubbed "standard" or "substandard" is, though rooted in an array of historical and political factors not easily overcome or escaped, arbitrary in terms of dialects' linguistic complexity and worth. The resolution has thus been used to argue for and enact a number of scholarly and pedagogical strategies for questioning the biased power of linguistic "standards" and advocating for unfairly marginalized dialects and unjustly marginalized students who use those dialects.[72] One noteworthy continuation of this well-established but oft-ignored work is "This Ain't Another Statement! This is a DEMAND for Black Linguistic Justice!"[73] Released by the Conference on College Composition and Communication in the summer of 2020 amidst a wave of anti-Black violence in the United States, the piece both builds on and critiques the 1974 CCCC statement. The authors point out that objections to addressing Black Language in writing classrooms don't hold water, including the long-disproven, fallacious, and racist notion that such language is linguistically or intellectually inferior to what April Baker-Bell calls "White Mainstream English."[74] Moreover, as the authors point out, concerns that teaching Black Language will undermine students' professional futures are both ethically and practically indefensible in a global marketplace where companies constantly appropriate and profit from the strategic uptake of Black Language.[75] The specific context of the 2020 demand—its emphasis on Black linguistic justice rather than students' language more generally—makes it clear that universalized opposition to notions of ownership over one's language risks heaping more disrespect on the already wrongfully disrespected. Depropriation marks an insufficient solution in the face of the simultaneous denigration and appropriation of Black Language as "one of those features of Black culture that white America loves to hate, yet loves to take."[76]

However, I would also argue that the assertion that one's language is one's "own" is connected to attitudes toward language—as something one masters and owns—that in some ways underwrite the self-satisfied power that would-be "owners" of dominant languages use to marginalize others. In a sense, this is an extension of what critical race theorist Cheryl I. Harris persuasively demonstrates in her article "Whiteness as Property." Through an examination of Supreme Court decisions spanning US history, Harris shows how whiteness itself—from the social standing historically granted to those deemed white to the ways that property rights were "defined to include only the cultural practices of whites"—has been and continues to be upheld as a kind of property that one owns.[77] As she succinctly puts it, "Owning white identity as property affirmed the self-identity and liberty of whites and, conversely, denied the self-identity and liberty of Blacks."[78] While Harris does not focus on language, her consideration of *Brown v. Board of Education* and the broader history of laws restricting Black people's rights to literacy and education implicates language in the history of white identity and, by extension, the intangible property interests whiteness affords.[79] That is, in the case of "standard" languages affiliated with power and privilege, the very language of ownership is connected to the fantasies of power and superiority that fuel linguistic prejudices and a variety of ethical, political, and physical forms of violence bound up with such prejudices. Just as those who've inherited a large amount of tangible property are easily persuaded that they've acquired and deserve said property by virtue of their own merits rather than unrecognized forms of privilege, so those who have acquired a disproportionately powerful language are easily persuaded that they rightfully possess and earned the often unrecognized power attached to that language. Thus, even though depropriative conceptions of language are not universal solutions, theorizing alternatives to the notion that language is something a self possesses and masters, and that reflexively grants a kind of self-mastery, is a significant ethical, theoretical, and pedagogical undertaking. The kinds and limits of imitation I have articulated in this chapter mark an interruption in that notion. In a critique of the hubris that attends colonial notions of languages as things to be mastered and possessed, Madina V. Tlostanova and Walter D. Mignolo state that "languages are not something human beings *have* but what human beings *are*."[80] In a slight extension of that critique, my suggestion here is that languages are not something human beings *have* but through which they are perpetually and prosopopoetically emerging.

Before circling back to imitation and *prosopopoeia* one last time, let me return to Judith Butler's *Giving an Account of Oneself*, which I drew on in this book's introduction, to flesh out the concerns with ownership and mastery toward which I'm gesturing. Butler argues that, in a number of "scenes of address" (e.g., courtrooms, psychotherapy sessions), what is expected of the interlocutor being addressed (e.g., the accused, the patient) is the ability to tell a coherent story (e.g., provide an airtight alibi, self-actualize). Questioning the virtue of coherence, Butler writes, "if we require that someone be able to tell in story form the reasons why [their] life has taken the path it has, that is, to be a coherent autobiographer, we may be preferring the seamlessness of the story to something we might tentatively call the truth of the person, a truth that . . . might well become more clear in moments of interruption."[81] Positioning the demand for coherence as a kind of ethical violence, Butler offers an alternative: "If, in the name of ethics, we (violently) require that another do a certain violence to herself, and do it in front of us by offering a narrative account or issuing a confession, then, conversely, if we permit, sustain, and accommodate the interruption, a certain practice of nonviolence may follow. If violence is the act by which a subject seeks to reinstall its mastery and unity, then nonviolence may well follow from living the persistent challenge to egoic mastery that our obligations to others induce and require."[82]

How might we unsettle approaches to rhetorical education that would pursue justice by extending ownership, by making more individuals the coherent masters of their respective discursive domains? As one way of interrupting such approaches, I have emphasized the fragility and vulnerability of pedagogical practices and relations as a key part, though not the entirety, of rhetorical and linguistic justice. *Prosopopoeia* in particular and imitation in general have, throughout their history, often been positioned as steps on the path to mastery. Guarded by authoritative teachers wielding canonical texts, students' imitative practices were premised on the promise that, should they sufficiently internalize the protocols of teacher and text alike, they themselves would grow into self-possessed masters all their own.

But throughout that history, the authority of teachers and texts has constantly been called into question, interrupted by the playful excesses of the students they sought to shape. Those students could have been Dido, but then again—

———

One obvious conclusion here might be to celebrate the agency of these playful students, the fact that the strictures of educational authority have never been able to fully extinguish their creativity and inventiveness. And yet, as Woods notes, even this playfulness can arguably serve the same ends as the imitation exercises themselves: shoring up the bonds between the next generation of self-assured masters. In conclusion, then, I hesitate in the face of student agency. Instead, I return one last time to the *Fun Home* exercise with which this chapter began. It is an exercise and attendant text that continue to interrupt my thinking about pedagogy nearly a decade later. Here is a sequence of rhetorical (and pedagogical, historical, and theoretical) questions to which the memory of that exercise has prompted me to respond, repeatedly and inconclusively: What if *prosopopoeia* is not just a masterable trope or exercise—one progymnasmatic step en route to rhetorical power? What if it is "not a power at all" but in fact "that which grants the effect of an I"?[83] Might this reposition *prosopopoeia* not as the exercise of encountering or appropriating an other on the way to mastery but as something that—acknowledged or not—characterizes all writing practices? In a curriculum that took these questions up, what could *prosopopoeia* do? How might it call into question the masterful notions of teacherly authority and student agency on which Western education so often depends, unsettling both vis-à-vis a relentless responsibility? So far, this chapter and this book have sought to undermine the purported stability of teacherly authority—including my own. But as this chapter has also suggested, the ethical limits of self-mastery extend beyond such authority and into the realm of student agency, to which this book now turns.

Online Education, the Limits of Agency, and the Dream of Education Without Responsibility

> Morality begins when freedom, instead of being justified by itself, feels itself to be arbitrary and violent.
>
> —EMMANUEL LEVINAS

In March 2020, as COVID-19 spread across the United States, the university at which I worked moved all courses online. The decision was announced during spring break, which was extended for an additional week so that faculty and students, many of whom had no experience teaching or taking online courses, could adjust to the new paradigm. During that break, I created a multitude of online discussion boards in our learning management system (to compensate for in-person discussions students and I would no longer be able to have), set up a server for each of my courses on a popular digital platform that supported text and voice chat (to facilitate real-time one-on-one communication with students), cut the amount of work students were required to do in each course (in an attempt at basic kindness in the midst of chaos), and redesigned remaining activities and assignments so they could unfold remotely and asynchronously (as a matter of necessity). I went to the grocery store and bought enough food to last for a few weeks. I responded to emails from students who'd be moving back home and wouldn't have reliable internet connections, and I offered advice to other teachers who had less experience with online and digital pedagogy. I tried to keep up with the news. I reconfigured part of my living space so I could work from home for the foreseeable future. I responded to student projects. I grew increasingly anxious. I corresponded with students who had symptoms of the virus, granting them extensions and trying to be as supportive as I could. I read discussion posts from other students claiming that public concern about COVID-19 was overblown.

I'm returning to this chapter to add these opening paragraphs and revise what follows in the wake of the 2020–21 academic year. While some of my colleagues spent that year teaching hybrid courses with in-person elements, all of the courses I taught were totally online. The shift to remote teaching was labor intensive and I missed face-to-face interactions with students, but I was immensely fortunate compared to many others who work in higher education: I had previous experience teaching online, I wasn't fired or left waiting for months to find out whether my contract would be renewed for the following year, and I was given the choice to teach online well before the 2020–21 academic year began. This was, of course, not the case for a lot of faculty. The working conditions faced by many who teach in the US public higher education system were already precarious prior to COVID-19, and as the pandemic exacerbated that precarity, the consequences were particularly dire for those already at the system's margins.[1] That included contingent faculty, graduate students, and undergraduate students without ready access to the digital resources necessary for online courses.[2]

For those who were working in higher education in 2020–21, the preceding paragraphs may sound all too familiar. Still, I rehearse these events because they have had a dramatic effect on a key component of this and the following chapter: online education. While people have been studying and implementing various forms of online learning for decades, many teachers and students still had no direct experience with fully online courses at the start of 2020.[3] Given the widespread shift online during 2020, that has changed dramatically. Revisiting a pair of chapters addressing online education in light of the last few years is thus a challenging task—and a potentially harrowing one.

But the crises that COVID-19 and its aftermath presented and will continue to present for public colleges and universities make it especially urgent to consider where online education might go from here. Consider this quotation from Sebastian Thrun, chairman of the for-profit education company Udacity, from a piece on the "opportunities" afforded by the coronavirus pandemic: "Crises lead to accelerations, and this is best chance ever for online learning."[4] Thrun's Udacity is a major player in this and the following chapter, the progeny of an arguably defunct, arguably persistent form of online education that was the initial motivation for the arguments I make here: massive open online courses, or MOOCs.

MOOCs blazed onto the educational scene in 2012, a would-be Silicon Valley panacea that aimed to disrupt higher education by personalizing student learning and democratizing access to educational content. MOOC advocates built the case for these courses on crises actual and imagined. On one hand, they pointed to the rapidly rising cost of higher education—a very real problem that intensified as states slashed higher-education budgets during and after the 2008 recession.[5] On the other, advocates relied on demonstrably false characterizations of higher education's stagnancy, making it sound as though faculty did nothing more than deliver pat, unresponsive lectures to rooms full of docile, unengaged students. As one venture capitalist and MOOC investor succinctly presented this fallacious and opportunistic viewpoint, "Education hasn't changed in 1,000 years."[6] Such claims would seem to reveal a profound ignorance, whether willful or blissful, of everything from the mere existence of computer classrooms to the extensive body of research on student-centered learning as well as the widespread implementation of student-centered practices in US college and university courses.

In many senses, MOOCs failed in their mission. They did not displace other forms of higher education, and they did not give rise to the "University of Everywhere."[7] Yet during the brief moment they spent in the limelight, they managed to affect state-level priorities for higher education, attract significant attention from the Obama administration and venture-capital firms, and propagate a powerful if often misleading and misinformed narrative about the purportedly static state of higher education.[8] Moreover, as Steven Krause notes in his book on the so-called MOOC moment, they are still with us in the form of skills-focused professional-development courses.[9] While MOOCs may have had a less significant effect on higher education than initially anticipated, they were far from ineffectual.[10] In short, MOOCs live on as one iteration of a longstanding, ongoing series of attempts to "disrupt" higher education via technological innovations that, regardless of their pedagogical merits, have persistent consequences for public colleges and universities.[11]

While COVID-19 engendered and exacerbated a range of technological, economic, and pedagogical challenges for public college and universities, it has not yet provided an opening for an online competitor to attract the level of hype afforded to MOOCs. It provided lucrative opportunities for technology companies to establish and expand contracts with universities, from video-conferencing platforms to online proctoring services, lecture-capture software to machine-learning tools.[12] While the ethics, effectiveness, and costs of these companies' services deserve intense scrutiny—especially given the well-established biases and inequities engrained in a host of popular digital technologies—they have primarily leveraged the pandemic to embed themselves in existing educational institutions rather than seeking to displace them wholesale.[13] Meanwhile, Silicon Valley initiatives like Google's recently announced Career Certificates program continue to generate hyperbolic, sometimes sponsored coverage, but that program is from the start emphasizing targeted, skills-focused courses closer to what MOOCs have become than to the earth-shaking educational force they were initially made out to be.[14]

However, despite some major differences between the rise and fall of MOOCs and the lower-profile tech-industry interventions that have unfolded amid the coronavirus pandemic, they share a key point of emphasis to which I want to draw attention: personalization. This recurring emphasis demonstrates a key point raised by Steven Krause: "The speed of the rise and fall of MOOCs was unprecedented, but the pattern is not."[15]

As I've argued in the preceding chapters, what I am calling "responsible" pedagogy resists taking teachers' authority over students for granted. While conventional notions of teacherly authority have shifted since the historical eras highlighted in chapters 1 and 2, the rhetorical power of appeals to such authority is still very much alive and well. Take, for example, pro-MOOC arguments that touted the possibility of students getting "free access to lectures and courses sourced from world leaders in their fields."[16] In exalting content tied to such leaders, MOOC advocates relied on a ratcheted-up reiteration of appeals to teacherly authority that have long been a staple of educational discourse. Even as MOOC advocates criticized higher education for being too reliant on outmoded lecture-based approaches to teaching, they also relied on more grandiose versions of just such approaches to promote their products, taking the thoroughly critiqued "sage on the stage" model of education to one logical extreme.[17] That said, pro-MOOC arguments that appealed to teacherly authority were relatively easy for skeptical educators to formulate responses to. Not only did those arguments often rely on clear mischaracterizations of contemporary pedagogical practices, but they were also at odds with well-established critiques of teacherly authority advanced by supporters of critical pedagogy and related educational philosophies.[18] But while teacherly authority remained an important variable in MOOCs' public-relations equation, their even more widespread and in some ways tougher-to-critique emphasis on "personalization," which remains an educational-technology buzzword, captures an important shift in the tropes used to justify education and frame teacher-student relations.

Specifically, this valorization of personalization exemplifies a shift in emphasis from teacherly authority to student agency.

While MOOC advocates and critics differed on a range of philosophical and pedagogical matters, they were in many ways united in their expressed commitment to student agency. To be clear, MOOC advocates did not explicitly use the phrase "student agency" as a regular selling point or rallying cry. However, the values to which they did appeal—student empowerment, personalized learning experiences, various versions of the sort of self-mastery I addressed in chapter 2—resonate powerfully with notions of student agency that commonly circulate among scholars in such fields as education and rhetoric and writing studies. Of course, one can argue that MOOC advocates were appealing to student agency in bad faith or without the pedagogical background or infrastructure to deliver on their often-extravagant promises. Yet the rhetorical challenge remains: How can those who see higher education as a public good and increased student agency as one of the values supported by that good differentiate their sometimes competing, sometimes surprisingly aligned commitments to student agency from those forwarded by private entities seeking to displace or undermine public education?

After all, appeals to student agency, including claims about personalized learning and student empowerment, continue to play a key role in privatized ed-tech "disruptions" emerging in the wake of COVID-19.[19] Moreover, they remain likely to recur in the context of inexorable and invented educational crises yet to come. Those interested in defending higher education as a public good must thus be prepared to counter not only MOOC-style appeals to teacherly authority but also more rhetorically vexed and vexing appeals to student agency. It is a matter not simply of separating our good appeals to agency from their bad ones but of being willing to question the limits of our own concepts of student agency. As I argue in this chapter and the next, if there is a good reason to argue against the agency-centered pedagogical claims made by MOOC advocates and their heirs, making that argument effectively may involve shifting the terms of the debate—moving from pedagogy as a practice of "fostering agency and empowering learners," as Sean Michael Morris and Jesse Stommel put it, to pedagogy as a practice of responsibility.[20]

In what follows, I pursue such a shift. Throughout the remainder of this chapter, I present and analyze arguments in favor of MOOCs and the notions of student agency and personalization on which those arguments were premised. I focus particularly on a 2012 panel during which key players in the burgeoning MOOC game made their respective cases to the President's Council of Advisors on Science and Technology. While the panel represents only a sliver of the debate around MOOCs, it provides a key window into how ed-tech advocates made the case for their product to public stakeholders and governmental decision-makers. The panel provides a detailed and at times surprisingly unvarnished glimpse into these advocates' pedagogical, philosophical, and technological assumptions. I consider where the conceptions of agency and personalization espoused by MOOC advocates overlapped with and diverged from the conceptions of their critics.

Next, in chapter 4, I elaborate on Emmanuel Levinas's positioning of responsibility as a necessary precondition for agency and propose a theory of pedagogical responsibility that challenges conventional conceptions of student agency. Finally, I demonstrate the implications of such a theory via a detailed description and analysis of the peer workshop practices I employ in online and in-person rhetoric and writing courses. In addition to providing concrete illustrations of a pedagogy of responsibility and the limits of student agency, these practices demonstrate what is lost in the purportedly personalized structures of MOOCs and their ed-tech offspring.

But before diving in, it's worth clarifying a few things these two chapters are *not*.

First, they are not unqualified, full-throated defenses of public higher education's current state. As I've mentioned, public higher education is embroiled in a number of real problems: rising costs driven by decreasing state appropriations, labor practices that leave many workers in profoundly precarious situations, and expansive vendor contracts that effectively redirect public funds and tuition dollars to such private entities as online program managers, video-conferencing companies, remote proctoring services, and learning management systems. Moreover, at the level of pedagogical practices, some fields and faculty still rely on notions of teacherly authority similar to those I've critiqued in the preceding chapters.[21] So, while these chapters are especially critical of the rhetorical claims, technological utopianism, and pedagogical approaches forwarded by MOOCs and their advocates (and, by extension, critical of many other for-profit models of higher education), my case for pedagogical theories and practices premised on responsibility also challenges some commonplace assumptions and practices in public higher education.

Second, these chapters do not offer a universal repudiation of online education. In rhetoric and writing studies alone, scholars have done extensive work researching and developing reputable frameworks for online courses.[22] And, despite the barriers to accessibility and affordability that online courses can present and that well-funded public institutions with in-person courses and other resources can help ameliorate, disability scholars and activists have pointed out that, when crafted with accessibility in mind, online courses can be "profound . . . teaching and learning experiences," especially for students and teachers for whom in-person classes are not accessible.[23] As these chapters make clear, the concerns I have about MOOCs and the ed-tech industry's subsequent attempts to "disrupt" and appropriate online education are specific. They do not extend to all forms of online education, many of which should have a place in a diverse, well-curated public educational ecosystem that attends to the needs of students and faculty alike.

Finally, these chapters are not an attempt to dismiss student agency from the pedagogical scene. As I discussed in this book's introduction, agency is a complex and powerful concept. While these chapters refigure the relation between responsibility and agency in the context of educational practices and philosophies, they offer a rethinking—not a rejection—of student agency.

ON THE RHETORIC OF MOOCS

In 2012, Sebastian Thrun—erstwhile professor at Stanford University, artificial-intelligence researcher, designer of award-winning self-driving cars, and cofounder and CEO of the for-profit education company and MOOC provider Udacity—became a central figure in what the *New York Times* dubbed "The Year of the MOOC."[24] In November of that year, Thrun was invited to speak to the President's Council of Advisors on Science and Technology (PCAST), one of four presenters on a panel entitled "Massively Open Online Courses & STEM Education."[25] The other members of this panel were Daphne Koller, another Stanford professor and cofounder of the for-profit MOOC company Coursera; Anant Agarwal, professor at the Massachusetts Institute of Technology and president of the nonprofit MOOC provider edX; and Frank DiGiovanni, director of training strategy and readiness for the Department of Defense.[26] Thrun spoke first, and one of his primary questions was this: "How can we open up and democratize education and make it available to people who presently can't partake in high-quality education?" Unsurprisingly, MOOCs were his primary answer. Though Thrun acknowledged some challenges, his tone was overwhelmingly optimistic as he argued that MOOCs afforded "a massive opportunity for this nation to redefine pedagogy in the online age." Koller built on Thrun's claims, arguing that MOOCs provide "access to education to a population that [otherwise] will never have that access," offering, in the face of rising tuition costs and government disinvestment in public education, a "richer, broader curriculum at a very low price point."[27]

Thrun's proposed redefinition of pedagogy was premised on restructuring the significance and responsibilities of those we've traditionally called "teachers." That is, the "low price point" invoked by Koller required circumventing the cost of teachers by redistributing and rethinking their work. As Thrun put it, "The reason why we all believe in small classrooms is because we know that learning is individually different, and small classrooms have the economic disadvantage that you need a teacher. Teachers cost money, and it has to be a good teacher, so [you need a lot of] money."[28] The titular massiveness of MOOCs, Thrun argued, would temper this economic difficulty.

This rethinking of teachers and their relational responsibilities was arguably *the* key issue raised by MOOCs. In his introduction to *Invasion of the MOOCs: The Promises and Perils of Massive Open Online Courses*, writing teacher and scholar Charles Lowe put it like this: "The teacher's role has been greatly reduced [in MOOCs] compared to the traditional classroom, mostly to that of a course instructional designer who administrates the class in progress. Not surprising, since it is impossible for the teacher to have individual interaction with even a small percentage of students in MOOCs. . . . What is lost without these student-teacher connections? That's the question that has yet to be answered."[29]

Another way of putting Lowe's question: what, if anything, justifies the 20:1 student-teacher ratio recommended by the National Council of Teachers of English, or the 25:1 ratio the National Communication Association recommends for such "performance courses" as public speaking, if MOOCs can radically reduce the cost of higher education by simultaneously centralizing and outsourcing the work traditionally attended to by teachers while spreading the cost of courses across thousands of students?[30]

While the structure of MOOCs themselves may have "disrupt[ed]" the ways in which "student-teacher connections" traditionally functioned,[31] Jeff Rice notes that arguments *about* MOOCs tended toward two conventional extremes: "alarm and enthusiasm," both of which "depend a great deal on the repetition of previous positions, commonplace situations in which to anchor our responses."[32] Moreover, Rice argues that many aspects of MOOCs themselves were in fact relatively commonplace and not nearly as disruptive as both advocates and opponents claimed. In MOOCs, Rice claims to "find a pedagogy that is familiar to me, . . . a pedagogy I have critiqued previously."[33] More precisely, he argues that MOOCs reiterated many of the acontextual, generic, relatively undisruptive pedagogical practices that have long been common—textbook, one might say—in face-to-face classrooms. "What we are talking about," he concludes, "is . . . a conversation that should be about pedagogical sameness."[34] In all, while advocates and opponents alike have positioned MOOCs and related varieties of "reform" as "disrupting" higher education, certain aspects of such courses and the controversies around them are remarkably conventional.[35]

As I stated above, I approach the ways MOOCs purported to disrupt and refigure the responsibilities and significance of teachers alongside a particular aspect of such courses' "pedagogical sameness": their proponents' insistent association of education with various tropes of agency, empowerment, and personalization. This association is one that's arguably spanned millennia. Despite the "collective" quality of Roman rhetorical education, its proclaimed end goal was typically a self-sufficient individual whose educational experience would allow them to exert greater power over themselves and their circumstances.[36] Consider Quintilian's famous description of the outcome of rhetorical education as the "good man speaking well."[37] Going back even further, Henri I. Marrou describes the sophists of ancient Athens as creating a "new education intended for all free men" aimed at "produc[ing] capable statesmen."[38] As Marrou's emphasis on "free men" and "statesmen" suggests, collective and political outcomes were tied to the "transformation of an individual"—in most cases, an individual who was part of a specific class of men. That transformation might have been wrought by collective educational processes, but it is a capacitated and self-possessed states*man*, a transformed *individual*, that Marrou positions as the educational deliverable par excellence.[39]

As is clear from ongoing debates about rhetorical agency, such tropes remain commonplace in and around contemporary pedagogy.[40] That is, many teachers proceed under the assumption that education, including civically oriented rhetorical education, is important because it enables students to be more free, that education's democratizing function has to do with its empowerment of at least *potentially* agentive students.[41] The uneducated student is, troublingly, often envisioned as "disabled," an incapacitated agent whose latent autonomy can be awakened by an engagement with the appropriate pedagogical structures.[42] A particular kind of agency remains a, if not *the*, key educational outcome and democratic good. As Diane Davis puts it, the notion of self-sufficient freedom, "often circulating under the name 'rhetorical agency,'" is "very frequently pegged as the fragile link between rhetorical practice and civic responsibility."[43] Even if "civic responsibility" is seen as a goal, it is often positioned as a secondary structure built on the ground of agency.

Despite the tensions and differences between MOOC proponents and their critics, similar assumptions about agency undergirded key arguments made by those advocating for MOOCs.[44] In fact, defenses of MOOCs read like a limiting case in the use of agency as an educational trope. That is, the hype that unfolded around MOOCs often turned on hypertrophied reiterations of tropes of agency that have been used to ground and justify pedagogical practice for millennia.[45] Their pedagogical approaches and their advocates' arguments were and are not necessarily so different from ones that have long circulated in educational spaces. They were just made at a higher volume.

The exaggerated quality of these arguments, however, brought out implications and resonances that are tacit in their less far-flung iterations. I emphasize the sameness in these arguments to indicate that, if we wish to continue defending the particular affordances a local teacher brings to the pedagogical scene—if there is something that sets the sort of person we've historically called a "teacher" apart from the various substitutions and concentrations offered by MOOCs—claims about agency may no longer cut it. In the face of this sameness, I argue that we might reimagine teachers not as empowered agents tasked with capacitating or liberating increasingly autonomous individual students it is hoped will go on to enact civic responsibility but as pedagogues responsible for attending to the limits of agency—the places, in other words, where one's agency, "instead of being justified by itself, feels itself to be arbitrary and violent" as it encounters the limit of responsibility.[46] Moreover, I argue that this reimagining offers a way for those teaching in smaller-scale pedagogical spaces to separate themselves from the pedagogical structures of MOOCs.[47]

Given my line of argument, it is worth noting the well-documented but frequently forgotten fact that Thrun and company were not the first ones on the MOOC scene. Earlier iterations of what came to be called MOOCs emerged in Canada as a manifestation of "connectivism," and they put less of an emphasis on agency and a great deal more emphasis on community.[48] After the 2012 MOOC "revolution," advocates of connectivist MOOCs used the label "cMOOC" as a way to distinguish their courses from "elite hyper-centralized Coursera- and Udacity-style MOOCs," which they labeled "xMOOCs."[49] Education and technology researcher George Siemens distinguished the two as follows: "cMOOCs focus on knowledge creation and generation whereas xMOOCs focus on knowledge duplication."[50] For example, cMOOC proponent and facilitator Dave Cormier designed courses in which "the community is the curriculum"—courses that positioned the relations formed and exchanges between participants as more important than any static course content, an approach Cormier linked with Gilles Deleuze and Félix Guattari's concept of the "rhizome."[51] Deleuze and Guattari famously present the rhizome—a variety of tuber with no discernable centralized point of origin—as operating on "principles of connection and heterogeneity."[52] In a rhizome, "There are no points or positions . . . such as those found in a structure, tree, or root. There are only lines."[53] The rhizome also operates on a "principle of multiplicity": none of its "lines" are privileged or more essential than others. In the network of the rhizome, "All multiplicities are flat, in the sense that they fill or occupy all of their dimensions: we will therefore speak of a *plane of consistency* of multiplicities, even though the dimensions of this 'plane' increase with the number of connections that are made on it."[54] In Cormier's theory of rhizomatic learning, then, the focus is not on individual, atomistic students, which would emphasize points or positions, but on the lines and connections between such would-be points. The focus is on relations or networks.

Though cMOOCs merit attention, offering an alternately anarchic and collectivist vision of education that differs significantly from the libertarian-inflected approach of xMOOCs, I won't have much more to say about them here. I focus on xMOOCs in what follows because of their singular influence on how MOOCs were discussed, figured, and structured in the United States. Nevertheless, I foreground the differences between cMOOCs and xMOOCs because it's worth noting that MOOCs are not monolithic. In fact, there's compelling work happening in their more experimental and less commodified iterations. It's just work that has had a harder time getting a foothold in US educational discourse and media coverage.[55] To draw attention to this fact, I use the term "xMOOC" throughout the rest of this chapter to highlight that I'm talking about one specific, if singularly influential, kind of MOOC.

According to what quickly became the US media's dominant narrative of MOOCs' rise to power, the catalyst was Thrun's "Introduction to Artificial Intelligence," a MOOC that attracted 150,000 enrollees and led to the founding of Udacity.[56] The key players in this narrative—one deployed even by writers skeptical of MOOCs' merits—are Udacity, Coursera, and edX; elite institutions such as Stanford and MIT; and, along with a few other Silicon Valley power players and STEM professors, Thrun himself, who often plays the father figure in this mythical history.[57]

The peak of the hype cycle surrounding xMOOCs included numerous profiles of Thrun and his peers in national newspapers and magazines, high-profile investments from venture capitalists, and the PCAST panel referenced above.[58] In the panelists' presentations, a common claim is that xMOOCs will radically democratize education, making affordable courses facilitated by the leading lights of the age available to anyone with an internet connection.[59]

As noted above, xMOOCs' affordability depended on simultaneously centralizing and redistributing various aspects of educational labor.[60] In Thrun's and Koller's views, xMOOCs would make it possible to centralize the role of the lecturer-teacher (frequently someone affiliated with "elite" institutions in the vein of Stanford), whom students would now access via videos that can be paused and replayed at will. This was paired with the decentralizing and outsourcing of responsive engagement to two networks. One of those networks was a collection of automated games, quizzes, and other "pedagogical instruments" that could supposedly "measure student outcomes in minutes" and subsequently adapt, or allow their designers to adapt them, to their pupils.[61] The panelists' investment and background in artificial intelligence shines through here. The second network consisted of students. A "peer-grading pipeline" and "peer teaching" are presented as key means of "circumventing the one thing that doesn't scale, which is instructor time." Koller gets a laugh from the PCAST when she notes that, in Coursera's xMOOCs, "students are actually answering each other's questions, and it turns out that's actually beneficial because students have a lot more time than the instructor."[62]

In short, these xMOOC advocates' arguments about empowering students assume that greater access to affordable content is key while access to a responsive teacher is not.[63] Teachers' responses were thought to be readily outsourced to a combination of peer networks and adaptive, artificially intelligent technologies.[64] In fact, Thrun suggests that asynchronous access to a teacher via recorded lectures holds advantages over synchronous instruction: "People, if they're given more time to exercise longer or watch the professor again [by replaying a video lecture], learn significantly better." (Though Thrun's earlier comments about small classrooms tie such classrooms' value to the fact that they allow teachers to adapt to the needs of individual students—perhaps, though he doesn't say so explicitly, through discussion or other forms of responsive engagement—his point here reduces the teacher's role to that of a lecturer. This bait and switch occurs frequently in xMOOC advocacy: higher education needs to be disrupted because its purportedly widespread lecture-based model of teaching is outmoded, and yet xMOOCs' disruption of higher education is largely premised on giving students access to video lectures.) Building up to the claim that xMOOCs would make it possible to circumvent the limitations of small classrooms by "redefin[ing] one-person classrooms," Thrun claims that xMOOCs could entail "a radical departure from classrooms where we force students onto a single path" and instead open up a proliferation of "individual learning paths." Thrun seems confident that such learning paths will be open to all comers and dwells on the example of two particular students:

> There's a pilot study we're running with a charter school in Texas with at-risk students. The students have to be fired from other [high] schools . . . to be admitted to this school, and they're typically economically challenged—often Latino, Hispanic, and so on. The charter school gave our classes to 24 students and two of those students finished a semester-long assignment in two weeks. They got into the Udacity system, they felt like playing a video game, and in doing so all of a sudden learned about physics and geometry at a level . . . that is a more polished level than at the high-school level. . . . Both of them were girls, both of them had nothing in common with STEM, and in both cases there's been a path for them in life that brands and marks them as failures for life even though both of them are actually plenty smart. The current education system in this nation is failing many of our students and it's failing to include many other students.[65]

Other panelists place a similar emphasis on individual standouts who, otherwise hampered by a variety of environmental and systemic variables, might have their educational progress and opportunities accelerated by xMOOCs. Koller positions xMOOCs as well suited for "independent learners": high schoolers who have facility with computers and can direct themselves through Coursera's online offerings. The Department of Defense's Frank DiGiovanni adds that he is interested in xMOOCs, particularly the artificial-intelligence technologies such courses were already making use of and might help generate in the future, because the military is "looking for autodidacts, people who are self-learners . . . who can operate in high levels of ambiguity" similar to the "highly unstructured" environments of xMOOCs.[66] Eventually shifting to long-term speculation, DiGiovanni imagines a "wearable . . . Aristotle- or Socrates-like tutor." His hope is "that each individual" in the military "would have a personal system for learning that would be with them for their entire life."

In short, despite a number of references to collaboration as both something that happens in xMOOCs via peer interaction and a desirable skill to be inculcated in those who participate in xMOOCs, the panelists repeatedly depict such courses' ideal input and outcome as the individual, already-agentive learner who encounters an increasingly individualized, personalized educational interface.[67] Collaboration is ultimately positioned as an adjunct to the individual learner's self-paced mastering of skills and content knowledge. Though xMOOC critics might raise an eyebrow at aspects of such claims—for instance, that content knowledge equals education—recall that there are points of overlap here. To reiterate, the notion of education as empowering, as a process of enabling individuals to exert greater agency over their political and professional circumstances and in turn fostering responsibility and collaboration by shoring up the foundation of agency, is in many cases the stated goal of educators critical of xMOOCs *as well as* xMOOCs and their supporters. The means may differ in myriad ways, but the ends resonate.

That said, the specific ways in which xMOOC advocates position *themselves* as individual agents in need of liberation is a point of departure from the self-positioning of many teachers. Near the end of the panel, moderator and PCAST member Eric Lander asks, "What if anything should the federal government be doing with respect to this movement [i.e., xMOOCs]?" For Lander, supporting the Department of Defense's efforts is a foregone conclusion, but he asks—given the other sectors involved—whether the PCAST and the federal government should "help it," "ensur[ing] it gets out" to such hard-to-reach targets as "the many job seekers in the United States who might like to have . . . advanced manufacturing jobs but are unqualified for them" or "figuring out the barriers with regard to K-12 education—a complicated marketplace to reach even if you have great products." Or, Lander proposes, "It could be that we should just sit back and let this creative disruption happen and kind of do nothing."[68] The panelists prefer Lander's final option: Koller suggests that government agencies should "basically get out of the way," while Agarwal argues that a variety of governmental regulations are stymieing the xMOOC movement and need to be relaxed or rescinded. In his words, "It's a tiger. Let it loose."[69]

These xMOOC advocates thus use the values of freedom, autonomy, and agency to frame not only what is expected of incoming and outgoing students but what should be afforded those who structure xMOOC students' educational experiences—a wide array of parties (e.g., companies, nonprofits, web and course designers, researchers, data miners) that are left responsible for much of the structural and pedagogical work traditionally afforded to teachers. In the case of students, it's assumed that the relative free*ness* and increasing prevalence of xMOOCs will give a massive number of students greater free*dom* to complete increasingly personalized courses at an individualized, relatively unstructured and nonlinear pace—all at once allowing, expecting, and inculcating a greater degree of agency as students undertake educational and professional pursuits. In the case of xMOOC facilitators, the argument goes that the best way to encourage the movement is to deregulate both the courses themselves and the individuals behind them.

To put it another way, the panelists claim that granting students the freedom *to* enroll in cheap, massive courses gives them a better shot at exercising and developing the agency they're presumed to already possess. Meanwhile xMOOCs themselves, as well as those involved in designing, promoting, and implementing them, need to be granted freedom *from* the regulatory strictures that govern higher education in the United States.[70] The task of external government entities, according to Koller, should not involve holding xMOOCs to certain accreditation standards (in a reply that highlights a key gap in Koller's knowledge of how higher education functions, Lander notes that the federal government already isn't responsible for accrediting institutions of higher education) or expecting or helping xMOOCs to reach certain goals with certain audiences (e.g., accessing the K-12 "marketplace"). Instead, the government should set xMOOCs and their creators loose, allowing them to help marginalized student populations precisely by not obligating them to do so. Questions of responsibility are quickly swept aside, trumped by the values of agency and autonomy. Let me note, however, that this drive for deregulation is paired with a desire to still have access to the sympathetic ear of government agencies in case the courses and their creators find themselves in need of assistance.

This dream of the unencumbered xMOOC pioneer resonates with a profile of Thrun in the magazine *Fast Company*. The 2013 piece, the title of which refers to Thrun as the "Godfather of Free Online Education," includes his infamous admission that Udacity doesn't "educate people as others wished, or as I wished. We have a lousy product."[71] But the piece ends on a far less dour note. Two days after a vigorous bike ride with Thrun, the profiler

return[s] to the Udacity offices, where Thrun is rerecording a seg-
ment for his statistics class. He'd mistakenly used an incorrect
notation in writing out a math problem, and he's returned to the
studio to get it right, spending an hour or so alone in the dark room,
talking into the microphone and scribbling on a tablet. "It's kind of
like being onstage, where you have all these lights in your face and
can't see the audience, but you still have to be able to excite them,"
he says. "So I think of the football stadium full of people that I'm
facing. I get a kick out of that." Thrun's taken the red pill. There's no
going back.[72]

What excites Thrun here is the challenge of moving an audience to which
he cannot respond. In his own words, the xMOOC instructor is figured as
a star: a performer on the stage, perhaps, or a quarterback energizing fans
as he coordinates a dynamic play. Though Thrun implies that this is a rhetorical obstacle—"you *still* have to be able to excite them" despite being
sensibly, geographically, and temporally disconnected—he ultimately
frames this disconnect as a pleasure.

In other words, what Thrun details in the profile—and what he, Koller,
and Agarwal were advocating for a year earlier—are the advantages of a
certain sort of irresponsibility, the pleasures set loose when one isn't bound
to respond but is instead free to bathe in the limelight reliant only on one's
own vision of what will strike others as exciting. I don't want to suggest that
irresponsibility is Thrun's conscious motivation—unlike some critics, I'm
hesitant to paint Thrun as "an oily charlatan" motivated solely by profit and
uninterested in if not hostile to improving educational structures and institutions.[73] Thrun's indirectly expressed pleasure in irresponsibility is arguably
not intentionally malevolent, and perhaps not so different from the pleasurable self-indulgence I occasionally experience when I have a few moments
to immerse myself in a non-teaching-related research project in the midst of
a busy semester. But, intentions aside, this is not *just* research and experi-
mentation happening here. This is, presumably, pedagogy—pedagogy that
unfolds under the assumption that the teacher-lecturer's inability to
respond to students based on those students' own responses to the teacher's
words is an exciting challenge with which to wrangle rather than an abdi-
cation of pedagogical responsibility.

The requested liberation of the innovator/experimenter/facilitator/ teacher is much more curious, and in some ways much more exclusive to xMOOC discourse, than such courses' purported liberating of students— students who are, as we've seen above, presumed to be already-autonomous agents who just need access to cheap content and the right pedagogical instruments and structures. And, despite my resistance to casting xMOOC proponents and practitioners as villains, this liberating of teachers from certain sorts of responsibilities and relations makes me at least equally hesitant to cast them as heroes.[74] In fact, it is in emphasizing unglamorous and nonheroic pedagogical responsibilities—responsibilities that put significant limits on one's agency—that I would seek possible justifications for teachers of nonmassive courses.

To set the stage for such justifications, let me summarize the case for xMOOCs documented throughout this chapter: By democratizing access to educational content, peer networks, and pedagogical instruments, xMOOCs will empower already-agentive students to become more agentive. In so doing, their advocates argue, xMOOCs will radically disrupt the educational status quo, and the best way to allow them to do so is to loose their creators from external regulations and responsibilities.

In a sense, this amounts to a claim that a combination of deregulation and individual agency generates democratic symmetry in terms of both access and opportunity. Consider an analogy Koller offers during the question-and-answer session at the end of the PCAST panel—one that both complicates and reaffirms this claim. In discussing the significance of on-campus peer networks, Koller offers a two-tiered description of such networks' benefits. For those she classes as "remedial students," she argues that the small-scale interactions with teachers and peers afforded by on-campus, face-to-face education ameliorate the risk that such students will drop out; such interactions also allow teachers to sort "remedial" students into smaller peer groups based on the particular topics with which those students are struggling. For "elite" students, on the other hand, engaging with "a star faculty member" and "a network of peers that are of equal stature" constitute important preparatory steps for those Koller hopes will be the leaders of the "science, government, business of tomorrow." One PCAST member responds by asking Koller whether the combination of xMOOCs and her tiered view of in-person higher education will simply "make elite institutions even more elite." Koller responds, "I think elite institutions are elite. It's a fact of life. But I think it will make all institutions better.... I think it will make all boats float higher. It won't necessarily make everyone equal; I think that's probably too ambitious of a goal. People aren't necessarily born equal in terms of their abilities, but I think it [the xMOOC movement] will make everyone achieve at a much higher level than where they currently are."[75]

Koller's reiteration of the old saw that a rising tide lifts all boats, not to mention her eyebrow-raising hierarchy that presupposes inherent distinctions between "remedial" and "elite" students, drifts from the rhetoric of parity she and her copanelists elsewhere espouse. It also sidesteps the question of "achievement gaps" and "education debt" in US education, including extensive evidence that such gaps are largely attributable to social inequities, not innate differences in individual ability.[76] Instead of considering the possibility that xMOOCs might close such gaps, helping address persistent inequities between the quantitative performance of and educational opportunities available to, for example, white students and students of color, Koller conveniently repositions these well-established gaps as a matter of decontextualized, ostensibly inherent intellectual disparities. For Koller, because the asymmetries that separate students and institutions are natural, it's not a matter of closing gaps. The analogy does, however, rely on a certain principle of symmetry: if a rising tide does in fact lift all boats, and presumably lifts them relatively equally, then it at least moves us closer to symmetrical distribution.

Students, of course, are not boats. What is the difference between a student and a boat? As I've suggested, in the case of the ideal xMOOC student, the difference is agency. Recall that Koller sees xMOOCs as a particularly good fit for "independent learners"—a view that resonates with DiGiovanni's interest in "autodidacts" as well as with Thrun's anecdote about the two girls in Texas. If xMOOCs are the metaphorical tide, what the panelists dream of are not in fact boats that will simply go with the flow but strong swimmers who, though they might benefit from connecting and collaborating with peers, can navigate the rising waters and communicate with those peers on their own. They don't need a dinghy or even a life preserver—just affordable access to the open ocean.[77]

Advocates of xMOOCs, in other words, depend on a figure that sociologist Tressie McMillan Cottom calls the "roaming autodidact."[78] In fact,

Cottom argues that many emerging varieties of for-profit online education rely on this figure: a "self-motivated, able learner that is simultaneously embedded in technocratic futures *and* disembodied from place, culture, history, markets, and inequality regimes."[79] Cottom contends that the decontextualized, generalized figure of the roaming autodidact doesn't account for the myriad past and present social variables and limitations that determine how students engage with educational structures and institutions. Measured against this idealized figure, then, most comers end up falling short. But that doesn't stop it from holding a prominent place in the rhetorical optimism around xMOOCs: the democratizing claims surrounding such courses depend on students who are roaming autodidacts readily able to make use of the instruments and networks provided by xMOOCs. Even Koller's simplistic "remedial"/"elite" distinction is effaced in such claims, which unmoor students and institutions alike from their social and intellectual contexts. It is assumed such distinctions will cease to matter in the coming xMOOC utopia, with xMOOCs erasing rather than exacerbating the troubled and troubling distinction between "remedial" and "elite." This assumption is precisely what Thrun's anecdote about the two girls in Texas seeks to forward, suggesting that xMOOCs allow students unfairly labeled as remedial (because of their gender, their ethnicity, the school they attend, their lack of success in traditional classrooms based on traditional metrics) to show that they were potentially elite all along. All the xMOOC does is allow them to exercise the agency they possessed the whole time. The panelists, then—some of them innovators in the realm of artificial intelligence who are otherwise attuned to distributed cognition and the networked factors at work in much of what we call intelligence—fall back on a valorized notion of human agency and describe technology as an instrument taken up by agentive humans. The symmetry they see xMOOCs facilitating becomes an essentially—and, in Koller's case, essentialist—humanist symmetry. (Note, however, that this is also Koller's view of conventional colleges and universities.)

———

This sort of symmetry—the notion that humans are first and foremost self-conscious, radically agentive beings—may seem democratizing but is in truth deeply atomizing, replacing fundamental democratic questions about what it means to learn and live together with questions about how one can become a more efficient individual learner, each in a boat of one's own, collaborating with and responding to one another only as means to an end. And this sort of symmetry, which remains central to the self-justifications of many companies still operating and emerging in the ed-tech sector, is precisely what Levinasian responsibility allows us to call into question in the pursuit of more just and responsible modes of teaching.

Peer Networks, the Limits of Symmetry, and the Possibilities of Responsible Education

> And who are we in the university where apparently we are? What do we represent? Whom do we represent? Are we responsible? For what and to whom? If there is a university responsibility, it at least begins the moment when a need to hear these questions, to take them upon oneself and respond to them, imposes itself. This imperative of the response is the initial form and minimal requirement of responsibility.
>
> —JACQUES DERRIDA

As I showed in the previous chapter, advocates of for-profit MOOCs, or xMOOCs, frequently premise their arguments on intertwined and variable notions of personalization, empowerment, and democratization. While I challenged some of those arguments in chapter 3, including pointing out places where they break down or get tossed aside, the fact that xMOOC advocates share a vocabulary with those committed to more circumspect approaches to higher education remains a rhetorical sticking point. This isn't just a matter of xMOOCs, either. Recall the University of Phoenix commercial described at the start of this book or the nonprofit and for-profit entities pitching personalized ed-tech solutions in the wake of the coronavirus pandemic.[1]

This chapter is not a brash rejection of democratized education, empowered students, personalized learning, or the guiding concept I'm arguing links those things together: student agency. Far from it. Rather, it is a challenge to a particular, all-encompassing notion of student agency that gets positioned as both the starting point for and the outcome of educational experiences. Rather than positioning student agency as something we can take for granted as a guarantor of symmetry in human nature and networks, I position agency as a relentlessly fragile thing—something premised upon an inherent vulnerability in human relations that points toward a similarly fragile notion of what it might mean to "democratize" education. I ask what might happen if we begin not by taking agency for granted but by considering that agency is founded upon something else. I begin, in a word, with responsibility.

Contra many of the implicit and explicit assumptions of xMOOC advocates, Emmanuel Levinas describes the subject as established by an *asymmetrical* relation. This relation calls the subject to a responsibility that is the condition for agency and freedom rather than the other way around. As Diane Davis puts it, "What Levinas is proposing is that a responsibility to respond, a preoriginary *rhetorical* imperative, is the condition for any conscious subject rather than the other way around. . . . [I]t is thanks to this preoriginary responsibility that there is consciousness and so the emergence of ego, which is now 'free' to enjoy all the pleasures and pitfalls of being-with-others-in-the-world."[2]

While this repositioning of responsibility and agentive freedom—which is not a simple flip—does not directly translate into specific pedagogical prescriptions, it does have implications for pedagogical relations that deserve to be drawn out. At the very least, the relation Levinas describes between "freedom" and "responsibility" exposes the fragility of a number of assumptions that xMOOC advocates make in their figurations of teachers' and students' relations to responsibility and freedom.

In many ways, xMOOC advocates' conception of the autonomous individual resonates with accounts of the subject spanning the intertwined histories of rhetoric and philosophy. These accounts, which I considered briefly in chapter 2, describe the human subject as an individual being that enters into relation with itself, then with the world and other people. As just one example, G. W. F. Hegel posits a sort of pure subjectivity that recognizes itself via a built-in capacity for self-reference.[3] The human becomes "his own property" by means of "*his self-consciousness comprehending itself as free.*"[4] The subject comprehends itself as free, and this freedom provides the foundation for responsibility. That is, only after recognizing myself as such do I take responsibility for myself and, through participation in the family and the state, for others. Responsible relations between selves are thus relations between self-conscious equals. As I discussed in the previous chapter, this sort of freedom prior to responsibility remains a common assumption in philosophical and rhetorical accounts of the structure of the human (and, more specifically, student) subject.

In *Totality and Infinity: An Essay on Exteriority*, Levinas describes the subject and its relation to responsibility and freedom very differently. Freedom is not the result of self-recognition or a self-made choice paving the way to responsibility; the primary encounter is not that of the subject with itself but the encounter with what Levinas calls "the Other."[5] The gathering up and identification of a "self" only occurs after I'm called by "the Other," an entity that exceeds comprehension, putting out a call that arrives before an "I" is even on the scene—a call, in other words, that precedes and exceeds the understanding of that "I" and opens the possibility of the subsequent realization that there is a something to be called "myself." "I" only am because I was called to respond to and be responsible for someone or something other than myself. It is only after and because of this responsibility that I can exercise anything that might be called "freedom" or "self-consciousness." A Levinasian self, then, emerges not as a virile, self-posited "I AM!" but as a response to a call: "Here I am." Or, perhaps even more hesitantly, "Who? Me?"[6]

We may seem to have strayed from pedagogical territory here. As one way to keep the connection open, let me note that Levinas often figures the relation with the Other in terms of teaching, contrasting the Other's "teaching" with that of Socrates: The "primacy of the same was Socrates's teaching: to receive nothing of the Other but what is in me, as though from all eternity I was in possession of what comes to me from the outside—to receive nothing, or to be free."[7] Countering Socratic teaching—anamnesis or maieutics, the reassembling of latent lessons I already contained—Levinas argues, "Teaching is not reducible to maieutics; it comes from the exterior and brings me more than I contain."[8] In short, the Other's teaching comes from outside of and is not comprehended by a "self." It does not reveal the free self I hadn't yet realized that I'd been all along but calls me to a responsibility that is the precondition for the self and its freedom.

It's worth emphasizing that Levinas *does not* position Plato's Socrates's maieutics-focused pedagogy as an ideal, particularly given the weird aspirational roles that Plato and Socrates played in the discourse around xMOOCs. For example, in a piece on the impact of MOOCs, journalist and scholar Owen R. Youngman echoed a philosopher's concern with whether "we could hold education in MOOCs to standards drawn from Plato"— standards the philosopher specifically derived from Plato's *Gorgias*.[9] Meanwhile, as noted in the previous chapter, the Department of Defense's Frank DiGiovanni imagined a "wearable . . . Socrates-like tutor" as the future of MOOC technology.[10] On both sides, then, Socratic pedagogy (as filtered through Plato) provided an ideal toward which education should strive. As laid out in chapter 1, that is not the ideal I'm after in this book. The fact that Levinas opens up pedagogical trajectories that do not take the principles of Socratic pedagogy for granted is a key part of what his work makes possible in this context.

That said, the teacher-student relationship isn't the definitive way to characterize one's irremissible, immemorial encounter with the Other even though it is one *Totality and Infinity* returns to again and again.[11] Rather, as Davis observes, the Levinasian relation with the Other can be described only as a "figuring of the unfigurable."[12] The Other is not a "teacher" in the everyday sense of the term: a human being who teaches a student or students a lesson. Far from it. It is in the encounter with this teacher's teaching, in the relation between a self that is not yet a self and the ungraspable Other, that one becomes an "I"—not by gaining enough self-distance to recognize oneself as such but by being pushed back onto oneself in the face of this incomprehensible, unfigurable relation. What makes the relation "asymmetrical" is that one doesn't encounter the Other on a level playing field of free, self-possessed subjects. Instead, the Other is encountered as a magisterial "'You' in a dimension of height."[13] From this dimension, the Other issues a call that demands a response. And yet the Other, issuer of a call that precedes and exceeds "me," is extremely vulnerable as well—and here the pedagogical figuration takes another turn: the Other is at once "hostile, my friend, *my master, my student*."[14]

Though Levinas describes the initial encounter with this "master"/ "student" as anarchic (without origin, "*an-*" plus "*arche*") and preceding memory, he provides examples of ways it resounds in everyday existence: he identifies a trace of the hospitality one extends to the Other—that one cannot *not* extend to the Other—in every small act of generosity, even something as simple as holding the door for someone else and saying, "After you."[15] Moreover, I—no longer in scare quotes—often find myself undone in daily life, put back in question, by what Levinas calls "the face." Davis describes this "face" as "neither a natural phenomenon nor the figure that is given in prosopopoeia: it names instead the dissolution of that figure. . . . 'face' here operates as a (para)figure for disfiguration."[16] Levinas compares the face to "someone who opens a window on which his figure is outlined. His presence consists in divesting himself of the form which, however, manifests him."[17] The face of the Other could be manifested by a stranger or by someone with whom I am familiar: in the gesture of a partner, the utterance of a friend, or a student's writing assignment—any event that shatters my concept of that person and renders me unable to figure them.[18] Suddenly I am again the responsible party in an asymmetrical relation.[19]

Before turning back toward xMOOCs, let me trace out an example. Imagine you're a teacher sitting in your classroom just before class starts. A student pops in with a draft of a writing assignment she wants feedback on. "I'm not sure I'm doing what I'm supposed to do with this assignment," she says. She passes the draft to you and you start to read. As you read, you find yourself unable to get your head around what's unfolding on the page. It's not that it's sublimely good or incoherently terrible—it's that you, a teacher with years of experience dealing with student writing, cannot figure it out. Perhaps later on you'll make sense of the draft by figuring it as a new genre or an unorthodox combination of rhetorical approaches, or you'll realize that it's written in a dialect or modality you couldn't recognize in the moment. In the here and now, however, none of your prefigured responses to student writing suffice. Moreover, when you glance up from the draft and look back at the student, you are suddenly unable to figure her within the taxonomy of students that you've developed over the course of your career—unable to figure her *as a student* at all. Maybe yesterday you thought of her as a slacker with a knack for first drafts but little patience for revision, or a formalist who can generate perfectly structured five-paragraph essays but is just beginning to experiment with other genres, or a future academic who keeps piling on examples and questions without ever getting to the point. In any case, whatever distance separates you now feels inadequate. This student, who suddenly seems to have taken on a position of mastery over you, demands that you respond—but that demand is attended by vulnerability. Lofty and exposed, this unfigurable student and her ungraspable writing await your response.

Of course, you can just tell her to go the writing center or that the draft needs a little bit more work before you can respond to it. You can decline to respond, but you can't decline the *invitation* to respond, the disfiguration that precedes and prompts the declension. That disfiguration is what Levinas calls the "face to face." This relation does not consist in a masterful "teacher" extending rhetorical agency or discursive power to a latently agentive student. It is not an encounter that leaves the so-called teacher in a position of authority, occurs between equals, or simply recenters the pedagogical scene around an agentive student. It is an encounter in which the figures and figurations that delimit everyday roles and expectations—the sagacious teacher, the earnest student—break up. The face of the Other looms above you with immense vulnerability. And suddenly you recognize the two of you aren't alone anymore, in fact were never alone in the first place: you're sitting in a classroom full of students, and how you respond to this face-to-face encounter has ramifications not only for this singular student but for a whole slew of third parties, of other others.

The introduction of these third parties is a key moment. For Levinas, it is their presence that takes one from "the limit of responsibility" to questions of justice. When the third party arrives, I'm no longer responsible only for the Other but find myself having to balance obligations to a multitude of others: "The responsibility for the other is an immediacy antecedent to questions, it is proximity. It is troubled and becomes a problem when a third party enters.... [This entry] put[s] distance between me and the other and the third party.... The third party introduces a contradiction in the saying whose signification before the other until then went in one direction. *It is of itself the limit of responsibility and the birth of the question: What do I have to do with justice?* A question of consciousness."[20]

Only now, with the arrival of a third party, do questions of justice, of balancing obligations, enter the picture. Let me note something about this "arrival," however. As with the admittedly simplistic classroom example above, it isn't the case that third parties arrive in the wake of the encounter with the Other. They were in fact there all along, issuing a sort of double depropriation. Not only am I depropriated in the face of the Other; I am simultaneously faced with a number of others, the result of which, in the variable and conflicting demands they issue, is that I can never totally fulfill my obligation to the singular Other.

Again, there is no chance for the entity who isn't yet a self-conscious being to refuse the encounter with the Other, to say "no." Davis glosses this situation in terms of a phone call: "you pick up the phone, and your first word is 'yes?' Even if you say 'hello?' it means 'yes?' Before you can say, 'yes I will take your call' or 'no, I won't take your call,' you have taken the call, *in order* to get the chance to decide. Already in picking up you have responded, welcomed the other in."[21] It is only after the primary "yes?," which I can't avoid uttering, that I get the chance to decide whether to say a second "yes" or to hang up. It is in the wake of this first inescapable "yes?" that I recognize the third party's presence on the scene and things shift from the asymmetrical relationship between the proto-"I" and the Other to the political realm in which equality, justice, and morality become concerns. Yet, just as there is no period of introspection in the encounter with the Other, there is no respite that intervenes between that encounter and the arrival of other others. As Levinas puts it, "If the other can invest me and . . . my freedom, of itself arbitrary, this is in the last analysis because I can feel myself to be *the other of the other*. But this comes about only across very complex structures. . . . Morality begins when freedom, instead of being justified by itself, feels itself to be arbitrary and violent."[22]

No longer the unquestioned ground of subjectivity, nor an innate possession of the self that is justified in and of itself, freedom is resituated as a consequence of responsibility—a fragile symmetry that is invested and justified in the synchronous wake of an asymmetrical relation. In her rhetorically oriented exposition of Levinasian responsibility, Davis concludes by reflecting on this re-/disfigured relation between freedom and responsibility: "If rhetoric has a specifically ethical task today, it surely would not involve revving the engines of virility and mastery all over again. Perhaps it would involve the deconstruction of heroic thematizations and the exposition of exposedness, the nonheroic ethical structuring of subjectivity."[23] What I'm arguing here is that both the rhetoric and the structure of xMOOCs (1) are built on the amoral ground of a freedom detached from responsibility and (2) depend precisely on "revving the engines of virility" in ways that don't account for the "complex structures" across which freedom becomes justifiable, arbitrary, even violent.

Just consider how the language of speed figures into xMOOC advocates' descriptions of the "disruptions" that are and could be brought about by their movement. Thrun highlights the speed at which the two girls in Texas tore through courses in physics and geometry: they "finished a semester-long assignment in two weeks" and were "all of a sudden" propelled beyond high-school competency levels. Or consider Agarwal's "tiger," his xMOOC movement that just needs to be let loose. Both Thrun's students and Agarwal's tiger constitute figures of acceleration dependent on the idea that autonomous agency is *the* preeminent educational value, a value that is justified in and of itself and that fundamentally characterizes both students and course facilitators. "Disruption," in the case of xMOOCs, means acceleration. One can almost hear the virile revving of the virtual engines.

The disruptions of the face, however, mark breakdowns and breakups rather than accelerations. Whereas the xMOOC movement's disruptions sought to speed things up, blowing past responsibility in order to get to freedom, Levinas takes us back to a responsibility that never stops interrupting and affecting the ways in which freedom manifests itself. From this perspective, the issue isn't that xMOOC advocates can escape responsibility's irruptions—one can imagine Sebastian Thrun facing a moment of abject depropriation, a fleeting moment of irremissible exposure, a primary "yes?" before he was able to conceptualize the extent of Udacity's failure. Again, such depropriations can be swept aside, but only as an after-the-fact form of addressing them. The issue, rather, is that they are perceived only as momentary interruptions, hitches that signal things are about to kick into a higher gear. In the world of xMOOCs, figures of speed reign supreme: in a magazine with the title *Fast Company*, Thrun is described as a vigorous cyclist, a dynamo, an immodest man about whose efforts one thing is certain: "There's no going back." Any disfiguration is quickly refigured and recuperated as another sign of the need to go faster still.[24] Even if a slight course adjustment is required, maintaining the freedom to accelerate is the main thing. And that drive is still with us. Recall Thrun's claim, uttered in the midst of the coronavirus pandemic, that crises "lead to accelerations, and this is best chance ever for online learning."[25]

As one final example, consider Agarwal's description of his encounters with education scholarship. Despite the PCAST panel's titular focus on "STEM Education," Agarwal pauses to offer this relatively generous nod to education scholars: "People may say . . . MOOCs are doing something radical and new. I just want to give a plug to some of our colleagues in education, who have been slogging away on learning for decades, for hundreds of years, and what I am finding is that I thought I was a really cool kid on the block doing some cool stuff, but . . . every single thing that I thought was cool, I was able to find a paper that demonstrated this was a good idea."[26]

Rhetorically speaking, Agarwal makes a curious double move: He lauds a non-STEM discipline, affecting an air of humility. At the same time, however, he seems less humble when he positions education research as legitimating "every single thing that [he] thought was cool." The suggestion here would seem to be that, though education research is a valuable and difficult undertaking with a robust and oft-overlooked history, Agarwal has been able to intuit the findings of education researchers without having to actually do the research. He is grateful, in other words, that a scholarly tradition exists to offer retroactive justification for the "good idea[s]" he—a STEM researcher—had already arrived at on his own.

What this "plug" demonstrates is a resistance to interruption. It strikes me as unlikely that Agarwal didn't encounter at least a few pieces of educational scholarship that ran counter to his vision of learning. Perhaps what he needed was an education scholar, maybe even a rhetoric and writing scholar, to interrupt his smoothly ordered world and ready-to-hand conceptions of teaching, learning, and the students that shape that world—to call attention to unrecognized interruptions and open the possibility that, rather than surging forth from the educational archives with the energy of a tiger finally set free, the xMOOC movement itself might need to spend some time slogging. The possibility that may need to be held open is that educators, from xMOOC lecturers to small-time teachers, cannot be responsible if they always remain in the position of the masterful teacher. Responsibly investing both my freedom and the freedom of others, whether in reading and applying others' scholarship or in structuring and inhabiting pedagogical spaces, involves the relentless possibility of being knocked off one's feet in the face of alterity, disrupted in a way that is not just a momentary hiccup or slowdown in the smooth, friction-free communication of educational content or the inevitable progress of educational technologies. It is to acknowledge, rather, that the very possibility of being taught *depends* on such disruption.[27]

Such an acknowledgment does not necessarily mean that one can recuperate disruption in a productive manner. Again, the disruptive depropriation of the first "yes?" occurs whether one acknowledges it or not. Putting off the urge to reassert the stability of the teacher's or student's capacity for understanding in the wake of that "yes?," however—holding open a space for a second "yes?"—is what I'm arguing provides a significant alternative to the simultaneously humanist and inhuman assumptions about student agency that underpin the designs of xMOOCs and the claims of their advocates. Exposing this alternative, however, means abandoning some of rhetorical education's traditional assumptions about communication and human agency, "to [instead] approach speaking and writing, any form of the address, not simply or firstly as the *means* of communication (as servants of the said), but *as* communication itself, as modes of the saying, expositions of an ethical relation that precedes identity, intellection, and intentionality."[28] It entails shifting our own assumptions about rhetorical education's relation to freedom and autonomy in order to attune ourselves to encounters with exposure and vulnerability that are not simply momentary interruptions to be overcome en route to empowerment and rhetorical agency but constitutive of the pedagogical scene in relentless and inescapable ways. Such relational encounters are, rather, the only justification for investing one's freedom and the freedom of others—justifications xMOOCs are designed to downplay if not ignore. It's not that small-scale rhetorical education and educators are better at fostering agency and autonomy, more empowering, more liberating. Instead, while Thrun dials up the power and takes the stage, we humble teachers might leave openings for power failures, for interruptions in agency and our own mastery, for anxiety and vulnerability. Such openings, I'm arguing, are a constitutive part of responsible, democratic pedagogy: the possibility of acknowledging that the "imperative of the response is the initial form and minimal requirement of [university] responsibility."[29]

THE RHETORICAL RESPONSIBILITIES OF PEER NETWORKS

I'll now conclude this pair of chapters by illustrating the ethical and rhetorical limitations of the agency-centered pedagogy espoused by xMOOC advocates, then providing a counter-illustration that highlights the possibilities of a pedagogical approach that prioritizes responsibility and, in doing so, does not take agency for granted as the simultaneous starting and ending points for classroom interactions. I do so by turning my attention to a component of xMOOCs that I haven't spent much time discussing so far: peer networks. I emphasize them now for two main reasons: First, because they are frequently situated as one of the key elements that allow xMOOCs to operate successfully without the smaller teacher-student ratio of nonmassive college courses. Second, to begin to complicate what many rhetoric and writing scholars have framed as "the" question raised by xMOOCs: "What is lost without . . . student-teacher connections?"[30] While this is an important question, the way it's phrased risks sidestepping many of the contextual factors that determine how, when, and why student-teacher connections happen. Even within the confines of a conventional public university, different kinds of courses involve different kind of connections. In a two-hundred-student course held in a tiered lecture hall with giant projector screens and multiple teaching assistants, students connect with a teacher and each other differently than they do in a twenty-student course taught in a computer classroom with no teaching assistants and a lot of small-group discussions, which is different still from a fifteen-student online course in which almost if not all exchanges between the parties involved take place asynchronously. In short, student-teacher connections are not easily abstracted from the specific educational infrastructures in which those connections develop, and though xMOOC advocates often paint higher education with a broad brush, those infrastructures vary widely from campus to campus, even from department to department and course to course. In the remainder of this chapter, then, I contrast the way peer networks are positioned as key components of xMOOCs' educational infrastructures with the way they might specifically figure into smaller-scale rhetoric and writing courses.

Doing so requires an initial clarification about the intended trajectories of xMOOCs. In the PCAST panel, Thrun argues that xMOOCs afford students a proliferation of "individual learning paths."[31] Because, as Thrun claims, the courses' "pedagogical instruments" can adapt tirelessly to students' multifarious needs and learning styles, students are no longer stuck with a one-size-fits-all approach to education. I would note, however, that all these paths lead to the same end: mastery of the particular skills and/or content knowledge represented by a given course's lecturer-teacher. All roads lead to Rome—or, in the case of xMOOCs, Silicon Valley and its intertwined educational, professional, political, and economic values.

The peer networks of xMOOCs are not designed to let students diverge from what I'm arguing are such courses' singular aims. Rather, they are simply there to open additional paths that lead to a course's preset destination, another set of means to an end. In fact, during the question-and-answer portion of the PCAST panel, Daphne Koller acknowledges that xMOOCs' peer networks were something of an afterthought. Initially, xMOOCs' STEM-focused developers only included peer response and assessment in the courses "because of very strong pressure from the humanities faculty that are working with us who did not respond well to the suggestion that multiple-choice is underrated."

Of course, peer interaction in rhetoric and writing courses can also be something of an afterthought, a lowly means to a predetermined end. Take one of the most commonplace forms of such interaction in writing-intensive courses: peer workshops. Students read each other's works-in-progress, offer each other feedback on those works-in-progress, and then make use of the feedback they receive as they revise. As Anne Ruggles Gere has pointed out, "college instructors brought writing groups into 'regular' composition courses" as early as 1895.[32] While early adopters might have been motivated less by high-minded pedagogical goals and more by the possibility of reducing their workload—"offload[ing] onto students some of the drudgery associated with" correcting student writing—by the 1980s, peer workshops were embraced as part of "a specific view of collaborative learning in which learning occurs best among a 'community of status equals' or 'peers.'"[33]

Despite a rich history and myriad pedagogical justifications, peer workshops are something many students in my first-year writing courses dislike or dread. It can take a lot to convince students to see such workshops as anything other than a nuisance. There are a variety of reasons for this, three of which I identify here and circle back to throughout this section. Students might (1) view peer response as redundant or unnecessary because they see teacher feedback as always trumping peer feedback, (2) consider themselves worse writers than their peers and thus unable to offer worthwhile feedback to others, which can come with a side of anxiety about sharing their writing with other students whom they perceive as superior writers, or (3) consider themselves better writers than their peers and thus unable to benefit from peer response.[34] For teachers attempting to assuage such concerns, claims about increased agency offer one way forward: responding to your peers' writing makes *you* a better writer, as demonstrated by research on the benefits of such response.[35] Whether you're a self-proclaimed "good" writer who can't or won't learn anything from your peers' responses or a self-proclaimed "bad" writer who feels incapable of offering anything to your peers, the relational work of peer response—as luck would have it—turns out to improve the individual's writing and communication skills.

But for reasons explained and implied throughout this and the preceding chapters, I hesitate to crystallize response, peer or otherwise, as a means directed toward the end of increased self-mastery. In some ways, my interests align with those of Kory Lawson Ching, who traces a history of peer response in college classrooms that "moves beyond the prevailing authority/autonomy binary."[36] According to Ching, Gere's history of writing groups presents peer response as emerging "out of a move to decenter classroom authority" and, in a manner modeled on "extracurricular settings like literary societies, writers' clubs, and self-improvement groups," extending authority and agency to the student writers and respondents who populate the groups.[37] However, while Ching acknowledges that peer response has developed into a robustly theorized component of rhetoric and writing pedagogy, he offers an alternative genealogy that grew "as a way for students to share some of the teacher's burden" for responding to student work—which, as we've seen, is precisely how peer networks are positioned by xMOOC advocates.[38] One of Ching's alternatives to Gere's history is based on the fact that she figures authority as "a finite commodity, a resource that one either does or does not possess. Under this view teaching authority and student autonomy balance each other in a zero-sum game, in which students gain freedom as teachers lose influence."[39] In place of this zero-sum view, Ching argues, "we might more profitably think of authority not as something one *has*, but rather as something one *does* or *enacts* in practice. From this perspective authority ceases to be a static quality and becomes instead an index of a person's capacity to act in a particular sphere of activity."[40]

It is here that my line of argument breaks with Ching's. While I am also interested in "mov[ing] beyond the prevailing authority/autonomy binary," I am not interested in reinscribing the commonplace move of extending authority and agency to more individuals.[41] It's not that I think this is a bad move to make. However, as Ching notes throughout his piece, responding to others' writing is not simply the potentially infinite enactment or extension of a capacity—it is a constraint, a responsibility, perhaps even a tacit recognition of a teacher's incapacities: "In none of these early discussions do teachers completely abdicate their own *responsibility* for correction";[42] "What the alternative genealogy for peer response suggests, in its vision of teachers and students sharing *responsibility* in the classroom, is a third way to understand learning processes."[43] To respond to others is quite literally a responsibility, as Ching acknowledges. But in challenging the authority/autonomy binary by making both terms part of a non-zero-sum extension of authoritative agency that empowers teachers and students alike, he sidesteps some of the more vexing connotations, challenges, and limitations involved in taking responsibility for another's writing—the incapacities that are bound up with responsibility as I have tried to articulate it.

Instead, I am interested in peer response as an opportunity to interrupt the procedures that teachers and students alike often rely on in responding to others' writing. This includes questioning the priority granted to authority and agency themselves in discourse around peer response. I propose interrupting this priority by calling into question the singular authority of teacher feedback—the reason labeled (1) a few paragraphs back—and emphasizing the vulnerability of teachers and their writings in tandem with the entropic tendencies of dialogue, which is not necessarily opposed to extending agency to students.

Like xMOOCs, writing courses often flow toward a singular end, no matter what diversions students pursue along the way: the teacher's conception of and preferences regarding writing can direct the course, even as those preferences also reflect those of broader academic, civic, or professional communities. In such courses, I can understand why students would be skeptical of peer workshops. Given that the teacher is the one who ultimately assesses students' writing, why should students care about anyone else's feedback?[44] This is especially the case if the teacher also provides feedback on the drafts to which peers respond, as I typically do. Why listen to anyone else in such a case? For students, the best-case scenario might seem to be that peers' advice echoes the teacher's and is thus redundant. Worst case: it contradicts the teacher's, potentially throwing the student off the trail of the revisions most likely to get them a good grade on the final product. If the teacher doesn't give feedback on peer-workshopped drafts, then peer response can seem like an imitation game, with student respondents doing their best to intuit what feedback the teacher *would* offer based on the assignment prompt, the syllabus, prior feedback, and so on.

A challenging exercise in *imitatio*, perhaps, but not particularly engaging as rhetorical decision-making goes.

More to the point, I would argue that such conceptions of peer response efface what Levinas calls the "third party." Even if it seems as though students are being asked to engage in complicated rhetorical and ethical work—both in the feedback they give and how they respond to the feedback they receive—they are only being asked to inhabit and exercise the protocols of a single "other": the teacher. In terms of the history of rhetoric and writing pedagogy *and* in terms of xMOOCs, this is just more of the same: ideally, a multiplicity of respondents merely highlights a singular end.

A pedagogy of responsibility asks for something different. Bearing in mind Davis's call "to approach speaking and writing, any form of the address, not simply or firstly as the *means* of communication (as servants of the said), but *as* communication itself," I position peer response in a different and more significant way.[45] Rather than echoing the voice of the teacher or pointing toward a predetermined end, peer response can open a proliferation of paths that do not reconverge.

Let me provide an extended example, some of which may sound familiar to experienced rhetoric and writing teachers. In Fall 2020, the first full semester following my university's widespread shift to online courses due to COVID-19, one of the courses I taught was ENGL 1010, the first of two courses in our first-year writing sequence. In past iterations of ENGL 1010 and first-year writing courses I'd taught at other institutions, I typically assessed student work using what is now often referred to as "ungrading."[46] Combining elements of contract grading, portfolio-based assessment, and other cumulative, evidence-based approaches to evaluating students' writing and learning, those courses would unfold as follows:[47] Students begin by writing a short statement of goals in which they outline how they want to develop in the course based on learning objectives stated in the syllabus and elaborated on in supplementary course documents. For example, the current objectives for ENGL 1010 are "composing processes," "reading," "rhetorical knowledge," "integrative thinking," and "information literacy."[48] Students pursue these goals in subsequent coursework, including things like reading notes, longer individual and collaborative writing projects, and peer workshops on drafts of those longer projects. Along the way, I provide extensive qualitative responses to the writing they're doing but no quantitative grades. At the midterm and the final, students use a detailed but flexible set of grading criteria to compose a written argument in which they argue for the grade they have earned in the course. Those arguments are based on the course's learning objectives as well as specific qualitative evidence drawn from the body of work the student has done in the course; how they've achieved, altered, or even failed at the goals they set at the start of the semester; and the amount of coursework they've completed. Thus, while students are self-assessing in extensive, meaningful ways, they are doing so in response to a system I've developed based on programmatic and institutional values and constraints as well as assessment schemes developed by others in and around my field. These are approaches meant to emphasis responsive exchange between students, between students and me, and between students and their reflective, nonidentical selves.

One of the first major writing projects I usually assign in ENGL 1010 is a literacy narrative, a common assignment in first-year writing courses.[49] My current prompt for this assignment begins as follows:

Summary
Write a personal narrative about your experiences with and attitudes toward literacy, reading, and writing.

Purpose
To reflect on the factors that have influenced your habits, feelings, and mindset when it comes to the work you'll be doing in this class, and to give me and your classmates a sense of who you are as a reader and writer.

Detailed Description
For this assignment, you will write a literacy narrative of 1000–1250 words in which you'll reflect on and narrate your relationship to writing, reading, and literacy. We'll read and discuss some examples of literacy narratives, but here are some key questions you might consider for this particular assignment:

How would you describe your relationship to writing and read-ing? What feelings (comfort, anxiety, boredom, etc.) do you associate with different kinds of reading and writing? What key events, people, or communities have shaped how you write/read and how you feel about writing/reading? What media and genres do you write in (a journal, social media, school essays, etc.)? What do you see as your strengths and weaknesses as a writer, including but not only in classroom settings?

You won't be able to answer all those questions, and you don't have to answer them in order. Ultimately, this should be a *narrative*, a true story about your development and background as a writer and reader. It shouldn't be a long list of unconnected memories or statements. The questions are just potential starting points.

As that last paragraph suggests, one of my primary concerns when introducing students to literacy narratives is familiarizing them with the genre conventions of narratives. While many students have had to write personal and fictional narratives for past classes, in the face of what is likely one of their first major college writing assignments, they often fall back on the conventions of the five-paragraph essay. That is, they begin with a paragraph stating what they'll be writing about, frequently including some sort of thesis statement. They then write three paragraphs in which they address three relatively discrete aspects of their experiences with reading and writing, and they conclude with a fifth paragraph in which they summarize what they've written. As John Warner writes, "The five-paragraph essay has taken root for explicable reasons, even if they are not good ones. They are easy to teach for the purposes of passing standardized assessments. The standardization makes them easier to assign and grade for teachers who are burdened with too many students."[50] In other words, students often fall back on the conventions of a genre they've been habituated to write in for a busy, standardization-focused, relatively unresponsive audience rather than adopting and adapting different conventions for a writing prompt that—while still constrained by genre norms and my guidance as a teacher—is meant for slightly more varied and responsive readers.

To be clear, my point here isn't to belittle students' tendency to fall back on the five-paragraph essay. Because it is such an effective genre in the context of standardized testing and other assessments that can be immensely consequential for students, it makes a lot of sense that students are socialized into the genre and fall back on it in the face of unfamiliar writing situations.

But as I point out regularly when working with students on literacy narratives, the five-paragraph essay doesn't always translate well to telling stories. An opening paragraph consisting of abstract statements about the importance of literacy doesn't necessarily serve as a compelling start to a narrative, even if it might be a perfect fit for the start of a five-paragraph essay written for a standardized test and, by extension, for those charged with assessing massive piles of test essays in a short timeframe for a little extra income. Instead, I suggest to students, they can jump right into the narrative itself via an illustrative anecdote, provide a detailed description of a person or object that influenced their relationship to literacy, establish a guiding metaphor that they'll return to throughout the piece, or offer a tongue-in-cheek metacommentary on why it's so hard for them to get started on a writing assignment.

In ENGL 1010, I typically have students write two drafts of their literacy narratives. Students workshop the first draft in groups of three or four and also receive feedback on it from me. For the workshop, students both provide feedback for and receive feedback from two of their classmates. As with the literacy narrative itself, I provide detailed guidelines for the peer workshop. In in-person courses, students spend part of a class session meeting with their small groups to share two key aspects of their drafts on which they would like feedback to help guide their revisions—aspects that their peers are responsible for addressing. Based on earlier class discussions about the difference between revising and editing, I ask them to avoid presenting such editorial matters as grammar, spelling, formatting, and citation as their key concerns. From there, students post their drafts and two key concerns in a discussion forum, then read and respond to the drafts of two other members of their small group. I typically provide a forty-eight-hour window, beginning during class on the day drafts are due, for students to complete the workshop. The current instructions for the workshop are as follows:

> You should offer feedback to your two peers by replying to their initial posts, copying and pasting in the material below the dashed line, and filling in your answers. You're welcome to write your answers in Microsoft Word, Pages, etc., and then paste them below. That can help keep you from losing anything if there's a glitch with [the learning management system] or your browser. . . .

> **NOTE: SIMPLE "YES" AND "NO" ANSWERS ARE NOT SUFFICIENT. YOUR RESPONSE TO EACH QUESTION SHOULD BE AT**

**LEAST 3 FULL SENTENCES LONG. WHETHER YOU'RE COMPLI-
MENTING OR CRITICIZING, ALWAYS POINT TO SPECIFIC
EXAMPLES FROM THE PAPER AND EXPLAIN YOURSELF TO
THE WRITER. FIRST PERSON ("I") AND SECOND PERSON
("YOU") ARE FINE.**

———————

Provide feedback about the two main things the author wants feedback about (not including editorial concerns like grammar or formatting):

  1. [insert your feedback here]

  2. [insert your feedback here]

In general, does the writer do what the assignment prompt asks? If not, or if their focus seems to drift away from the prompt at any point(s), what changes might they make? If they do stick to the prompt, what parts of the paper do an especially good job of addressing the prompt's requirements?

  [insert your feedback here]

The intended audience for these projects is, basically, the writer's classmates and teacher. But you can also think about it as the broader audiences who might be interested in some of the sample literacy narratives we've read for class.[51] With that in mind, is the paper appropriate for its intended audience? For example, does the writer provide enough details about/descriptions of their experience to allow you to follow along? If not, what additional narrative elements or alternative writing strategies might they adopt as they revise?

  [insert your feedback here]

In terms of organization, is the paper structured in a way that engages you as a reader and allows you to follow along with the narrative the writer is providing? How and/or how not?

[insert your feedback here]

Are there any aspects of your group member's narrative that you found especially compelling or difficult to follow? How could they expand on, build on, or revise based on those aspects?

[insert your feedback here]

Provide a final additional piece of feedback you think would help the writer as they revise.

[insert your feedback here]

As students began reading and responding to one another's drafts, I began doing the same. As I mentioned above, one of the first things I often notice when reading students' literacy narratives is whether the writer is hewing to the conventions of the five-paragraph essay or experimenting with the conventions of a narrative, which is often apparent from the introductory paragraph: does it summarize what the writer is going to write about and offer a broad thesis about the importance of literacy, does it begin to tell a story, or does it combine those approaches or go in a different direction entirely? By way of illustration, let me recount a recent student's introductory paragraph and the network of responses and rhetorical decisions it generated. In their introduction, this particular student made a brief allusion to Two-Face, a popular nemesis of Batman, as a metaphor for their experiences with literacy. In various Batman comics and films, Two-Face starts out as a well-meaning district attorney named Harvey Dent who, after an acid attack damages half of his face, becomes a villain preoccupied with binary chance, making many of his decisions with the flip of a coin.⁵² The student aligned reading with Harvey Dent, positioning it as literacy's more familiar and supportive visage. They positioned writing as Two-Face—the other side of the literacy coin, more malevolent and unpredictable. In my feedback, I gave the student some advice on revising how they used the metaphor: introduce Two-Face more clearly for readers unfamiliar with the character and world of Batman; think about whether the metaphor might be fleshed out to become the entire introduction, structuring and setting up the rest of the narrative rather than serving as a throwaway line in the opening paragraph. But overall, I suggested the student keep it. It was a distinct and evocative way for them to frame their attitudes toward and experiences with literacy.

The advice the student received in the peer workshop was similar, with classmates appreciating the metaphor but explicitly expressing uncertainty about whether it was appropriate for an academic setting and how I, the teacher, might react to it. After reading the responses from me and their peers, the student had to set three revision goals, one of which had to be connected to my feedback and one of which had to be connected to their peers' feedback. After comparing my feedback with their peers' and talking about it with me outside of class, the student chose to keep the metaphor and to expand on it to make it more integral to the paper. Alongside the revised draft of the paper, students were required to turn in a short reflective note explaining and justifying the revisions they made. The student spent a couple of paragraphs discussing their decision to keep and expand on the introductory metaphor, referencing my feedback, the peer workshop, and a taxonomy of types of introductions they'd read as part of the class.[53] In particular, the student noted that they'd revised to make the introduction less of a "funnel." As the aforementioned taxonomy puts it, "The funnel introduction moves from abstract generalizations to the most specific statement, which is assumed to be the thesis statement. . . . This is very much 'student' writing—while it is very common in school (and even required by many teachers)—it's very unusual to see any non-student writing that uses this kind of introduction."[54]

Admittedly, this is a somewhat rose-colored example that was largely a matter of consensus: the student wrote an introduction that their peers and I both appreciated, then chose to revise and build on that introduction accordingly. But the process of developing that introduction nevertheless involved a number of third parties: their peers, me, past teachers who may have instilled in them the value of the "funnel" introduction and the five-paragraph essay, the student's own reflexive perspective on their writing, their peers' perceptions of me as a college writing teacher who might see certain things as appropriate or inappropriate in the context of "academic" writing, the authors of the textbook from which I drew descriptions and examples of literacy narratives, the author of the taxonomy of introductions who helped give the student a vocabulary for the kind of introduction they wanted to avoid. It is also a process that involved a balancing act between authority and agency: I exercised my authority as a teacher to structure the writing process in ways meant to give students room to exercise agency in the decisions they make as writers—and that, perhaps paradoxically, are meant to give them space to set aside my potentially authoritative commentary in pursuit of other paths.

And in other cases, that is precisely what students do when revising and reflecting on their revisions: they prioritize their peers' suggestions above my own, they address things I misread or overlooked entirely, or they offer justifications for why they chose not to make a revision I or their peers suggested. While these may not always be decisions with which I concur completely, the process is meant to take writing beyond authority or agency—to position it as a matter of responsibility. In some ways, this approach resonates with that of Timothy Oleksiak, who positions peer response as a matter of "building relationships," "guid[ing] students through the ethical practice of recognition of the labor others invest in them" without "limit[ing] the ways in which they might respond."[55] And yet, I would note, the approach is limiting. While I admire Oleksiak's description of "slow peer review" as a practice through which "writers and peers become dependent upon each other as individuals who are compelled to live together," my approach to peer response involves tweaking the phrasing slightly: as I attempt to situate it, peer response is a process through which parties who are dependent upon one another experience fleeting moments of individuation in the face of divergent responses from a number of others. While responsibility, in the Levinasian sense, is a condition for freedom and agency that cannot be summoned forth by individual choice or force, these pedagogical processes are designed to expose students to the rhetorical and ethical challenges involved when neither one's own self-certainty nor the singular, unquestionable authority of another is sufficient grounds for a decision. It is a pedagogy that is meant to leave space for the possibility of disruption and depropriation, not because of some malicious drive I possess as a teacher but out of a commitment to positioning writing *as communication itself*—an ongoing disruptive and disrupting process of exchange in which agency emerges from response.

It is also a pedagogy that is itself susceptible to outside influence. To return to Fall 2020—a semester during which, as I've mentioned, I taught all my courses online—I again taught two sections of ENGL 1010. Anticipating the unpredictable demands and stresses many students would be facing, from illness to caregiving to limited internet bandwidth to lost or new jobs to lack of ready access to a computer, I scaled back the amount of work I expected.[56] I made all assignments pass/fail and made it clear in the syllabus that I would be willing to accept any late work without penalty. However, in the syllabus, I included the following:

I have deadlines in my classes for three main reasons, which I think it's worth taking a moment to explain as a way of helping you understand where I'm coming from as a teacher:

1. Because of my own limitations. If I have every student turning in every assignment at a different time, it gets easy for me to overlook things, which can delay my feedback and cause confusion for you all.

2. Because you all will be learning to write together. As much as we sometimes think of writing as a solitary activity (a lone author sitting in their room typing away at a novel or essay), learning to write is a deeply social experience. We'll discuss this point a lot more in this course. But for now, it means you'll be planning and developing writing projects in conversation with each other, and you'll be providing each other feedback on what you're writing. For that to work, you'll need to be working on writing assignments at roughly the same time as your classmates.

3. Because the writing assignments in this class build on each other. That means you'll apply things you learn from writing earlier assignments while you're working on later assignments. If you try to do everything in the last few weeks of the semester, then you won't be able to build on what you've already learned. It would be like trying to climb a ladder by immediately jumping to the highest step—a difficult if not impossible task.

So there will be deadlines in this class, which you'll be able to see using the course calendar. I ask that you stick to those deadlines as much as possible. But because I know that personal emergencies and technological problems pop up, I am more than willing to offer extensions as needed and will not penalize late work.

In short, while I was open to students working at their own pace based on personal interruptions and crises, I wanted to emphasize that the deadlines I set in the course were not meant to be punitive mechanisms for enforcing moralistic, nigh-unattainable notions of personal responsibility in the face of a collective crisis. Instead, they were about the particular social and ethical conditions made possible by a group of students learning and writing together with a teacher. Thus, while those online courses enacted personalization of a certain sort, "using personal approaches/elements that invite students on a journey of learning together,"[57] their design was in many ways inimical to the kind of personalization and individual agency championed by xMOOCs and their descendants. That's not to say there aren't many things one can learn from courses offered by Coursera, Udacity, edX, or Google. It is to say, to the extent that they are designed to lead toward individual mastery of static, authoritative content—with peer networks as, at best, an adjunct to rather than a formative, responsive part of the learning process—such courses do not offer an experience that meaningfully resembles a *democratic* education or the deliberation among and between vulnerable, *responsible* beings (teachers included) involved in such an education.

CONCLUSION: TOWARD PEDAGOGICAL ENTROPY

A recollection from chapter 1: near the start of *The Writing of the Disaster*, Maurice Blanchot describes "the disaster" as something that is "always already past," only recognizable via after-the-fact figurations that cannot capture the unfigurable excess of the disaster itself.[58] In *The Writing of the Disaster*, as in his earlier book *The Infinite Conversation*, Blanchot invokes Levinas and acknowledges that any dialogue about "the disaster" commits an inescapable violence.[59] The disaster cannot but be reduced, disfigured by being figured within language. To ignore or deny it, however, is also to commit a sort of silencing, a dismissive violence.[60] Moreover, it is not just events or texts that are reduced and silenced in this way—others are also victims of such dialogue's reductive violence, dismissed or captured in being figured. Yet, Blanchot notes, we often proceed as if humans are simply and stably equals in the "interrelational space" of "dialogue" and as if dialogue tends toward understanding and equality. For his part, Blanchot emphasizes that "in the interrelational space, dialogue, and the equality dialogue presupposes, tend do to nothing other than increase entropy."[61] Instead of assuming that dialogue inherently or ideally fosters equity, he proposes this: "Let us suppose that it falls to speech not to reduce [this entropy], not to turn away from it by declaring it unsayable, but rather to present it."[62] Blanchot's proposal resonates strikingly with points raised by Stephanie L. Kerschbaum in a book analyzing students' peer-review processes: "These analyses reveal the claims to authority" performed by students are "interactionally contingent," "accret[ing] over time" and "demand[ing] considerable attention to and involvement with others."[63] In other words, peer response is complex relational work, and even if it "occurs best among a 'community of status equals' or 'peers,'" as many advocates of peer response have argued, such equality of status is an exceedingly rare occurrence, and not a state likely to occur naturally in the vast afterthought of xMOOCs' peer networks.[64]

The approach to peer response I've proposed is one that resists reducing the entropy of dialogue. It is an approach that asks students to dwell with the significance of writing as more than a means to an end. It emphasizes that writing unfolds as and in response, as a relation in which one encounters limits and obligations—obligations that often conflict. In short, it emphasizes the presence of the "third party" on the rhetorical and ethical scene. Students can no longer respond simply and totally to the demands of the teacher but must respond to a number of others. Moreover, because the teacher's feedback is not all that guides students' revisions, the responses students extend to one another take on additional significance: how they respond *will* have consequences for others in the class. Such an approach to peer response does not erase agency entirely: students still go on to revise their "own" papers. But the decisions they make as they revise are framed as decisions made in response—as a responsibility rather than an act of individual, agentive creation.

This is an approach to peer response that requires a great deal of oversight, organization, and scaffolding, which is a key point: If we accept Ching's historical account in which peer response grew out of writing teachers' attempts to navigate an unmanageable workload by passing some of their responsibilities to students, then the case for peer response starts to sound quite a bit like the case for xMOOCs. For example, Armando Fox argues that one of the benefits of MOOCs is that "TAs and professors . . . are freed from the drudgery of grading."[65] I won't deny that responding to student writing—which is not the same as grading student writing—is demanding work. But if rhetoric and writing teachers want to present small-scale peer response as something that doesn't inadvertently dovetail with a defense of xMOOCs, we must be prepared to speak to the delicate balance of meaningful pedagogical *responsibilities* on which thoughtful peer response depends—from the importance of framing the process for students in a careful, responsive way to ensuring students notice the divergences as well as points of sameness in the feedback they receive; from the complex challenge of framing response as important in its own right rather than a mere means to an end to holding students accountable for the tough decisions involved in how they decide to take up or set aside diverse and potentially contradictory feedback. Some may experience this work as drudgery, but it is complex, demanding, *responsive*, and, if done carefully, significant ethical and rhetorical work.

———

As I've described it, peer response is a process dependent on a teacher who holds open space for a manifestation of the second "yes?" described earlier—a teacher who is responsible and who can be questioned and, by virtue of that exposedness, works to call students' attention to questions of response and responsibility. I am not arguing that such an approach to peer response couldn't hypothetically unfold in a digital space, be overseen by a "pedagogical instrument," or be coordinated by someone who doesn't match the description of the figure we typically call a teacher.[66] I am arguing that, as xMOOCs and their progeny are currently described and structured, it could not unfold in such a course. Such an approach depends on students *not* taking personalized learning paths or moving at their own pace but instead encountering and responding to one another and their teachers as they navigate a divergent network of learning paths *together*. It depends on teachers and courses that don't use a variety of paths to shuttle students toward a particular end. And it is the sort of approach I would argue those in rhetoric and writing studies are distinctly well positioned to speak to, argue for, and design—not because of their innate capacities but precisely because of their exposedness to students and the interrelational asymmetries of the networks in which learning takes place.

CHAPTER 5

From Thesis Statements to Hedge Mazes

> But that is the essence of humility: in the midst of no clarity, no certainty, no assurance of your adequacy, you respond.
>
> —KENDALL GERDES

Near the end of *Otherwise Than Being*, Levinas offers the book's "thesis": "This book interprets the subject as a hostage and the subjectivity of the subject as a substitution breaking with being's essence."[1] Without further ado, he notes that this "thesis [*thèse*] is exposed imprudently to the reproach of utopianism [*au reproche d'utopisme*]."[2] In other words, Levinas is quick to acknowledge that *posing* a thesis involves *exposing* that thesis. This acknowledgment follows from Levinas's theory of subjectivity: the thesis, like the subject, can never remain absolutely sovereign, perfectly posed and poised without the risk of exposure, of reproach, of response. For the thesis as for the subject, it is "an impossibility to remain at home."[3] In fact, it is precisely by acknowledging this "impossibility" that Levinas attempts to resist "the reproach of utopianism": "by recalling that what took place humanly has never been able to remain closed up in its site."[4]

Levinas's readers might recall here the double meaning of "utopia" as both "good place" and "no-place." Because Levinasian ethics positions no person, no place, no *topos* as sealed off from others' affection, Levinas argues that the very act of exposing a thesis moves it out of the realm of utopianism: once stated, it is no longer nowhere, no longer out of touch.[5]

If it ever did occupy a "non-site," which Levinas doubts, it doesn't any longer.[6] To put it otherwise, even if readers see Levinas's "thesis" as overly idealistic, the simple fact of that thesis being exposed in the text has moved it out of the intangible, inviolable realm of ideas and into the realm of reproach and response. No utopia, once posed and exposed, remains a utopia—and so, Levinas argues, *Otherwise Than Being* "escapes the reproach of utopianism—if utopianism is a reproach, if any thought escapes utopianism."[7]

In this book's final chapter, I trail Levinas by exposing a thesis of my own—specifically, a thesis about the thesis statement, which remains a pervasive rhetorical device in higher education. The thesis statement made a cameo appearance in the previous chapter as the taken-for-granted element that students are often taught is indispensable to an effective introduction. In this chapter, I zoom back in from the massive scale of MOOCs to a narrow focus on this singular statement. And yet this chapter's pursuits double back to paths this book has previously traveled. Rather than concluding with a clear-cut pedagogical assertion, I end with one more roundabout challenge to authority and agency alike—more to the point, a challenge to the forms of academic certainty that are sometimes presumed to accompany the acquisition of authority and agency. Such certainty, I argue, is distinctly, perhaps definitively, captured in the rhetorical power attached to the thesis statement.

I'll put my thesis in bold so it is not missed: **Many of those who teach writing put too much emphasis on the *posing* of thesis statements and not enough on the *exposedness* that attends any act of stating, claiming, or asserting.** Bearing in mind Levinas's response to the "reproach of utopianism," I proceed topographically, using the hedge maze as a *topos* to structure what follows.

Let me not delay in acknowledging a paradox: I'm questioning the emphasis placed on thesis statements in contemporary pedagogy, but I've already stated a thesis of my own. I'm going to argue for more attention to hesitation, hypothesizing, *hedging*—to enactments of self-doubt and uncertainty—in pedagogy and scholarship. I make this perhaps antithetical claim because I worry that, in foregrounding and emphasizing thesis statements, those who teach writing risk reinforcing chauvinist approaches and attitudes toward argument, privileging posing over exposing. In exploring alternate routes, I am not presuming to dismiss or dodge thesis statements entirely. In writing this chapter, I have already failed to do so. I am just suggesting, tentatively, that a strongly posed thesis statement is not the be-all and end-all it's often cracked up to be.

But what do I mean by "thesis statement"? You know, the thesis statement: that one sentence—two might be okay, but one is probably best—that lays out the argument you're making in your paper. It doesn't *have* to be the last sentence of your introductory paragraph, but you want it place it pretty early so that readers don't get lost before it arrives. Not *too* early, though, because that doesn't let you build any rhetorical intrigue. So yes, putting it at the end of your first paragraph is probably the best bet. You'll really grab your readers' attention if you put it there.

At least that's how I've often found myself talking to students about thesis statements, especially in my less reflective moments, smack in the middle of a jam-packed semester with hundreds of pages of student writing to respond to. Though I'm not quite so explicit about any fatigue I might be feeling, I give them the same advice that I've been given for writing proposals for academic conferences: You're writing for tired people, so keep it straightforward. State your argument early and plainly, but not so generically that it'll melt into the massive pile of documents through which your reader is sifting. But if I—and, I assume, the vast number of writing teachers who are responsible for many more students than I am in the heavily adjunctified realm of postsecondary writing instruction—feel worn down by the work of responding to reams of student writing semester after semester, I also feel worn down by the commonplace moves we've embraced to cope with and manage the work of response.[8]

I'm not the first writing teacher "maxed out" on "impersonal, thesis-driven essays."[9] In *Experimental Writing in Composition*, Patricia Suzanne Sullivan nods to a number of teachers and scholars who—motivated by a variety of ideologies and aspirations—have tried to throw a wrench in the thesis-mobile's gears. For instance, in *The Rhetoric of Cool*, Jeff Rice writes, "Any critique of the thesis or topic sentence, no doubt, will irk a long-standing tradition within composition pedagogy that has depended on these items in order to teach first-year writing students how to order their ideas."[10] According to this tradition, "The student, obviously too scattered in thought and undisciplined in structure, needs the thesis to put everything quickly in its place (and, we might note, to be put, herself, in place)."[11] As evidence of composition's preoccupation with theses, Rice cites Edward

P. J. Corbett's influential essay "The Usefulness of Classical Rhetoric": "I find my students are most likely to produce a unified, coherent piece of writing when they are forced, before they begin to write, to state their thesis in a single declarative sentence."[12] Countering Corbett, Rice states, "Single, declarative sentences leave too much information out; they restrict thought in unnecessary ways."[13]

While I agree about the restrictiveness of "single, declarative sentences," I am interested not just in the "information" they leave out but in the attitudes toward writing, toward others, and toward one's own position and subject matter that such declaratives delimit and disallow. In emphasizing hedging, I hope to call attention to the affective as well as informational restrictions that thesis statements impose, and thus to do more than retread the arguments of the thesis skeptics in whose winding footsteps I'm otherwise following. I dwell on alternatives to thesis-driven, persuasion-focused arguments as a way of broadening what counts as argument in pedagogical contexts, as well as how those arguments are permitted to unfold.[14]

But because I've already stated my thesis so boldly, there's a risk that I've lost the attention of thesis advocates. As Patricia Roberts-Miller notes while describing common strategies for structuring written arguments, "It is an understatement to say that" a thesis-driven list of reasons "is unpersuasive to an intelligent and informed opposition audience."[15] Moreover, argues Roberts-Miller, lots of people—writing teachers included—don't even have a clear idea of what is meant by the word "thesis":

> So many people (at least in America) confuse the thesis and the partition. The thesis is the proposition the paper argues; it is the underlying principle. The partition is the statement of what the text will do—and the tense here is important. A partition establishes expectations about a text by saying what the topic will be and often how that topic will be handled—it may be a hypothesis, but it is not a thesis. In contrast to what *The St. Martin's Guide to Writing* . . . says, in most published writings, the thesis (if anywhere in the text at all) is stated at the end of the text, and it usually takes more than one sentence. In many texts, especially ones presented to students as models of good writing, there is no single thesis sentence.[16]

Roberts-Miller counters the advice of many writing teachers and textbooks by discouraging student writers from opening with a thesis, arguing that

doing so is bad practice for most other rhetorical situations, in which starting with a strong claim can establish an ethos of closed-mindedness.

It is as part of an attempt to maintain an ethos of open-mindedness that
I decided on the hedge maze as a conceit for structuring and partitioning
this chapter. In unfolding this conceit, I hope to make the most of resonances between the "hedge" as both a rhetorical movement and a network
of plants that can be used to construct not just barriers but complex pathways and labyrinths. And so, despite the thesis exposed above, I'll try to
move through most of this chapter unequipped with any thesis-powered
shears that would allow me to cut to the chase with minimal hesitation—
not for the sake of wanton obtuseness but out of an abundance of certified
uncertainty. I'll wander as I wonder about this question: What might come
of emphasizing hedging and the performance of uncertainty over the thesis
statement and the performance of certainty, both in pedagogy and in scholarship? En route to some final expositions, I now turn toward some of my
reasons for questioning thetical certitude.

A PEDAGOGICAL DIVERSION

Certainty talks. In the advice offered by many textbooks, in US political
discourse, even in much scholarly writing, I am arguing that this is the case.
To elaborate just a bit: certainty talks, hesitance walks. And so I walk. To
elaborate again: I am going to walk through some examples of the rhetorical
arenas—pedagogical, political, scholarly—in which I hear certainty talking
too boldly, in which audacious surety steamrolls nuanced hesitation.

First, to textbooks. In her article "A Textbook Argument," A. Abby Knoblauch offers a detailed rundown of popular writing textbooks' attitudes
toward argument. Knoblauch claims that, while contemporary textbooks
are giving increasing attention to understanding and compromise as rhetorical modes and goals, persuasion still wins out: ultimately, most textbooks
position convincing others of *your* position as the general goal of written
argumentation.[17] A quick survey of some of the best-selling handbooks
meant for use in postsecondary writing courses reveals a similar attitude
toward thesis statements in particular. *A Pocket Style Guide*, for instance,
advises writers to "read a variety of sources" and then "form a working thesis—a one-sentence (or occasionally a two-sentence) statement of your
central idea. The thesis expresses not just your opinion but also your
informed, reasoned judgment. Usually your thesis will appear at the end of

the first paragraph. . . . Your ideas may change as you learn more about your subject through reading and writing. You can revise your working thesis as you draft."[18] In other words, a strong thesis is not just a rhetorical structure that helps writers persuade readers but evidence of the writer's own journey toward rhetorical confidence.

A "working thesis" is also the name of the game in the similarly popular handbook *Rules for Writers* (which, I should note, shares the same authors and publisher as *A Pocket Style Guide*). A working thesis "will need to be revised as the student thinks through and revises his paper, but it provides a useful place to start writing" and can eventually crystallize into an unqualified thesis.[19] The authors claim that a "thesis should be an answer to a question, not a question itself."[20] When it comes to the thesis's placement, the advice in *Rules for Writers* goes like this: "Although the thesis frequently appears at the end of the introduction, it can just as easily appear at the beginning."[21] In other words, you can choose whether to use your thesis to introduce your paper or to use it to introduce your introduction. *Rules for Writers* assures its readers that, in either case, foregrounding your thesis won't offend your audience. Don't worry that stating it as "directly as possible" will make you come across as "unrefined or even rude," the authors write—at least as long as your audience is based in the United States, where "readers appreciate a direct approach; when you state your point as directly as possible, you show that you understand your topic and value your readers' time."[22] Let me recall Roberts-Miller and note how quickly the handbook's advice moves from thesis to topic here. Even if it doesn't exactly conflate proposition and partition, *Rules for Writers* places them in close proximity.[23]

That's all I want to say about handbooks, especially since going after them could be a dead end. To mix botanical metaphors for a moment, the claims of handbooks might seem like low-hanging fruit in the hedge maze we're currently navigating—an easily accessible diversion from the more complex puzzle facing us. But as we start to move in other directions, I want to restate how easy it is for even a well-intentioned, well-informed teacher to indulge a certain taste for this fruit.

Let me nest a mini-maze within the broader trajectory of this chapter to illustrate what I'm talking about. Textbook advice about thesis statements positions them as the exit to a rhetorical maze that students are charged with solving, with students certain of their thesis only at the *end* of the writing process. And yet this exit then becomes the entrance point to a passage of students' own devising: now certain of where the labyrinth leads, students can use that end as the (arguably unpersuasive) beginning of their own attempts to lead readers to the same position. This is advice that I, at least, fall back on all too readily.

And isn't a similar process often projected onto rhetoric and writing courses more broadly? Students are expected—by most handbooks and many teachers, though perhaps not the teachers who are actually in charge of the courses in question—to proceed through a series of rhetorical tasks and puzzles, eventually exiting with the certain knowledge that they are now officially Good Writers, a conviction they can use to retroactively understand the paces through which the course has put them. Just as a cautious, careful writing process produces greater certainty about one's topic and position and thus a more confident written product, so a carefully structured writing course produces a more confident writer. Or maybe not. I'd imagine most who teach college writing have received student evaluations that suggest a few pupils still feel mystified about the point of the paces through which the course put them. And, given the wide body of rhetoric and writing scholarship demonstrating the extent to which what counts as "good writing" varies from discipline to discipline, situation to situation, and job to job, we have plenty of reasons to be uncertain about the relative generalizability of rhetoric and writing courses' desired outcomes.[24]

So here we reach another bend in the path: those of you reading this, the final chapter of a book largely focused on rhetoric and writing pedagogy, may be all too aware that the thesis statement is only one rhetorical tack among a variety of others. Rhetoric and writing scholars may recognize that the rules for writers presented in a book titled *Rules for Writers* are really more like guidelines, meant to be broken after having been learned, and so forth. But the authors of *Rules for Writers* aren't exactly *wrong* when they say that lots of US audiences may in fact see a strong thesis, stated early and often, as *the* way to argue. In fact, a quick spin through the realms of political and academic discourse turns up a variety of writers who've been vilified not for confidently asserting a thesis but for daring to hedge—for having the audacity to perform uncertainty. Trouble is, neither does that mean that Patricia Roberts-Miller is wrong about the unpersuasive quality of arguments that put their thesis statements front and center.[25] To meander further into this convoluted web of conflicting writing advice, desires, and rhetorical persuasions, let me trace out two quick examples—one political, one academic.

OVER THE HEDGE WITH NATE SILVER AND JACQUES DERRIDA

First, the case of statistician Nate Silver. In the months leading up to the 2012 US presidential election, Silver was blogging for the *New York Times* and predicting up a storm, applying his experience analyzing baseball statistics to election polls in order to forecast the election's probable outcomes.[26] By the end of October, he had President Barack Obama's reelection chances at over 70 percent. Political reporter Dylan Byers, writing in the outlet *Politico*, was unimpressed: "For all the confidence Silver puts in his predictions, he often gives the impression of hedging. Which, given all the variables involved in a presidential election, isn't surprising. For this reason and others—and this may shock the coffee-drinking NPR types of Seattle, San Francisco and Madison, Wis.—more than a few political pundits and reporters . . . believe Silver is highly overrated."[27]

Byers was not alone in claiming that Silver "g[ave] the impression"—but only the *impression*—of "hedging." To support his argument, he cited MSNBC pundit Joe Scarborough: "Anybody that thinks that this race is anything but a tossup right now is such an ideologue, they should be kept away from typewriters, computers, laptops and microphones for the next 10 days, because they're a joke."[28]

In a response to critiques of Silver, then-*Atlantic* blogger Ta-Nehisi Coates described Byers's jab at "coffee-drinking NPR types" as "the most bizarre slur I've ever read" and then quoted a similar insult from Dean Chambers, a would-be rival of Silver's. In a piece that experienced a moment of viral popularity and was published on the now-defunct website *Examiner.com*, Chambers wrote, "Nate Silver is a man of very small stature, a thin and effeminate man with a soft-sounding voice."[29] Between Byers and Chambers, Coates was at a loss: "I don't really know. Anyway, Byers goes on to quote David Brooks and Joe Scarborough, manly-men who can't find San Francisco on a map and are so macho that they chew coffee beans whole, leaving the French press for you wimpy-ass, Terry Gross-listening, Steve Urkel-looking motherfuckers." Coates goes on to acknowledge that, though he's "nobody's tough guy, as someone who spent a significant portion of my life seeking ways to not get punched in the face, it's really amazing how much interaction—even now—boils down to . . . 'Can you kick my ass?'"[30]

The controversy surrounding Silver's predictions about the presidential election, at least until those predictions proved correct in every one of the fifty states, demonstrates a complicated set of attitudes toward certainty and confidence in US political discourse: For Byers and Scarborough, Silver's hedges were—couldn't *not* have been—artificial diversions allowing him to sneak irresponsible and overly confident claims past his readers. While Byers and Scarborough were certain of the race's uncertainty (and, as political pundits, professionally invested in attracting audience share by boldly proclaiming that uncertainty for as long as possible), they were convinced that Silver's methodical and methodological uncertainty betrayed an excess of certainty.[31] The statistician drew the derision of his less equivocal colleagues not because he was perceived as self-assured but because he was allegedly masking his faulty certainty with a veneer of uncertainty, which paradoxically granted Silver's veiled convictions a greater, and thus more pernicious, power over his audience. It was this purported disingenuousness that Silver's chauvinistic and sometimes overtly homophobic critics used to dismiss him as an "effeminate" interloper in the virile realm of political punditry and prognostication. That is, these critics weren't concerned with Silver's presumed certainty but with his presumed duplicity—because, as guys like Byers and Scarborough saw it, Silver's hedges and hesitations couldn't possibly be offered in good faith.

Such critics might have felt a sense of vindication four years later, when Silver's predictions for the 2016 presidential election went the other way. By then, Silver had departed the *Times* to create the website *FiveThirtyEight*. The site's final preelection predictions put Donald Trump's odds of winning at only 29 percent; the candidate Silver gave the smaller statistical chance won.[32] But despite the difference in the outcome, the arguments leveled against him in 2016 were remarkably similar in tone to those leveled against him in 2012—it's just that this time, they were concentrated after the election instead of before it. In a piece published the day following the election, media reporter Brian Flood noted that in the lead-up to the 2012 election, "Democrats took to tweeting the slogan 'Keep Calm and Trust in Nate Silver.'"[33] But in the wake of his 2016 predictions, another media reporter quoted by Flood stated, "'The title of "'guru'" is now gone.' . . . Silver's career will survive, but 'never again will he be held in any revered regard.'"[34] But in dismissing Silver, media commentators—as well as Democrats who had taken unqualified solace in his predictions—went awry in their frequent claims that Silver was *wrong*. A 29 percent chance is, of course, a long way from a 0 percent chance, and Silver noted a few days after the election that "FiveThirtyEight's forecast gave Trump much better odds than other polling-based models."[35] Could his models be improved? Certainly. Is Silver infallible? Certainly not, as his critics on Twitter frequently point out, especially as he took to issuing sweeping, unqualified epidemiological claims during the COVID-19 pandemic. However, in the case of the 2016 election, Silver did not claim otherwise, and the backlash against him arguably said less about Silver himself and more about his audience's failure to hedge their own bets and to consider the hedges built into statistical models—to consider the inherent uncertainty in probabilities less than 100 percent. In short, the backlash again betrayed an unwillingness or incapacity to take hedging and hesitation seriously.[36]

In a curious way, such critiques of Silver are surprisingly resonant with one of the most popular definitions for "postmodernism" posted to *Urban Dictionary*, an online dictionary in which competing definitions are ranked based on how many votes of support they receive. Though the dictionary is focused primarily on slang terms, it includes a number of definitions for "postmodernism." The following definition—which ends by equating the tenets of "postmodernism" with those of Adolf Hitler—has so far attracted 859 "upvotes" and 337 "downvotes," exceeding the upvote and downvote totals for any of the other competing definitions on the site:

> Postmodernism: pseudo-intellectual Trojan Horse of tyrants everywhere in the western world. Began in Arts faculties in various universities under "thinkers" like Derrida, Baudrillard, Foucault and Irigaray, and spread like a cancer into at least the "soft" sciences, if not further afield. Works insidiously by establishing in the minds of the faithful that there are no ultimate truths in either a moral or a scientific sense, and dressing up bullshit in flowery language. . . . [T]hese matters are brought up in the midst of reams and reams of tendentious twaddle which constitute a dreadful waste of perfectly good trees, and the most notable effect of postmodernist

(un)thinking is not the freeing of anyone's mind from conservative tyranny, but the scrapping of the very idea of objective truth.[37]

Just to make sure I'm not taken for a pseudo-intellectual, I should probably skip the hedges for a moment: I'm arguing that this definition's critique of "postmodernism" is of a piece with the aforementioned critiques of Silver. Both presume that the objects of their critiques are tyrannically certain of their conclusions but use inconclusiveness as a rhetorical diversion in an attempt to bury the lede. Both Nate Silver and Jacques Derrida only *pretend* to hesitate in order to shut down debate, effetely "dressing up bullshit in flowery language" instead of just manning up and saying what they mean.[38]

Given the supposedly tyrannical takeover "postmodernism" has achieved in the arts and "'soft' sciences" (the "hard" sciences being, one assumes, resistant to postmodernism's perfumed seductions), perhaps someone with a penchant for hedging would find more sympathy in the esoteric realms of academia than the bare-knuckle rings of political punditry. After all, diatribes about the state of academic writing often turn on its supposedly windy and long-winded tendencies. Then again, perhaps not: enter example number two. In a 2001 interview, Slavoj Žižek— himself the poster child for certain strains of "postmodernism," though not necessarily the ones described in that *Urban Dictionary* definition— identifies a "certain ruthlessness" characteristic of his writing process: a "pure, cruel self-instrumentalization" that he contrasts with the writing of Derrida.[39] Žižek writes, "I sometimes have this problem: even though I admire a lot of [Derrida's] essays, I nonetheless tend to skip the first third of them—which, as you know, is usually the part before he passes on to the argument. Before finally getting to the point, you have to go through certain ballet pirouettes, like 'Am I writing this article or is this article writing me?'"[40]

Though that Žižek interview was published in 2001, his dismissal of such "pirouettes" remains in style. Consider linguist Steven Pinker's 2014 *Chronicle of Higher Education* op-ed "Why Academics Stink at Writing."[41] Among other things, Pinker blames the bad odor emanating from "academese" on an "agonizing self-consciousness," an excessive defensiveness on the part of academics about how their colleagues are going to receive them and their arguments. According to Pinker, one of the "symptoms" of this self-consciousness is "hedging": "Academics mindlessly cushion their prose with wads of fluff that imply they are not willing to stand behind what they say." Pinker goes on to admit, in what may or may not be a hedge, "Sometimes a writer has no choice but to hedge a statement. Better still, the writer can *qualify* the statement—that is, spell out the circumstances in which it does not hold rather than leaving himself an escape hatch or being coy as to whether he really means it." For Pinker, "It's not that good writers never hedge their claims. It's that their hedging is a choice, not a tic." In other words, Pinker's "good writers" are aware of themselves, their decisions, their own writing, and the needs of their readers. When they do hedge, it's because they're self-conscious in a good way—a way that is generous, reflective, and healthy—while bad writers hedge because, as Pinker sometimes claims and sometimes just implies, they are defensive, unhealthy, and only aware of their readers as a potential threat to the integrity of their arguments.

In short, in attacks on Nate Silver, in *Urban Dictionary*'s and Žižek's characterization of Derrida's writing, and in the "academese" that Pinker diagnoses as unwell, bad writing smells both rotten and too sweet. It's bloated, flowery bullshit. It stinks even if, or maybe because, it's so pretty and—at least on the surface—so carefully wrought. The indulgent hedges of seemingly uncertain writers, who are generally presumed to be all too certain, are a flagrantly fragrant mess rather than a carefully crafted web of thoughtful qualifiers.

Of course, there exist writers that I don't particularly like, and it's tempting to just flip the script: *they're* the ones whose hedges are unjustified, misplaced, or insufficient while the people *I* like get it right. In places where those writers telegraph a point, they should have written more. In places where they pause to explain something, they should have written less. It's tempting to chide Pinker, for instance, for engaging in a reductive, ahistorical generalization when he identifies the "*classic style*" of "17th-century French essayists such as Descartes" as self-evidently superior to other styles of writing. But, to be fair, Pinker goes on to hedge this claim: "For all its directness, classic style remains a pretense, an imposture, a stance. Even scientists, with their commitment to seeing the world as it is, are a *bit* postmodern." It's also tempting to note that Judith Butler, whose writing Pinker quotes as paradigmatically bad, has responded at length to critiques of their style, which renders Pinker's op-ed somewhat redundant in its lack of engagement with copious responses to the commonplace criticisms its author is once again reiterating.[42] Pinker may have cause to disagree with Butler's responses, but he, like a number of other defenders of "common sense" and the classic style, writes as if the "badness" of Butler's writing speaks for itself.[43]

I don't want to browbeat Pinker, though—at the very least, it seems irresponsible and uncharitable to do so.[44] After all, I agree with him that there are hedges that function defensively and inhospitably. Instead, I want to dwell on his gloss of "hedging" in light of the various examples I've considered throughout this chapter so far—examples that show just how rare it is for hedges to be respected in pedagogical, political, and even academic discourse. From there, I want to suggest a different characterization of "hedging," playing around some more with the various meanings of "hedge" and, in so doing, offering an alternate conception of hedging that diverges from Pinker's without entirely dismissing it.

A FLOWERY DETOUR

Before proceeding, let me turn back to Žižek for a moment. Specifically, I want to reiterate that he characterizes the first third of Derrida's essays *not* as a peculiar, indirect mode of argument but as *not argument*, as prelude to argument.[45] To my mind, Derrida's most direct response to this sort of characterization happens in his introductory remarks to *Who's Afraid of Philosophy?* Writes Derrida, in a passage I considered briefly in chapter 2:

> Certain people are always impatient to *access-the-things-in-themselves-directly-and-reach-right-away-without-waiting-the-true-content-of-the-urgent-and-serious-problems-that-face-us-all-etc.* Thus, they will no doubt judge an analysis that deploys [a] range of meanings and possible sentences playful, precious, and formal, indeed futile. . . . Of course, one can share this impatience and nonetheless think, as I do, that not only do we gain nothing by immediately giving in to it, but that this lure has a history, interest, and a sort of *hypocritical* structure, and that one would always be better off to begin by acknowledging it by giving oneself the time for a detour and analysis.[46]

As I've tried to show, one way of dismissing what Derrida calls "detour and analysis" is to call it "bullshit dressed up in flowery language."[47] Rather than arguing against this label, I want to make the most of it. After all, bullshit can make for some pretty fertile soil. So, in the spirit of hedging, let me work through an allegory derived from the plant kingdom and the fanciful realm of fairy tales.

A hedge, at least in the world of landscaping, is a network of plants that can be cultivated to create a variety of structures. One of the most common plants used to create hedges is blackthorn.[48] On one hand, blackthorn can be used to create barriers: for English farmers, the plant has long been a popular option for constructing cattle-proof hedges. As a hedge, then, blackthorn offers a quite literal way to confine and define the limits of bulls' shit. In Steven Pinker's gloss of "hedging," bad writers are unscrupulous farmers who don't want their neighbors to recognize the stink coming off their property. The function of the hedge is not to keep cattle and their manure in but to keep interested parties out and prevent them from noticing or identifying the odor of decomposition. Like *Sleeping Beauty*'s evil fairy, who installs a thorny hedge around the castle where the torpid princess's body rests, blackthorn can be used in pursuit of maleficent exclusions.

Then again, blackthorn, which is also known as "sloe," can be used to create networked boundaries that are less exclusionary: not fences but mazes. While hedge mazes can disorient, that is not necessarily their purpose. As Adrian Fisher writes in *Mazes and Follies*, the hedge mazes of seventeenth-century England "were originally designed not to confuse, but merely as a means of taking a long walk in a short space."[49] It is only over time that such mazes have grown more convoluted. Consider the labyrinth at Longleat House in Wiltshire, England, which was designed in 1978: "Six bridges create a three-dimensional puzzle, spiral junctions add confusion by repetition, and although elongated fork junctions help visitors to 'conserve their momentum,' the whirling lines and lack of any rectangular grid add further disorientation."[50]

But where was I going with all this? Specifically, that hedges can be cultivated not only to bar inquiring minds or guard the premises of putrid arguments but to help one move through a line of thinking more carefully, more reflexively, a little more sloe. Let me return to Sleeping Beauty by way of *Maleficent*, the revisionist 2014 film that repositions the "evil" fairy as the story's protagonist. In that film, the thorny hedge serves as much-needed protection against the hubris and violence of sword-wielding men who would hack through any other obstacle blocking their path. It is still a barrier of sorts but one that provides the wakeful young princess—in this version, caringly preserved rather than held captive by the fairy—with ample room and time in which to wander as she explores, develops, and grows.

What I am trying to move toward, in other words, is the possibility that hedging can preserve spaces for writers to ruminate and wander without being compelled to reach immediate, unqualified certainty regarding "*the-true-content-of-the-urgent-and-serious-problems-that-face-us-all-etc.*"[51] That is not to say the conceit of the hedge maze that I'm outlining here is all about unserious fun and games—though it may be in part. Mapping a maze's twists and turns can be frustrating for designers and inhabitants alike. Moving slowly, operating in a different register than hasty hubris, navigating a hedge maze involves slouching uncertainly toward decision. Like Victor J. Vitanza's "*dissoi* para*logoi*," this is a hedging that, though it "speaks no logical course of action," "does, nevertheless, urge us to *act* in our uncertainty."[52] Like the first third of Derrida's essays, this is a hedging that I would argue is neither poorly cultivated nor interminable but that detours, taking the discursive equivalent of a long walk in a small space because of the possible exclusions that often occur when judgment takes shortcuts. Such hedging does not seek to erect barriers for the sole purpose of keeping out well-intentioned *readers* but acknowledges in part that even well-intentioned *writers* who proceed too rapidly risk razing the terrain in their pursuit of clear-cut arguments.

But then this is all merely a hypothesis, just a starting point—or not a point, but a winding path that I am not satisfied to condense into a point. A hypothesis nevertheless, however, and it is toward uncertain connections between the hedge and the hypothesis that I now turn. These connections lead us back to the terrain of rhetorical education.

A PARALLEL PATH

Long before Francis Bacon helped make the hypothesis *de rigueur* in the sciences, rhetoricians were talking about it. Hermagoras, a Roman rhetorician working in the first century BCE, "divided 'political questions' into two broad kinds, 'theses' (*theseis*) and 'hypotheses' (*hypotheseis*)."[53] Jeffrey

Walker notes that this division was forwarded by some of ancient rhetoric's most influential figures: Cicero reiterates the two categories as "*quaestionae* and *causae*, 'propositions' and 'cases'. . . . Theses/propositions were general issues for debate that, as Quintilian would later describe them, did not involve specific 'persons, times, places, and the like.' Hypotheses/cases, in contrast, were issues for debate involving such particulars. . . . The hypothesis/case, in other words, is a particular instantiation of a thesis/proposition within a specific set of social, legal, political, and historical circumstances."[54]

The "thesis" features prominently in the *progymnasmata*, the series of rhetorical exercises I discussed in chapter 2. In Aphthonius the Sophist's progymnasmatic treatise, for instance, it is the second-to-last exercise in the series. Aphthonius writes that "thesis differs from hypothesis in that an hypothesis has attendant circumstances, where a thesis is without particulars"—for example, the question of "whether one should marry."[55] While this might seem to suggest that historical students of rhetoric were engaged in abstract philosophical speculation, Walker argues that the Hermagorean thesis/hypothesis division in fact marks a "lack of interest in the metaphysical speculations of the philosophic schools. . . . Insofar as *thesis* literally means 'position' or 'seat' (even in modern Greek, one can buy a ticket for a *thesis* in a train), and insofar as *hypothesis* means 'under-position' or 'foundation,' the implication seems to be that 'theses' must rest on, be grounded in, or arise from the practical real-world situations of 'hypotheses.'"[56]

As Walker interprets it, thesis exercises were built on hypothetical foundations—"foundations" not as in unshakable metaphysical underpinnings but as in contextual exigencies that granted abstract theses some sort of practical justification. A thesis needed a hypothesis to keep it grounded and prevent it from drifting into philosophical speculation.[57]

Given that many pragmatically inclined scholars see Derrida's writings as exemplifying speculation and theoretical abstraction, it might seem odd to link him to "the practical, real-world situations of 'hypotheses.'"[58] And yet that is the connection I am about to attempt. In "Interpretations at War," Derrida "gives focus to a key element of testing: the hypothesis."[59] Discussing the Protestant Reformation (which Derrida emphasizes was not just a religious and metaphysical event but at least also a political one) and its entanglements with antisemitism and questions of German and Jewish identity, Derrida demonstrates how "hypothesis and [scientifically inflected] testing band[ed] together to undermine dogma" in the case of the Reformation.[60] The work of "undermin[ing]" might smack of "deconstruction" and thus be seen as antithetical to rhetoric's more practical and constructive aims, but note what is being undermined by the sort of hypothesis Derrida describes: transcendent metaphysical certainties. In "Interpretations at War," Derrida, so often positioned as an enemy of science, does riff on a "scientific *idealism*" outlined by the philosopher Hermann Cohen. But that "*idealism*," like a progymnasmatic thesis, is driven by practical concerns— by, in a word, hypotheses: "As hypothesis, the idea is then by no means the solution of the problem but only the exact definition of the problem itself."[61] Though it may be the particulars of the *problem* rather than a particular, pragmatically oriented *solution* that are elaborated in the sort of hypotheses that Derrida describes, such hypotheses remain dedicated to what might be called rhetorical particularity.

And so here the boundaries of thesis/hypothesis, idealism/pragmatism, and theory/practice are perhaps beginning to blur. This may be my fault—I may have either wandered away from or too deep into the narrow, winding strictures of the hedge. In fact, I may have been wrong about the thesis all along. Perhaps the kind of thesis statement that is so central to contemporary writing instruction is, like its premodern forerunners, built on defensible practical exigencies that are part and parcel of rhetorical education. What would it mean, at this point in this chapter, to say that I have grown uncertain about my dismissal of thesis statements' resolute certainty—a kind of certainty that may be undergirded, not undermined, by practical concerns? Have I wandered and speculated only to loop back around to a certain kind of certainty? Then again, in inserting the phrase "a certain kind," have I moved from the realm of thesis to hypothesis, proposition to case, zeroing in on an intensely qualified (one might even say "hedged") statement that calls thetic certainty into question? Is that a rhetorical question? And insofar as rhetoric is a pedagogical tradition, does it remain a *pedagogical* question?

To turn once more to pedagogy: If I have written ten thousand words of this chapter only to find myself less certain than when I began, can there be a rhetoric and writing pedagogy that would allow students the same leeway? Moving away from authoritative certainty, away from mastery, what could such a rhetorical education be?

GARDEN OF FORKING PEDAGOGIES

And now here I find myself at a curious point in this maze of hedges—a point that demands decision. English aristocrats may have had countless afternoons in which to design and navigate elaborate hedge mazes. I, a rhetoric and writing teacher, do not, nor do most of the students I encounter. And so the meandering uncertainty I have so far pursued now reaches a point of decision. Like the tension Derrida posits between "*the* law of hospitality," an unconditional commitment to welcoming the other, and "the laws (plural) of hospitality," which condition and delimit hospitality so that the singular ideal does not remain inconsequentially or irresponsibly abstract, my anxious, idyllic uncertainty risks insignificance if it is not instantiated—if I do not, having dwelt in the crucible of undecidability, *decide* what to do about it.[62] Ahead, the maze bifurcates again and again, and above each diverging path is suspended a gate that will drop once I pass beneath it. Some paths may intertwine again on the other side, some may not.

It seems allowable to reflect for one last moment, given that there are no agents that I'm aware of on my trail. The routes arrayed before me are pedagogies that proceed from the pathway I've traced up to this point. They are pedagogies that, although they comprise a certain sort of practice, do not aim at certainty as an endpoint. They are pedagogies, you might say, that are *hypothetical*—not in the sense of "suppositional" so much as "conditional." They are not purely theoretical or speculative. They are hypothetical because they are practical. But let me take a moment to speculate about what might await me down these various pathways. In the spirit of undecidability, rather than proposing *a* pedagogy, I wish to emphasize that careful theorization of pedagogy can lead a teacher in multiple directions.

Path 1

The first path appears to widen into more intricate, interwoven subpaths as it progresses. It reminds me of past experiments with telescopictext.org, a browser-based writing platform that allows users to write texts that expand when readers click on specific words or phrases. These texts consist of black words on a white background, with certain words and phrases highlighted in gray, indicating that clicking on them will result in textual expansions.

For example, a writer might start with this initially simple sentence: "Hedges are good." From there, they could make it so clicking certain words adds to the sentence. Click on "Hedges" to unfold it into "Hedges, a means of expressing uncertainty or noting situations in which a claim might not hold." Click on "are" to unfold it into "can be." Click on "good" to unfold it into "a significant act of rhetorical humility." Click again on "can be" to unfold it further: "can—when not used as defensive measures intended to bar an audience's engagement with an argument—be." All told, those initial three words could unfold into a much more complex statement: "Hedges, a means of expressing uncertainty or noting situations in which a claim might not hold, can—when not used as defensive measures intended to bar an audience's engagement with an argument—be a significant act of rhetorical humility." Clearly more clarifications could be added to expand the text further.

In a sense, telescopictext.org is one of many digital reiterations of ancient exercises in amplification or those described in *Copia*, a rhetoric textbook by the Renaissance humanist Desiderius Erasmus.[63] Erasmus endorses the teaching of "the abundant style" because, in students' writing, "excessive growth can easily be cut back by criticism . . . while it is impossible to do anything to improve a thin . . . style."[64] Critics might write off copious compositions as "tendentious twaddle that constitute[s] a dreadful waste of perfectly good trees," but I would argue there is more at stake here than mere stylistics.[65] Rather than just adding colorful adverbs or more descriptive noun phrases, such platforms as telescopictext.org can be used to insert hedges, qualifications, and doubts into a thesis statement that initially appeared forceful, invulnerable, direct. Imagine a statement that took a position on Aphthonius's question of "whether one should marry." A straightforward "one should not marry" could unfold into a nuanced, hypothetical paragraph addressing cultural and social variables, Supreme Court decisions about gay marriage, financial concerns, and the writer's own biases. Airtight declaratives might turn into fragments, anacolutha—even into questions. Rather than starting with a working thesis or thesis question and moving toward a thesis *statement*, this sort of composition would begin with a thesis only to move toward questioning, conditional hypothesizing, and hedging. Certainty would move toward a sort of entropy rather than uncertainty crystallizing into orderly argument.

Path 2

To the left of the widening path is another. This one proceeds precisely ten meters before diverging in various directions. Each of the three diverging trails is marked with a methodological signpost: the first "Psychological Attachment Research," the second "Social History," and the third "New Historicism."[66] Beyond those signs, it looks like the pathways continue in a series of crisp, well-marked turns. I recall here writing in the disciplines (WID) research and its findings. By identifying the context-specific rhetorical principles that guide argumentation in particular disciplines, workplaces, or fields, WID research can offer students argumentative and rhetorical moves that are carefully contextualized in terms of the values and goals of particular academic and professional fields. These principles are hypothetical and practical, with scholars, teachers, and students keenly aware that they only apply given certain conditions in certain communities of practice.

Path 3

Down another path to the left of WID's smartly delineated lanes, I can glimpse a series of mechanical obstacles—machinic hedges and turnstiles that raise and lower, emerge and recede at odd intervals. Whether those obstacles are automated or managed by unseen human hands I don't know, but they remind me of Steven LeMieux's hedging machine.[67] The hedging machine requires a two-person team. One member of the team writes an argument in a word processor. Using a microcontroller called an Arduino, the other member is able to insert stock hedges (e.g., "perhaps," "according to some people," ellipses) into that argument. LeMieux goes so far as to envision an automated version of the second team member—a "mechanical gadfly" that would insert hedges based on such environmental variables as room temperature, the amount of ambient light, and the writer's heart rate. While LeMieux, like Steven Pinker, acknowledges that some hedges are little more than "white noise," the product of nervous tics or thoughtlessness, he suggests that the machine's collaborative approach to hedging could help writers develop a "rich ethos of care." Its hedges could serve as reminders to both writers and readers that the argument articulated in the text "doesn't speak for everyone or . . . doesn't apply in all cases, that even while this is an argument worth making there might be room for disagreement."[68]

Path 4

The next way forward is marked by another series of somewhat similar and yet still distinct collaborative games, material activities, and interruptive challenges that face those who choose it. Here one might recall the multitudinous pedagogical approaches presented by feminist rhetoricians: Laura Micciche's case for play as a "deliberate and valuable method influencing writing pedagogy"; Sonja K. Foss and Cindy L. Griffin's notion of "invitational rhetoric," which reframes rhetoric as more than powerful persuasion by accounting for "the potential of the audience to a contribute to the generation of ideas"; Gloria Anzaldúa's conception of writing as a kind of "mosaic pattern (Aztec-like) . . . a weaving pattern, thin here, thick there" that resists Western artforms that seek to "move humans by means of achieving mastery in content, technique, feeling" and remaining "whole and always 'in power'"; the innumerable ways in which "women have manipulated the material world" in ways that emphasize the embodied, interruptive, playful, collaborative, and creative aspects of our theoretical, compositional, and pedagogical practices and expand traditional notions of rhetoric and writing alike.[69]

Path 5

The next artery I glance down in fact resembles a human circulatory system in its manner of progression. I count one path, two paths, and some more but soon lose track. These numerous and unevenly sized passages diverge and multiply like the veins that extend from a human heart. They even loop back on one another from time to time. I affirm that this path would seem to resemble Victor Vitanza's "*dissoi-paralogoi*," with its many channels indicating "affirmative deconstructions that point to the excess flying around, to the leftover that's busily shattering the border zones of thought."[70] Expanding on the ancient rhetorical practice of *dissoi logoi* (i.e., contrasting arguments), in which sophists and students would practice arguing both sides of an issue, *dissoi-paralogoi* dispenses with the assumption that arguments merely have two sides, instead proliferating ever-more rhetorical positions as a way of interrupting the binary ways in which controversial issues are often conceptualized and debated (e.g., good vs. bad, us vs. them, rhetoric vs. philosophy, left vs. right, etc.).[71]

And, as I continue to look to the left, I see more and more options, more and more pedagogical paths extending like an additional plurality of *dissoi-paralogoi*—ancient and mechanical and feminist and queer and material and decolonial and some more avenues, all twisting and turning and beckoning me forward. Before I can explore them, however, I hear a murmuring. I turn to find that students have arrived and are discoursing with each other. Or were they here all along and I am only now noticing them? Selecting a path is no longer, if it has ever been, my solitary choice. It is time to take others along and to be taken along by them. I can let them choose among the variety of options before us and hope our paths all cross again on the other side of the gates. I can guide them into one, knowing that some will dislike my choice, perhaps even find ways to link to other paths on their own. It is time to decide: to choose *for* these students, to choose *with* them?[72] The paths diverge. It is time to decide, uncertainly.

EXPOSITION

As I mentioned at the beginning of this chapter, Levinas, near the end of *Otherwise Than Being*, states the book's thesis one last time. *Otherwise Than Being* is made up of three primary sections—"The Argument," "The Exposition," and "In Other Words"—and the final statement of its thesis occurs on the penultimate page of "In Other Words" (in French, "*Autrement Dit*"). To put it otherwise, even though Levinas emphasizes that the thesis is "exposed"—specifically, "exposed imprudently to the reproach of utopianism"—he ends the book not with definitive exposition, but with other words.[73] Prioritizing the fluid, unsettled modality he calls "saying" above the static "said," Levinas ends by restating his thesis in a way that draws attention to its vulnerability and its lack of finality. In fact, *Otherwise Than Being* ends with a meditation on the significance of vulnerability: "For the little humanity that adorns the earth," writes Levinas, "a relaxation of essence to the second degree is needed, in the just war waged against war to tremble or shudder at every instant because of this very justice. This weakness is needed. This relaxation of virility without cowardice is needed for the little cruelty our hands repudiate."[74]

The "relaxation of virility without cowardice." A weakness that is necessary to the repudiation of cruelty. In many ways, such a weakness informs my roundabout approach to thesis statements throughout this chapter. As I tried to show along the way, an obsession with direct, virile, strongly stated theses drives many arenas of Western, and particularly US, rhetorics. Hedging, hesitation, the relaxation of virility, weakness: such rhetorical approaches are frequently read as duplicitous. Even in the stereotypically milquetoast towers of academia, champions of rhetorical directness often engage in arguments that link hesitance with a lack of conventionally masculine bona fides, lumping hedging on the side of feminized disingenuity. Like border guards asking for your passport, such figures demand to see your thesis up front before they'll let you in.

One of my concerns throughout this chapter—really, this whole book—is the self-satisfied chauvinism of such demands and the argumentative styles they perpetuate. I have in mind cases where putting your thesis front and center (or asking others to do the same) is not an act of charity, a generous offer meant to help your audience follow your train of thought, but something akin to an act of violence. I state my thesis, or demand that you tell me yours, so that I don't have to listen to anything that follows. I can hack off any warrants or reasons you offer in support of your thesis, deem any nuanced attempts at persuasion insignificant because I know I disagree with your primary point. In such contexts, the demand for an up-front thesis attempts to keep my position inviolable, sealed up in itself and closed off from affection or revision.

Of course, moving the thesis to the end of an essay, book, or verbal exchange doesn't necessarily constitute a relaxation of argumentative virility. For those who think that getting the theoretical pieces in the right place will lead to an airtight practice or endpoint, holding off on a thesis can be just as much about establishing and preserving inviolability.

In the case of rhetoric and writing pedagogy, I have argued that we often emphasize the starting points of arguments (especially in the case of written products) and the endpoints (especially in the case of writing processes) as moments ripe for thetic confidence—a confidence that evinces the writer's movement toward increased certainty regarding their rhetorical position. In this view, rhetoric and writing pedagogy, as well as the processes, products, and subjects it produces, is a movement that in a sense begins *and* ends with clear-eyed confidence.

But what if such pedagogy were to position thesis statements like rhetorician Kendall Gerdes positions humility: "In the midst of no clarity, no certainty, no assurance of your adequacy, you respond. You read, then you read again, prolonging your approach toward the limit but opening the possibility of still another reading, another saying"?[75] In this view, the thesis might be positioned as an exposed response issued "in the midst" of a prolonged approach rather than as a beginning or an end. Neither entrance nor exit, such a thesis would be issued in the midst of the hedge maze. Like the thesis Levinas offers at the end of *Otherwise Than Being*, which unfolds so as to call attention to its vulnerability, weakness, and fragility, such a thesis would be offered *as* a response and as *open to* response. Uncertain, unassured, unsovereign.

The thesis that I am working to *ex*pose here, uncertainly, is this: our thesis-driven pedagogies risk irresponsibility in teaching students to get in and get out of rhetorical dilemmas as directly as possible. While we may hope to empower marginalized subjects to be more efficient and efficacious rhetors, we often do so by privileging certainty and confidence—which I'm arguing are already overblown, at least in dominant rhetorical practices in the United States—at the expense of hesitation and self-doubt, contributing to an atmosphere that fosters further marginalization insofar as it allows those who already do and/or will go on to exercise all manner of economic, political, and material power to rest assured that the lack of hesitation and self-doubt that keeps them in power is the just and justifiable coin of the rhetorical realm. Yes, some of our students may need more rhetorical confidence. But some may need less. Moreover, the same is surely true of *us*, of teachers. Some of us are too certain, too confident when it comes to our assessments of our students, ourselves, and the outcomes of our pedagogies. Some of us are likely not confident enough. But in foregrounding thesis statements, both in our own writing and in the way we teach students, we lop off much of the rhetorical nuance that might allow both ourselves and our students to address more thoughtfully the multifarious concerns at issue in our courses. What if we were to hedge? I leave off here, still in the midst of the hedge maze, with a thesis that may be exposed imprudently to the reproach of utopianism—a thesis that calls for response. I finish, in other words, "in the midst," which is also where I'm arguing we might allow our students to leave off. Careful thinking so often leads to greater uncertainty. Why shouldn't our pedagogies account for that possibility, acknowledging that, while hesitation is not always the most effective tactic in public discourse, our classrooms could also open room for a rhetorical humility that—who knows—might seep into public discourse?

What if the end of a composition was not a confident bang but a rhetorical question?

Epilogue

On the First Day of Class

The ethical task is never quite accomplished.

—GAYATRI CHAKRAVORTY SPIVAK

A common classroom scene: It is the beginning of the semester, the first day of classes. The teacher, having advance access to a roster of students' names—a roster that might also include majors, email addresses, photos—calls roll. Along the way, the teacher probably calls the names of a few students who aren't present and doesn't call the names of a few who are, butchers the pronunciation of a few names, and calls some students by names that they no longer go by. No big deal, though. Calling roll is just a formality, a very little thing, almost nothing. It is a task to get through as quickly as possible—after all, there's the real work of the course to get to.

But wait. In *Very Little . . . Almost Nothing*, philosopher Simon Critchley meditates on Maurice Blanchot's *La Part du feu*, or *The Work of Fire*. Critchley notes that, in *La Part du feu*, Blanchot seems to "advanc[e] the proposition that language is murder, that is, the act of naming things, of substituting a name for the sensation, gives things to us, but in a form that deprives those things of their being. Human speech is thus the annihilation of things *qua* things, and their articulation through language is truly their death-rattle."[1] Thus Adam, he who is responsible for naming all the animals in the opening pages of the Book of Genesis, "is the first serial killer."[2]

Critchley writes, "There is a paradox here: namely that the condition of possibility for the magical power of the understanding to grasp things as such entails that those things must be dead on arrival in the understanding."[3] Like the pin that affixes a taxidermied butterfly to the properly labeled spot in an exhibit case, a name allows one to grasp another by affixing that other to a particular linguistic locale.

Let us return to the scene of the roll call, with the possibility of a teacher "butchering" a student's name now taking on some additional connotations. Bearing in mind language's annihilating grasp, the commonplace procedure of calling roll takes on a certain rhetorical and ethical urgency. Consider some possibilities: A trans student whose dead name still appears on the roll sheet. A student who now goes by another name because of some estrangement from the family or person whose legacy is reflected in their prior name—a name that nevertheless continues to appear on official forms. A student whose name is routinely mispronounced by teachers and other officials, and who has taken to using a nickname to avoid the frustrations and embarrassments that can attend such mispronunciations—or who, unwilling to abandon their given name, deserves the opportunity to pronounce that name for others rather than beginning another semester by having someone else mislabel them.

What am I suggesting? In this case, not a difficult deconstructive displacement but a simple flip: at the beginning of a course, to let students state their names for themselves. Plenty of teachers already do so, of course. Plenty of teachers do even more, engaging students in various icebreaker activities meant to give students an opportunity to share details about themselves, to allow both their teacher and their classmates to learn something about them on their own terms.

What I'm suggesting, then, is somewhat banal, perhaps just as common as the roll call I described at the start of this epilogue. And that banality is perhaps true of many of the interventions outlined in this book's moments of decision. For readers desiring powerful proclamations, bold descriptions of a pedagogy of responsibility that would sweep away conventional pedagogical wisdom, what I've written here may seem to amount to a hill of beans: an exercise here, a hedge there, an approach to peer response that doesn't so much revolutionize the process as shift its emphasis a bit. To riff on Critchley's title, my suggestions may come to very little, almost nothing—pedagogical tweaks that unfold at an even more modest level than course design, assignment sequencing, or curriculum.

But part of my argument is that these very little things, which are bound up with much more expansive educational structures, institutions, and tropes, are also very *significant* things. These relational moments, exercises, workshops, and rhetorical devices that we either overlook or try to crystallize because they escape our thinking and our attempts at mastery—these are things that matter. I began this book with some meditations on pedagogical authority, but I have tried to focus much of what followed on the small things that resist that authority, refusing to be grasped by teachers, companies, textbooks, or students themselves.

So: It is the beginning of the semester. The giving of names is turned over to students, turned into a series of questions offered by the teacher rather than a series of unilateral pronouncements demanding curt responses: "Here." "Present." Of course, it's true that asking for someone's name is also a sort of demand, not just a form of generosity. Derrida considers this in *Of Hospitality*: "Now the foreigner, the *xenos* ... who has the right to hospitality in the cosmopolitan tradition . . . is someone with whom, to receive him, you begin by asking his name; you enjoin him to state and to guarantee his identity, as you would a witness before a court."[4] Derrida describes this enjoinment as "a question," an "address," and "a demand, the first demand, the minimal demand being: 'What is your name?'" Then again, he observes, it is a question that "seems very human and sometimes loving." In various forms, it is a question "we sometimes tenderly ask children and those we love": "what is your name? tell me your name, what should I call you, I who am calling on you, I who want to call you by your name? What am I going to call you?"[5]

I'm arguing for structuring the giving of names that begins so many courses as a series of relatively open-ended, perhaps even relatively tender, responses rather than a more constrained call and response. I am arguing that this common ritual, which so often sets the tone for a course's relational dynamic, might constitute or be constituted as a "scene of address."[6] Doing so opens the possibility of certain detours, interruptions, and delays as the teacher crosses out certain names and writes in others, matching or mismatching the names students give with those given by the institution. It is a less efficient approach than the teacher just ripping through the names as written. And yet it makes the first day of class a more open rhetorical exchange, and that is a small thing that is perhaps no small thing.

As I've acknowledged, plenty of teachers are already willing to introduce this bit of discursive disorder into the way a course begins. But as the semester picks up—as students' writing and projects pile up in teachers' inboxes, as some teachers balance pedagogical responsibilities with administrative, scholarly, and service work while others balance courses at multiple institutions and simultaneously attempt to cobble together a contingent slate of courses to teach the next semester—the daily vagaries of pedagogical disorder often begin to feel less allowable. It becomes prudent, even necessary, to rely on various means of delimiting a course's structure and the range of our responses to students: due dates, rubrics, thesis statements, course policies. It becomes more defensible (and perhaps more pleasurable) to rely on a professorial mantra that's become a meme—"It's in the syllabus!"—rather than taking a moment, time and time again, to consider *why* students keep bringing us certain questions, why they seem to encounter the syllabus as an inscrutable document, why they might have trouble mastering a course's procedures and protocols. Rather than making a singular decision in the face of every question or miscommunication, the time comes to defer the responsibility of decision-making to established authorities outside ourselves.

In fact, I would argue that the chaos of an unfolding course often prevents us from encountering many of its inevitable interruptions *as decisions to be made.* Denying a student's petition for a deadline extension can feel like a foregone conclusion rather than a decision *I* must make. In Levinasian terms, we outsource responsibility to "the said" without even recognizing the possibility of "the saying" that might render our response questionable.[7]

Which, again, is not to say that course policies or programmatic responses—whether they're instituted by a university, a department, a syllabus, a teacher, or an assignment prompt—are necessarily indefensible or unethical. As I argued early on, the establishment of policies and institutions can be a key part of what allows pedagogical questions and student challenges to be heard and allows the work of teaching to happen. What I am suggesting is that there are pedagogical questions to be heard in places where we tend not to hear questions. To return once more to a line that I cited earlier, "If there is a university responsibility, it at least begins the moment when a need to hear these questions, to take them upon oneself and respond to them, imposes itself. This imperative of the response is the initial form and minimal requirement of responsibility."[8] In short, I only wish to indicate the pedagogical cracks from which rhetorical and ethical questions might be sprouting—questions that, though we tend not to hear them *as* questions, perhaps need to be heard.

Unfortunately, the ways higher education treats its teachers and students are constantly foreclosing on rather than fostering the recognition of such questions. As John Warner argues in *Sustainable. Resilient. Free. The Future of Public Higher Education*, "We have reached the end point of what it means for colleges and universities to be run with what I call an 'operations on down' approach, rather than a strategy focused from the 'mission (pedagogy) on up.' This is because schools are not currently in the teaching and learning business. They are machines meant to capture education-related revenue."[9] Public higher education has been squeezed and cut over and over again in recent decades: By rankings and metrics that reward self-interested and well-funded private institutions. By state funding models that push public institutions to compete with rather than collaborate with and complement one another. By competition with the venture-capital-backed scions of the "MOOC moment," the self-styled innovators and promoters who seem to barely comprehend the complex and multifaceted pedagogical work happening at the local postsecondary institutions they continually seek to "disrupt." By political discourse that positions higher education as a waste of time and money rather than a meaningful public investment. By increasing tuition costs fueled by state disinvestment as austerity measures attributed to temporary crises (e.g., the 2008 recession, the coronavirus pandemic) quietly become permanent budget cuts.

In this context, it can be hard to teach, especially in the ways I've argued for throughout this book. I am, admittedly, one of the lucky ones: someone who graduated from a PhD program in the liberal arts in 2016 and still got a tenure-track position my first year on the job market. I would probably be making more had I gone into the private sector straight out of undergrad, but I've found a position that makes teaching a sustainable middle-class career. That is not the case for the majority of higher education's academic workforce, and I constantly wonder whether my search would have failed and I'd have ended up following another career path had I been on the increasingly narrow and competitive job market a mere two or three years later. According to the American Association of University Professors' 2020 statement on "Contingent Faculty and the Global Pandemic," contingent faculty now account for 70 percent of the academic labor force.[10] As I finalize this epilogue, it's also hard to forget that, despite the flexibility some universities extended to faculty during the 2020–21 academic year, in 2021–22, many of those same universities—some, to be fair, at the insistence of economically obsessed state governments unwilling to support measures to mitigate COVID—demanded a return to in-person teaching even as parts of the country hit record numbers of COVID cases. As Warner puts it, faculty and staff have been "asked to sacrifice their lives for the good of the stock market."[11]

Meanwhile students continue to face rising tuition costs that make it increasingly prudent to approach higher education with an eye toward maximum efficiency: getting through in the least amount of time possible with minimal debt, the best GPA, and the most market-focused degree (even if such degrees are often in oversaturated fields and thus leave graduates underemployed), often while working full- or part-time jobs to make ends meet. Obviously I don't hold this against students, but it creates a situation where the challenging work of learning and taking courses can feel like an impediment to rather than the substance of a degree. For both faculty and students, "we have managed to reduce the value of a postsecondary education entirely to its credential, while simultaneously leaving institutions starved of the revenue necessary to do their work."[12]

In the midst of all this, a contingent labor force and precariously positioned student bodies have continued to do remarkable work at public colleges and universities—often in spite of rather than thanks to the institutions responsible for coordinating and supporting that work. But these conditions make it harder to attend to the ethical and rhetorical work I've described and argued for throughout this book: instilling and valuing mutual uncertainty and vulnerability rather than solely valorizing authority and self-mastery; creating courses in which students engage with one another and the teacher rather than pursuing a fixed, content-driven end; not just teaching students to rely on pat rhetorical moves that make their writing easy to assess but ultimately unpersuasive and inflexible; addressing and practicing the complex challenges involved in living together rather than focusing solely or primarily on one's individual socioeconomic future.

Even this book itself is perhaps already an artifact of a vanishing state of educational affairs, particularly for faculty at regional comprehensive universities and other underappreciated, non-flagship public institutions. Given higher education's present reliance on contingent workers whose sole responsibility is to teach and who have minimal say in how universities operate and are governed, combined with the fact that the sort of pedagogical work I'm doing here is not a magnet for grant funding and course releases, the opportunity to reflect extensively on one's pedagogical theories and practices can be a rare thing. This is not to critique or dismiss the laudable, exhausting work that contingent faculty do at colleges and universities across the country on a semester-to-semester, day-to-day basis. It is to say that they deserve better and that (speaking from experience) studying, honing, and revising your teaching practices and extending hospitality to students is much more challenging when teaching five-plus sections of first-year writing with enrollment caps constantly creeping up than when you have the more stable, manageable teaching loads and employment situations that typically come with tenure-track and tenured positions. Because of the specifics of my position, even though finishing this book has involved working into the wee hours of the weekend on a number of occasions, I have had time in recent years not only to write it but to reflect on and experiment with the pedagogical practices, theories, and arguments laid out in its pages without constantly burning the candle at both ends.[13] And, perhaps most importantly, I have had the chance to get to know and *respond to* the students for and with whom I have pursued and developed these pedagogical materials. As of 2022, in the midst of current and looming crises unavoidable, manufactured, and imagined, my hope is that higher education will find ways to carve out spaces in which faculty and students can experimentally, supportively, thoughtfully, and collectively engage with one another without the specter of precarity constantly nipping at their heels. My hope is that public institutions of higher education can remain (to the extent that they are) and become (to the extent that they can) places where teachers and students can work together to create something better for each other and for those that such institutions have not yet welcomed—that higher education will not become an arena in which institutions, faculty, staff, and students grow ever-more competitive with and suspicious of one another in a scramble for ever-scarcer resources in the eyes of an increasingly incredulous or indifferent world.[14]

In short, I hope that higher education will remain a space for disorderly, messy, uncertain exchanges between teachers and teachers, students and students, teachers and students, and so on and so forth—exchanges that may not shore up our respective authority and agency, but that might give us the chance to be responsible to and for one another.

As one last illustration, let me return to the exercise that was at the crux of chapter 2.

It was a few days before the due date for that *prosopopoeia* exercise. As you may recall, the exercise asked students to compose something like a counterfactual history, to imagine what might have been said had Alison Bechdel and her father been granted entrance to the "notorious local night-spot" they visited after seeing the film *Coal Miner's Daughter*.[15] I was holding office hours and a student stopped by. She was unsure about her ability to complete the assignment. It wasn't that she didn't understand the prompt, had a big test in another class, or was hoping for a free pass. Rather, she was concerned that completing the assignment would constitute an irresponsible act. The event I was asking students to imagine had not in fact occurred, and she felt that the best way to honor that nonoccurrence was to leave it unsaid. She was, of course, theorizing. While I was channeling Levinas, she was maybe channeling Wittgenstein, compelled to pass over in silence that which she felt it would be unethical to state.

And so I found myself theorizing in return. This was, I had to admit, a response to the assignment that I had not anticipated. Then again, the perplexity the student was describing was exactly the sort of perplexity I'd hoped to call attention to through the assignment. There was a chance that her response to the assignment had something on the assignment. That is, in her loyalty to the protocols of both *Fun Home* and the prompt itself, she had perhaps traced an ethical horizon that the assignment had failed to consider. It crossed my mind that this student deserved an immediate A plus.

But I was mindful of the comparative complications that might arise if I gave her a pass on completing the assignment and word subsequently got around to other students (at which point her reservations, which I'm here taking at face value, could be reiterated by her classmates as an opportunistic gambit). I thus complimented her on the thought she'd put into the assignment but encouraged her to finish it anyway. Years later, I remain uncertain of whether this was the best response to her call. Why not allow her to swap the assignment itself for a piece of writing that described her hesitation? Why did I not at least make that hesitation a topic of conversation the next time that class convened? What a deceptively simple, immensely complex ethical and rhetorical situation.

Now, with another decade of teaching experience and a bit more professional stability, those questions point to alternatives I likely would have pursued—not because I have become more certain about one singular right way of teaching but because I have had pedagogical experiences and opportunities that have allowed me to better recognize and welcome particular kinds of ethical entropy, uncertainty, and contingency as indispensable, though not controllable, parts of what it means to learn, to teach, and to be taught.

Given that sort of contingency and the wide variety of contexts in which postsecondary rhetoric and writing courses happen, not to mention the wide variety of contexts faced by students and teachers involved in such courses, I have been and remain hesitant to prescribe one-size-fits-all solutions for the ways that relations between teachers and students, theory and practice, and so many other pedagogically relevant entities *should* unfold in such courses. But I end this book, end even this epilogue, by returning to the scene of the first day of class because even in a class's opening moments, a complicated and significant set of theoretical, practical, rhetorical, and ethical questions are at issue. There are countless justifiable ways in which to respond to and even dismiss these questions. But when the various authorities and institutions responsible for the ways and contexts in which higher education unfolds, including teachers and students, refuse to support the work that helps certain questions be heard—when certain questions cease to resonate *as* questions—the overlapping horizons of rhetoric, ethics, and education may begin to vanish.

What and whom does higher education represent? Are its practitioners responsible? To whom and for what are we responsible? There are many ways to answer such questions. I can only say that, over the course of this book's many turnings and returnings, I hope I've respected these questions' status *as* questions. I hope to have responded to them, bearing in mind that the "imperative of the response is the initial form and minimal requirement of responsibility," and that the devaluation of the rhetorical and ethical work of teaching makes even this minimal requirement—those messy and myriad, very little, almost nothing pedagogical exchanges that can unfold when courses are approached as scenes of address rather than just scenes of punishment, authority, self-mastery, efficiency, personalization, certainty—ever more rare and precious. Bearing in mind that the moment we assume, for instance, that the names given on a roll sheet are sufficient figurations of those we call "students," or that the aggregated or individuated names of faculty given in a budget line item are sufficient figurations of those we call "teachers," we may have to mark responsibility absent from the pedagogical scene. And yet, even as these figurations stubbornly define so much of education's past and present, responsibility is never totally absent. It lingers, awaiting the next time the Other's anarchic call resounds and we must figure our pedagogical relations anew. Until, again, we find ourselves responsible.

Introduction

1. Cottom, *Lower Ed*, 38–39.

2. Kahn, Lalicker, and Lynch-Biniek, *Contingency, Exploitation, and Solidarity*; Welch and Scott, *Composition in the Age of Austerity*.

3. Baca and Villanueva, *Rhetorics of the Americas*; Bernard-Donals and Fernheimer, *Jewish Rhetorics*; Campbell, "Rhetoric from the Ruins"; Wu, *Guiguzi*.

4. Kaster, *Guardians of Language*; Marrou, *History of Education*; Walker, *Genuine Teachers*.

5. Let me also note that because rhetorical education predates what we've come to think of as "higher education," it does not map perfectly onto the work or student bodies of colleges and universities. Nevertheless, given that it was the culmination of many ancient students' educations—a final step undertaken by some but not all students, and one that attracted a mixture of heightened respect *and* heightened suspicion compared to earlier educational stages—there are significant resonances between ancient rhetorical education and present-day higher education.

6. Cooper, "Rhetorical Agency," 426.

7. Ibid., 443–44.

8. Cribiore, *Gymnastics*, 47.

9. Arendt, "Crisis," 185. For more on Arendt's relevance to rhetoric and writing education, consult Restaino, *First Semester*.

10. Arendt, "Crisis," 187.

11. Ibid., 184.

12. Ibid., 187.

13. Arendt, "What Is Authority?," 91.

14. Ibid., 91–92.

15. Ibid., 141.

16. Ibid., 118.

17. Arendt, "Crisis," 178.

18. Ibid., 178.

19. Enders, "Rhetoric."

20. Ibid., 46.

21. Ibid., 46.

22. Ibid., 41.

23. Cribiore, *Gymnastics*, 158.

24. Ibid., 50.

25. Writing about classical grammarians, whose schools students occupied before moving on to the schools of rhetoricians, Robert Kaster observes, "The grammarian was one of antiquity's great middlemen" (*Guardians*, 7), "a threshold figure, exposed and ambiguous; his position of strength was vulnerable, capable of being chipped away on several sides" (31). Even when they fared better than Cassian, the authority of grammarians, rhetoricians, and the pedagogical structures they sought to create and inculcate was rarely seamless, as documented in Walker (*Genuine Teachers*, 4).

26. Maraj, *Black or Right*. See also Fares and Moon, "U.S. Campuses"; Randle, "Racial Slurs"; Seltzer, "Missouri 3 Years Later."

27. Arendt, "Crisis," 178. It's worth remembering that the decades during which Arendt wrote saw disparate and rampant challenges to traditional notions of educational authority, leaving a lot for a political theorist to wrangle with. To her credit, Arendt was a thinker who was willing to change her mind, revisit her arguments, and be persuaded by others (Roberts-Miller, "Fighting"). Of course, that does not simply erase her missteps.

28. Lebeau, "Unwelcome Child"; Steele, "Arendt Versus Ellison"; Warren, "Ralph Ellison."

29. Arendt, "Reflections on Little Rock."

50. Arendt apparently combines details from photos of Eckford, one of the Little Rock Nine, and Dorothy Counts (D. Allen, *Talking to Strangers*, 197; Lebeau, "Unwelcome Child," 54).

30. Arendt, "Reflections," 50.

31. Ellison, "Leadership from the Periphery," 343.

32. Ibid., 343–44.

33. Ibid., 343.

34. D. Allen, *Talking to Strangers*, 4.

35. Ibid., 5.

36. Arendt, "Reflections," 46.

37. Ibid., 50.

38. Pitkin, *Attack of the Blob*.

39. Ibid., 149, 159.

40. Ibid., 145. For instance, Pitkin claims that in *The Human Condition*, Arendt extrapolates "a general theory of free citizenship . . . from the experience of wartime resistance to the Nazis."

41. Conor Friedersdorf, "Campus Activists." In light of Friedersdorf's claims, it's worth remembering that US universities are never far from slavery and other historical and ongoing manifestations of institutional racism. As Craig Steven Wilder points out in *Ebony and Ivy*, not only were many US colleges literally built by slaves, but "the American college trained the personnel and cultivated the ideas that accelerated and legitimated the dispossession of Native Americans and the enslavement of Africans. Modern slavery required the acquiescence of scholars and the cooperation of academic institutions" (10; consider also Ore, "Black Feelings").

42. Halberstam, "You Are Triggering Me!"; Jackson, "Obama Rips into 'Coddled' College Students"; Lukianoff and Haidt, *Coddling*; Schlosser, "I'm a Liberal Professor."

43. Friedersdorf, "New Intolerance."

44. Intercultural Affairs, "Email."

45. Christakis, "Email."

46. Ibid.

47. Friedersdorf, "New Intolerance."

48. Wilson, "Open Letter."

49. Friedersdorf, "New Intolerance."

50. Cox and Love, "White Yalies in Blackface."

51. Vought, "Memorandum," 1.

52. Kruesi, "Tennessee."

53. SB 0623, 112th General Assembly. It is worth noting that this bill, along with others passed or proposed by state legislatures since the 2020 election, have also flipped student feelings from a specific threat to an abstract thing in need of protection. For instance, SB 0623 prohibits local education agencies from promoting the concept that an individual "should feel discomfort, guilt, anguish, or another form of psychological distress solely because of the individual's race or sex" (7). Or perhaps "bifurcated" is more accurate than "flipped" insofar as the bills, ostensibly motivated by a fear of critical race theory, seem specifically invested in protecting the feelings of *white* individuals from being threatened by the emotional legacy of racism in the United States.

54. On the tension between American ideals and actualities, and for a piece that helped inspire legislation banning the teaching of critical race theory by highlighting the contingencies and racial inequities of US history, see Hannah-Jones, "Idea of America."

55. On the contingency of racial inequities, consider Carbado and Harris, "Intersectionality at 30"; Harris, "Whiteness as Property"; Martinez, *Counterstory*, 14.

56. Christakis, "Email."

57. Ahmed, "Against Students." Consider also Orem and Simpkins, "Weepy Rhetoric."

58. Gerdes, "Trauma," 18. Gerdes's argument builds on concepts outlined by Mary Louise Pratt. In her oft-cited 1991 article "Arts of the Contact Zone," Pratt describes what she calls "safe houses": "social and intellectual spaces where groups can constitute themselves as horizontal, homogeneous, sovereign communities with high degrees of trust, shared understandings, temporary protection from legacies of oppression" (40). She contrasts these with "contact zones": "social spaces where cultures meet, clash, and grapple with each other, often in contexts of highly asymmetrical relations of power, such as colonialism, slavery, or their aftermaths as they are lived out in many parts of the world today" (34).

59. For a cross-section of such work, see I. Allen, *Ethical Fantasy*; Brown, *Ethical Programs*; Davis, *Inessential Solidarity*; Duffy and Agnew, *After Plato*.

60. Muckelbauer, "Implicit Paradigms."

61. I. Allen, *Ethical Fantasy*, 4.

62. Arnett, *Levinas's Rhetorical Demand*, 4; Brown, *Ethical Programs*; Davis, *Inessential Solidarity*, 2.

63. Butler, *Giving*, 14. Butler is summarizing, and Enders is building on, arguments from Nietzsche's *On the Genealogy of Morals*.

64. Ibid., 13 (emphasis added).

65. Ibid., 91.

66. Ibid., 83.

67. See Geisler, "How"; Geisler, "Teaching"; hooks, *Teaching to Transgress*; Reynolds, "Interrupting"; Yancey, "Writing Agency"; cf. Lundberg and Gunn, "Ouija Board."

68. *Framework*, 1.

69. Leff and Lunsford, "Afterwords," 62. My hope, in a sense, is to elaborate on a hedge that Adam J. Banks drops in his book *Race, Rhetoric, and Technology*. In the midst of arguing that rhetoric and writing teachers should engage in what he calls "design work," Banks pauses to note what he's *not* arguing: "This is not an argument that teachers can best serve students by simply creating spaces and then getting out of the way, an argument whose strongest versions are profoundly *irresponsible* to me" (84; emphasis added).

70. Lyon, *Deliberative Acts*, 24.

71. Ibid., 43.

72. Ibid., 49.

73. Ibid., 92.

74. For example, I would argue Butler does not present a "site of accusation and accounting" so much as they present the scene of accounting as an alternative to the Nietzschean scene of accusation. Moreover, I would question whether this scene of accounting is solipsistic insofar as Butler argues against the demand for complete understanding of one's self. Rather, Butler argues that there may be "a certain violence" in demanding that a subject "reinstall its mastery and unity" by offering a narrative account that demonstrates complete self-mastery (*Giving*, 64). In not demanding such an account, Butler is releasing the self from the solipsism of self-understanding and obliging others to leave room for the aporias that arise when someone is unable to explain themselves in a way that moves others toward shared narrative coherence or deliberative consensus. Butler may address "difficulties of difference"

in a different manner than Lyon does, but the difficulties are not escaped.

75. *Deliberative Acts*, 101.

76. Ibid., 101.

77. Ibid., 102.

78. Mapping the dominant gender ideologies with which Arendt grew up and lived, and which often informed her work despite the ways she pushed back on them, Hanna Fenichel Pitkin writes, "For a number of reasons, the father appears as the representative of adulthood and autonomy, while the mother remains that of infancy. . . . [T]he father tends to become both the symbol and the model of access to the larger world outside the family and of autonomous agency" (*Attack*, 172–73). Pitkin emphasizes the ways in which culturally constructed gender roles can calcify into abstract symbols of authority, noting how Arendt's particular context underwrote her tendency to tie such roles to generalized theories of authority.

79. Eberly, "From Writers."

80. Consider Kahn, Lalicker, and Lynch-Biniek, *Contingency*; Jarratt, *Rereading*, 64.

81. Chávez and Griffin, *Standing in the Intersection*; Ryan, "Rhetoric(s) of Becoming."

82. On the inequities experienced by women, consider El-Alayli, Hansen-Brown, and Ceynar, "Dancing Backwards." On inequities experienced by queer faculty and faculty of color, consider Kopelson, "Rhetoric," 119–20.

83. Kerschbaum, *Toward*, 101.

84. Levinas, *Totality*, 29.

85. Ibid., 29.

86. For a more detailed reconsideration of the entwinement of theory and pedagogy, see Detweiler, "Toward Pedagogical Turnings."

87. Hawhee and Olson, "Pan-Historiography," 103.

88. Driskill, "Decolonial Skillshares"; Meyerhoff, *Beyond Education*; paperson, *Third University*.

Chapter 1

This chapter has been revised from a previously published article: Eric Detweiler, "Disfiguring Socratic Irony," *Philosophy and Rhetoric* 49, no. 2 (2016): 149–72, copyright ©

2016 The Pennsylvania State University Press. This article is used by permission of The Pennsylvania State University Press.

1. Cribiore, *School*, 130.

2. Positioning Socrates among the ranks of rhetoric teachers may strike readers as a questionable move. For the moment, I'll just note that a number of texts have explored Socrates's sophistic tendencies and rhetorical impulses (Colebrook, *Irony*, 30; Henderson, "Introductory Note," 4; Kennedy, *New History*, 20).

3. Fredal, "Why Shouldn't the Sophists Charge Fees?," 150.

4. Isocrates, "Against," 1. Citations of Isocrates refer to line numbers; quotations are from the Mirhady and Too translation.

5. Isocrates, "Antidosis," 155, 39, 88.

6. Walker, *Genuine Teachers*, 4.

7. Cribiore, *School*, 139.

8. Walker, *Genuine Teachers*, 161. In addition to Libanius's complaints, consider the numerous satiric depictions of Roman teachers of rhetoric (Lucian, *Professor*; Petronius, *Satyricon*).

9. Cribiore, *Gymnastics*, 59.

10. American Association of University Professors, "Data Snapshot"; Edwards, McGuire, and Sanchez, *Speaking Up*; Kahn, Lalicker, and Lynch-Biniek, *Contingency*; Welch and Scott, *Composition*.

11. Crowley, *Composition*, 264.

12. hooks, *Teaching to Transgress*, 20.

13. To both avoid and risk falling into my own Platonism, let me pause to unpack that sentence's deployment of "Platonic" as an adjective that might itself be read as essentializing. "What is *x*?" questions "are" Platonic only insofar as Plato is, in our historical moment, regularly interpreted as a philosopher who saw the essence or nature of an idea or concept as metaphysical and not delimited by historical, rhetorical, and/or hermeneutic variables and variations. Such a question is not *essentially* Platonic given that, at some point, Plato's dialogues might be interpreted—however oddly—as nonessentialist and not purely metaphysical. As I preface this chapter's encounter with the *Gorgias*, then, I don't mean to suggest that Socrates (Plato's or otherwise) is an essentialist or idealist. I have in mind, rather, extensive hermeneutic traditions that read Plato's Socrates as such—traditions into whose interpretive certitudes I hope to sow some patches of uncertainty.

14. De Man, "Concept," 164.

15. Regarding more generalized considerations of these difficulties, see the fluctuations of the performative/constative split in J. L. Austin's *How to Do Things with Words*, in which Austin claims, "there can hardly be any longer a possibility of not seeing that stating is performing an act" (139). See also Derrida's further interrogations of this split, undertaken all over the place but perhaps most famously in *Limited Inc.*

16. De Man, "Concept," 164. Given this section's citations of de Man, I am compelled to note his antisemitic publications during World War II (Hamacher, Hertz, and Keenan, *Responses*).

17. Ibid., 164.

18. Ibid., 165.

19. One could go further; some scholars certainly have. In addition to the varieties of irony listed above, they've named "conditional irony" and "reverse irony" (Vasiliou, "Socrates' Reverse Irony," 221), "Platonic irony" (Nehamas, *Art of Living*, 44), and the sub-subdivided "Socratic verbal irony" and "Socratic dramatic irony" (Wolfsdorf, "Irony of Socrates," 176).

20. Biesecker, "Rethinking," 120.

21. Pareles, "Solipsisters."

22. Morissette, "Ironic."

23. *Oxford English Dictionary*, s.v. "irony." OED Online, https://www.oed.com.

24. De Man, "Concept," 179. De Man defines "parabasis" as "the interruption of a discourse by a shift in the rhetorical register" (179). Avital Ronell traces it back to the "lightning effect (*Blitz*) of provocative revelation occurring when the Greek chorus steps forward, crossing the line" (*Stupidity*, 139).

25. De Man, *Allegories*, 301 (emphasis added).

26. Ronell, *Stupidity*, 156. In 2018, a few years after I began revising this chapter for inclusion in this book, Ronell was suspended by New York University after a Title IX investigation found her responsible for sexually harassing a former graduate student (Flaherty, "Harassment and Power"). Because I recognize this chapter's reliance on her work may seem to elide that investigation's findings, and by extension playfully dismiss

the broader problem of teachers sexually harassing students, let me note here: I unequivocally condemn such harassment. I considered revising this chapter to omit citations of Ronell's work, but doing so seemed disingenuous. Whether or not such citations appeared, it is undeniable that reading her writing has influenced my thinking on the ethics of teaching. That is something I feel the need to account for rather than attempt to bury. You don't have to look too deeply into the history of education to find copious examples of the rationalization of sexual harassment and abuse under the guise of teacher-student intimacy or the master-novice dynamic often presented as an integral part of such relationships. I acknowledge that history as something that I, in writing a book on teacher-student relationships, have to reckon with. It is a real problem, and it is a persistent one. For my part, I will continue working to uproot such harassment and the harm it does to students rather than excuse or condone it, but that includes acknowledging the ways I am implicated in that history and its ongoing manifestations.

27. In "The Concept of Irony," de Man positions Booth's book, as well as "American criticism of irony" in general, as the *alazon*, noting in parentheses, "I recognize that this makes me the real *alazon* of this discourse" (165).

28. Booth, *Rhetoric of Irony*, 3.

29. Ibid., 3 (emphasis added).

30. Ibid., 227, 276.

31. Ibid., 177.

32. Colebrook, *Irony*, 2.

33. Ibid., 30.

34. De Man, "Concept," 167; Booth, *Rhetoric*, 177.

35. Felman, "Psychoanalysis," 21. Diane Davis paraphrases Felman's positioning of Socrates, placing him among a set of teachers who are exemplary insofar as they "know that they *do not know*" (*Breaking Up*, 224).

36. Cf. David Wolfsdorf's consideration of "Plato's intentions" as he works to define—and basically cancel out—"Socratic irony" (181).

37. Vasiliou, "Socrates' Reverse Irony," 230.

38. Ibid., 225.

39. Ronell, *Stupidity*, 121.

40. Vasiliou, "Socrates' Reverse Irony," 221.

41. Consider Latour, "Socrates' and Callicles' Settlement," 224.

42. Too, *Pedagogical Contract*, 76.

43. Foucault, "Discourse," 217.

44. Ibid., 218.

45. Ibid.

46. Gorgias, "Encomium of Helen," 20, 2, 8. Citations refer to line numbers, with quotations from George A. Kennedy's translation of the "Encomium of Helen" in Aristotle, *On Rhetoric*.

47. 449c. Unless otherwise noted, all quotations from the *Gorgias* are from Donald J. Zeyl's translation.

48. Kierkegaard, *Concept of Irony*, 25, 27.

49. Ibid., 25.

50. Ibid., 128.

51. Ronell, *Stupidity*, 146.

52. Kierkegaard, *Concept of Irony*, 128 (emphasis added).

53. Ibid., 153.

54. Regarding option (a), consider the totalizing, unity-driven Platonism Paul Ramsey maps onto "modern conservatives' curricular [and broader educational] agenda" ("Plato," 573).

55. Zeyl, "Introduction," xii.

56. Hauser, "Teaching Rhetoric," 40.

57. Plato, *Gorgias* 447a. For ease of reference, this section includes parenthetical citations for *Gorgias*, including locator numbers.

58. Latour, "Socrates' and Callicles' Settlement," 192.

59. Zeyl, "Introduction," xiii (emphasis added).

60. Consider *Gorgias* 449c, 505c.

61. Gorgias, "Encomium," 20. This would also correspond with the later rhetorician Athenaeus's claim that when Gorgias read the dialogue, he "said to his friends, 'How well Plato knows how to satirize!'" (quoted in Sprague, *Older Sophists*, 37).

62. In the context Plato is using it, *eirōneuēi* is closer to "dissembling" or "feigning ignorance" than to the more recent sense of "not saying what you mean," though it's not entirely distinct from the latter. For the glosses of Greek terms included in this

chapter, I am significantly indebted to Jeffrey Walker.

63. Consider Plato, *Gorgias* 455a.

64. Vasiliou, "Socrates' Reverse Irony," 226.

65. Plato, *Phaedrus* 276d.

66. On Gorgias's mood, consider 462a. Consider also the rhetorician Athenaeus's claim that Gorgias viewed the dialogue as a testament to Plato's abilities as a satirist (Sprague, *Older Sophists*, 37).

67. Kennedy, *New History*, 20.

68. Plato, *Seventh Letter* 341c. That the authorship of this letter remains uncertain further multiplies the possibilities outlined here.

69. Consider Callicles's reactions at *Gorgias* 505c and 521b.

70. Plato, *Gorgias* 523a.

71. Plato, *Lysis* 223b.

72. Ronell, *Loser Sons*, 9.

73. Consider the allusion to Socrates's trial at *Gorgias* 521c.

74. Ronell, *Stupidity*, 292.

75. Plato, *Gorgias* 276d.

76. Ronell, *Stupidity*, 298.

77. Plato, *Gorgias* 500b.

78. Ronell, *Stupidity*, 156.

79. *Limited Inc*, 72.

80. Latour, "Socrates' and Callicles' Settlement," 194, 198.

81. Ibid., 208.

82. Plato, *Gorgias* 483d.

83. Latour, "Socrates' and Callicles' Settlement," 231.

84. Ibid., 233.

85. Ibid., 233.

86. Ibid., 235.

87. Plato, *Gorgias* 507e–508a, quoted in Latour, "Socrates' and Callicles' Settlement," 235. Latour quotes Robin Waterfield's 1994 translation of the *Gorgias* and includes the bracketed Greek. Waterfield notes that the "experts" Socrates is speaking of are likely the Pythagoreans and some pre-Socratics, whom Waterfield claims "perceived the universe as in some sense an ordered whole" (160). Donald J. Zeyl, meanwhile, renders the same passage as follows: "Yes, Callicles, wise men claim that partnership and friendship, orderliness, self-control, and justice hold together

heaven and earth, and gods and men, and that is why they call the universe a *world order*, my friend, and not an undisciplined world-disorder" (Plato, *Gorgias* 507e–508a). Given Latour's championing of this passage, Waterfield's "ordered whole" certainly has a nicer ring than Zeyl's ominously italicized "*world order*."

88. Latour, "Socrates' and Callicles' Settlement," 234.

89. Ibid., 238.

90. Latour, "Socrates' and Callicles' Settlement," 237, 238. His interest in "conditions of felicity" arguably precludes Derrida's interest in "opportunit[ies] to transform *infelicity* into delight" (*Limited Inc*, 72; emphasis added).

91. Ronell, *Stupidity*, 121.

92. In the *Gorgias*, consider 454c, 493c, 506d.

93. Aristophanes, *Clouds* 1457. For ease of reference, this section includes parenthetical citations for *Clouds*, including line numbers.

94. Henderson, "Introductory Note," 4.

95. "General Introduction," xxxi.

96. Storey, "*Clouds*: Introduction," 3.

97. Ibid., 3–4.

98. Ibid., 7.

99. Ronell, *Stupidity*, 156.

100. Aristophanes, *Clouds*, 789–90.

101. Blanchot, *Writing of the Disaster*, 1.

102. hooks, *Teaching Community*, 9–10.

103. Lu, "Professing Multiculturalism."

104. Levinas, *Totality and Infinity*, 51.

105. Crowley, *Composition*, 225–26.

106. Ibid., 225.

107. Levinas, *Totality and Infinity*, 51.

108. Ibid., 45.

109. Boring, "Gender Biases"; Chávez and Mitchell, "Exploring Bias"; Esarey and Valdes, "Unbiased, Reliable, and Valid"; Gomes and Ma, "Engaging Expectations"; Kreitzer and Sweet-Cushman, "Evaluating Student Evaluations."

110. National Center for Education Statistics, "Characteristics of Postsecondary Faculty."

111. Derrida and Dufourmantelle, *Of Hospitality*, 77. While readers who associate Derrida with reductive notions of "postmodernism" or "deconstruction" may view him as

a destructive figure opposed to the building of systems, I would note, for instance, his role in establishing the Collège international de philosophie.

Chapter 2

1. Consider Detweiler, "Toward Pedagogical Turnings"; Dobrin, *Postcomposition*; Graff, "Pedagogical Turn"; Sánchez, *Function*; Worsham, "Writing."

2. Consider Lynch, *After Pedagogy.*

3. Derrida, *Gift of Death*, 51.

4. Blanchot, *Writing*, 110.

5. Spivak, "Translation as Culture," 240.

6. Ibid., 252.

7. Ibid., 253.

8. Ibid., 253.

9. Spivak, "Translating into English," 256–57.

10. Consider Davis, "Autozoography," 544.

11. For those who see literature and rhetoric as separate areas of study, my focus on an exercise from a course intended to teach students to write about literature might seem to diverge from this book's overall emphasis on rhetorical education. However, as Jeffrey Walker argues at length in *Rhetoric and Poetics in Antiquity*, the division of literary or poetic education from rhetorical education is a relatively recent phenomenon. The history of the imitation exercises I focus on in this chapter provides a case in point: though they frequently required students to imitate characters and styles from what we would now call "literary" texts (e.g., Virgil's *Aeneid* and Ovid's *Metamorphoses*), these exercises were considered part of students' *rhetorical* education. I elaborate on this history in subsequent sections of this chapter.

12. On the term "graphic narrative," consider Chute and DeKoven, "Introduction," 767; Chute, "Texture," 92.

13. Driscoll, "Alison Bechdel's Memoir"; McCammon, "Books." More recently, *Fun Home* met with resistance from a small number of incoming students at Duke University (Bady, "Against Students Stories"; Ballentine, "Freshman Skipping 'Fun Home'").

112. Morris and Stommel, "Open Education," 192.

113. Yergeau et al., "Multimodality in Motion."

14. "Alison Bechdel Interview."

15. Chute, "Interview," 1008.

16. In *Fun Home*'s narrative, this happens just after the two go to see the movie *Coal Miner's Daughter* and is followed closely by a trip home from college that marks the last time Alison sees her father.

17. Bechdel is here referencing the "Circe chapter" of James Joyce's *Ulysses.*

18. Spivak, "Translating," 256.

19. Crowley, "Composition"; Hauser, "Teaching Rhetoric"; Walker, "What Difference"; Welch, *Electric Rhetoric.*

20. Detweiler, "Sounding Out the *Progymnasmata*"; Fleming, "Very Idea"; Ray, "*Progymnasmata* for Our Time."

21. Kennedy, *Progymnasmata*; Libanius, *Libanius's "Progymnasmata."*

22. Enterline, *Shakespeare's Schoolroom*, 7; Kraus, "Rehearsing the Other Sex"; Ray, "*Progymnasmata* for Our Time," 204; Woods, "Boys Will Be Women"; Woods, "Weeping for Dido."

23. Aphthonius the Sophist, 115; consult also Enterline, *Shakespeare's Schoolroom*, 31.

24. Theon, *Exercises*, 47.

25. Enterline, *Shakespeare's Schoolroom*, 4.

26. Ibid., 6.

27. Ibid., 15–16.

28. Ibid., 19.

29. Ibid., 22.

30. Ibid., 18.

31. Woods, "Boys Will Be Women," 145. Going back further, Libanius's *Progymnasmata* includes a model *prosopopoeia* that takes up the following prompt: "What words would Niobe," a mythological mother famous for a boast that led two gods to kill most or all of her fourteen children, "say when her children lie dead?" (381). Aphthonius, who was Libanius's student, uses the same prompt as the sample *prosopopoeia* in his progymnasmatic treatise (Aphthonius, *Preliminary Exercises,*

116). Bear in mind that Aphthonius's treatise had a singular influence on rhetoric pedagogy in later eras, particularly in the Renaissance.

32. Austern, "'No Women Are Indeed,'" 85–86.

33. Woods, "Boys Will Be Women," 145.

34. Ibid., 146.

35. Ibid., 154.

36. Woods, "Weeping for Dido," 289–90. Even in scholarship celebrating or advocating the use of *prosopopoeia* as an opportunity to challenge conventional attitudes toward and performances of gender, these challenges are still often framed in terms of a gender binary. In the passage from Woods quoted here, I have replaced "him- or herself" with the bracketed "[themself]" as a small acknowledgment of students whose gender identities, roles, and performances extend beyond the conventional "male"/"female" binary. The recognition of nonbinary students is an ethical imperative intertwined with the broader arguments of this chapter. Consider Bey, "How Ya Mama'n'em?"; Hibbard, "Out in the Classroom."

37. Woods, "Weeping for Dido," 290.

38. Enterline, *Shakespeare's Schoolroom*, 56.

39. Ibid., 25 (emphasis added).

40. Ibid., 34, 152.

41. Ibid., 131.

42. Spivak, "Translation," 241, 252.

43. Ibid., 253. While not identical to the power imbalances between the versions of Bengali Spivak addresses, consider also the extensive body of work on Anti-Black Linguistic Racism—the various forces that have marginalized and stigmatized the languages of Black English speakers and lifted up the varieties of English historically spoken by white people in positions of power (Baker-Bell, *Linguistic Justice*; Smitherman, *Talking and Testifyin*; Young et al., *Other People's English*).

44. Ibid., 252. After all, Spivak's "Can the Subaltern Speak?" provides an especially thorough and oft-cited critique of the tendency to apply Western theoretical concepts in ways that position such concepts as universal.

45. Woods, "Weeping for Dido," 290.

46. Ibid.

47. Cvetkovich, "Drawing the Archive," 111.

48. Spivak, "Translating," 256–57.

49. Cvetkovich, "Drawing," 114.

50. Ibid., 124, 122.

51. Chute, "Interview," 1008.

52. Plug, "Translator's Note," ix.

53. Derrida, "Privilege," 1.

54. Ibid., 3. Like the English "right," the French *droit* has various meanings tied to direction and directness, legal rights, rectitude, and so on.

55. Ibid., 3–4.

56. Ibid., 4.

57. Blanchot, *Infinite Conversation*, 171.

58. Cixous, "Sorties," 68.

59. Ibid., 76.

60. Ibid., 77.

61. Ibid., 77.

62. Ibid., 99.

63. Ibid., 99.

64. Woods, "Weeping for Dido," 289.

65. Cixous, "Sorties," 74.

66. Davis, "Autozoography," 535.

67. Ibid., 541.

68. Ibid., 543.

69. Ibid., 544.

70. Committee on CCCC Language Statement, "Students' Right," 2–3.

71. For more on the legacy of the resolution, consult Bruch and Marback, *Hope and the Legacy*; Perryman-Clark, Kirkland, and Jackson, *Students' Right*; Smitherman and Villanueva, *Language Diversity*.

72. Baker-Bell, *Linguistic Justice*; Smitherman, *Talkin and Testifyin*; Young et al., *Other People's English*.

73. Baker-Bell et al., "This Ain't Another Statement!"

74. Baker-Bell, *Linguistic Justice*, 2.

75. Ibid., 13–14. As a case in point, consider the discussion of the novel *The Help* in Young et al., *Other People's English*, 15–16.

76. Baker-Bell, *Linguistic Justice*, 14.

77. Harris, "Whiteness as Property," 1721.

78. Ibid., 1743.

79. W. Banks, *Black Intellectuals*, 10; Harris, "Whiteness as Property."

80. Tlostanova and Mignolo, *Learning to Unlearn*, 61.

81. Butler, *Giving*, 64.

82. Ibid., 65.

83. Davis, "Autozoography," 546.

Chapter 3

1. Kahn, Lalicker, and Lynch-Biniek, *Contingency*; Marcus, "Most Americans Don't Realize"; Welch and Scott, *Composition*.

2. Flaherty, "Next-Level Precarity"; Kaiser Health News, "COVID Crisis"; Long and Douglas-Gabriel, "Latest Crisis"; Woolston, "Signs of Depression"; Zahneis, "Covid-19 Crisis."

3. Hawisher and Selfe, *Passions*; Haynes and Holmevik, *High Wired*; Hewett and Ehmann, *Preparing Educators*.

4. Thrun quoted in Lohr, "Remember the MOOCs?"

5. Archibald and Feldman, "Drivers of the Rising Price"; Marcus, "Most Americans Don't Realize."

6. Chafkin, "Udacity's Sebastian Thrun."

7. Krause, *More Than a Moment*, 122.

8. Chafkin, "Udacity's Sebastian Thrun"; "Massively Open Online Courses"; Straus, "83rd Legislature," 21.

9. Krause, *More Than a Moment*, 121. Consult also Lohr, "Remember the MOOCs?"; E. Porter, "Smart Way."

10. Losh, *MOOCs and Their Afterlives*, 2.

11. For an extensive history of such attempts, consult Watters, *Teaching Machines*.

12. LaBarre, "Zoom Is Failing Teachers"; Morrissey, "Using Technology"; Patil and Bromwich, "How It Feels." Many of these companies, along with remaining MOOC providers, resemble and can be usefully understood in terms of the platforms described in Srnicek, *Platform Capitalism*.

13. Cole, Kemple, and Segeritz, "Assessing the Early Impact"; Feathers and Rose, "Students are Rebelling"; Swauger, "Our Bodies Encoded." On matters of technological bias and inequity, consult A. Banks, *Race, Rhetoric, and Technology*; Benjamin, *Race After Technology*; Noble, *Algorithms of Oppression*.

14. Bariso, "Google Has Announced a Plan"; Weinberg, "Google Just Changed the Higher Education Game."

15. Krause, *More Than a Moment*, 4. On personalization and education technology, consult also Watters, "History of 'Personalization.'"

16. Boxall, "MOOCs."

17. King, "From Sage on the Stage."

18. Morris and Stommel, "Open Education as Resistance."

19. Consider the plagiarism-detection software Turnitin, which I inform students that I refuse to use due to a number of ethical objections. Despite the fact that it is often deployed as a means of policing student writing in a guilty-until-proven-innocent manner, Turnitin's homepage prominently features the slogan "Empower students to do their best, original work." Or consider Panopto, a company whose name seems to be derived from a type of prison layout and that makes lecture-capture and screen-casting software many universities adopted during the pandemic. In a video made by the company, entitled "Panopto for Education—Product Overview," the speaker foregrounds the fact that "Panopto indexes the instructor's speech and any text that that appears on screen. As a result, your students can find and fast-forward to any word spoken or shown in any video. This enables them to learn at their own pace, study more effectively, and engage in class without the need to scribble notes." As I discuss in this chapter, MOOCs relied on similar arguments about their ability to allow students to "learn at their own pace" by pausing, fast-forwarding, and searching through video content. It is not clear to me why this is revolutionary or noteworthy in a context where students and teachers already have the opportunity to learn at their own pace by doing Ctrl+F searches in text-based documents that are significantly more accessible and easier to create than videos (Friedner, Sanchez, and Mills, "How to Teach with Text").

20. Morris and Stommel, "Open Education as Resistance," 179.

21. Meyerhoff, *Beyond Education*, 15.

22. Borgman and McArdle, *Personal, Accessible, Responsible, Strategic*; Hewett and DePew, *Foundational Practices*.

23. On inaccessibility, consult Long and Douglas-Gabriel, "Latest Crisis." On accessibility, consult Friedner, Sanchez, and Mills, "How to Teach with Text."

24. Pappano, "Year of the MOOC."

25. STEM is an acronym for "science, technology, engineering, and mathematics."

26. Notably, edX—the highest-profile nonprofit MOOC provider—was bought by a for-profit company called 2U in 2021 (Lederman, "2U, edX to Combine"). 2U is a private contractor that assists colleges and universities with online program management and thus is an indirect beneficiary of public universities' tuition dollars and dwindling state funding.

27. "Massively Open Online Courses."

28. Ibid.

29. Lowe, "Introduction," xii. Consider also J. Porter, "Framing Questions."

30. National Communication Association, "National Communication Association's Guidelines"; National Council of Teachers of English, "Why Class Size Matters Today."

31. Lowe, "Introduction," xii.

32. Rice, "MOOCversations," 94.

33. Ibid., 95.

34. Ibid., 94.

35. On supposed "disruption," consider Christiansen and Weise, "MOOCs' Disruption"; Galer, "How MOOCs are Disrupting Education"; Pappano, "Year of the MOOC." On conventionality, consider Rice, "MOOCversations"; Watters, *Teaching Machines*. Some of the arguments made by MOOC advocates in fact sound remarkably similar to those of ancient rhetoricians. Consider the complaints lodged by Isocrates against the excessive fees of his greedy competitors or the ways Quintilian defends collective models of rhetorical education against one-on-one tutorial models: "If we talked to one person at a time," he writes, "there would be no such thing as eloquence in human life" (Isocrates, "Against the Sophists"; Quintilian, *Orator's Education* 1.2.31). It's not difficult to hear echoes of such arguments in MOOC advocates' claims about the prohibitive cost of higher education in the United States or the ways MOOCs can bring together networks of students that transcend localized borders and discourses. A key difference, of course, is that rhetoricians now find themselves in the shoes of the small fry, defending purportedly overpriced, narrow-minded, and

insufficiently democratic pedagogical institutions against a massive newcomer.

36. Mirhady and Too, *Isocrates I*, 17; Quintilian, *Orator's Education* 1.10.

37. Quintilian, *Orator's Education* 12.1.1. Quintilian attributes this description to the Roman senator Marcus Cato.

38. Marrou, *History of Education*, 39, 47.

39. Consider also Cribiore, *Gymnastics*, 46.

40. Rhetoricians are far from alone in this view, which is shared not only by many MOOC advocates but also by scholars and teachers in other fields. In a *Chronicle of Higher Education* editorial, history professor Steven Conn puts it quite bluntly: Conn argues that, for teachers, "the goal"—*the goal*—"is to produce independent and self-sufficient human beings." What we're talking about here is an educational trope that is perhaps singular in its ubiquity.

41. Geisler, "How Ought We to Understand"; Hauser, "Teaching Rhetoric"; Keith and Mountford, "Mt. Oread"; Leff and Lunsford, "Afterwords"; Lowe, "Introduction," xii.

42. Hauser, "Teaching Rhetoric," 52. On the prevalent and ableist assumption that students must "overcome" disability through writing education, consult Hitt, *Rhetorics of Overcoming*.

43. Davis, *Inessential Solidarity*, 87. In addition to rhetoric and writing scholarship, this emphasis on empowering the free self frequently appears in Marxist educational traditions forwarded and elaborated on by such writers as Paulo Freire, though such work is much more attuned to the ways that freedom is conditioned, constrained, and interpellated.

44. "Massively Open Online Courses"; San José Philosophy Department, "Open Letter"; Smith, "What Universities Have in Common."

45. In "What is Authority?," Hannah Arendt states freedom's rhetorical dominance in a way that stretches beyond the pedagogical scene: "There is hardly a school of political thought in our history which is not centered around the idea of freedom" (97).

46. Levinas, *Totality*, 84.

47. Here and throughout this chapter (and this book), I have in mind a Levinasian linkage—one traced out by Jacques

Derrida—between "response" and "responsibility." In "Mochlos, or The Conflict of the Faculties," Derrida asks, "what does university responsibility represent?" (83). Within the context of the university, he argues, "If there is a university responsibility, it at least begins the moment when a need to hear these questions, to take them upon oneself and respond to them, imposes itself. *This imperative of the response is the initial form and minimal requirement of responsibility*" (83; emphasis added). For Derrida, then, responsibility is at least response-ability: the willingness to respond to "the call of responsibility." Let me emphasize, however, that I, following Derrida and Levinas, am not arguing for the total erasure of agency, nor for the wholesale replacement of rhetorics and "narrative[s] of [pedagogical] emancipation" with rhetorics of pedagogical responsibility (Vitanza, "Three Countertheses," 157). "Responsibility" is not agency's opposite.

48. Downes, "Introduction"; Downes, "What Connectivism Is"; Kop, "Challenges to Connectivist Learning"; Kop and Hill, "Connectivism."

49. Siemens, "MOOCs." Consult also Caulfield, "xMOOC Communities"; Morrison, "Ultimate Student Guide."

50. Siemens, "MOOCs."

51. Cormier, "Rhizomatic Learning"; "Your Unguided Tour."

52. Deleuze and Guattari, *Thousand Plateaus*, 7.

53. Ibid., 8.

54. Ibid., 9.

55. Consult Koh, "Feminist Pedagogy"; Rault and Cowan, "Haven't You Ever Heard"; Zamora, "Reimagining Learning."

56. Pappano, "Year of the MOOC."

57. For examples of journalism forwarding this history, see Leckart, "Stanford Education Experiment"; Pappano, "Year of the MOOC"; Webley, "MOOC Brigade." For skeptical takes, see Marcus, "All Hail MOOCs!"; Weller, "Dangerous Appeal."

58. In the PCAST panel itself, the xMOOC/cMOOC distinction, which was fairly new at the time, isn't used or acknowledged. I use the distinction in writing about the panel because many of the structural features and problems I'm discussing are particular to the xMOOC model.

59. Lewin, "Instruction for Masses"; "Massively Open Online Courses." I say "affordable" rather than "free" here because it's debatable whether the sort of MOOC popularized by the "Year of the MOOC" is in fact "open" (i.e., free of charge and open to anyone interested in enrolling), given that many xMOOC platforms found ways to attach fees to their courses (Fain, "Paying for Proof"; Kolowich, "MIT Will Offer MOOC Curricula").

60. Lowe, "Introduction," xii; "Massively Open Online Courses."

61. "Massively Open Online Courses."

62. Ibid. While Koller's claim may be true in aggregate, it raises important follow-up questions: *Which* students have more time that instructors, and what of students who don't? Is a network of students who *can* respond to their most overburdened peers a substitute for a teacher who is professionally tasked with such response?

63. Cf. Borgman and McArdle, *Personal, Accessible, Responsive, Strategic*; Fedewa et al., "Thinking about Thinking," 176.

64. Lewin, "Instruction for Masses"; "Massively Open Online Courses."

65. "Massively Open Online Courses." More deserves to be said about Thrun's describing students as having been "fired" from other schools.

66. DiGiovanni's description of xMOOCs as "highly unstructured" is a noteworthy if potentially inadvertent counterpoint to the other panelists' emphasis on "personalization," and it raises questions about how many/which students would actually be well served by xMOOCs.

67. As a supplementary example here, consider a Department of Defense program entitled "Education Dominance," which DiGiovanni references repeatedly during his presentation ("Massively Open Online Courses"). A collaborative undertaking involving the Department of the Navy, the Defense Advanced Research Projects Agency (DARPA, creators of the internet and the M16 assault rifle), and a team called Acuitus, the program was described on the Acuitus

website as "focused on the end-goal of education—becoming the expert in your field"
(Acuitus, "DARPA"). The individual "expert,"
then, is seen not only as the desired output
of "Education Dominance," but of education
as a whole.

68. "Massively Open Online Courses."

69. Public universities and their faculty
have of course put in their own bids for various forms of agency and freedom (Skinnell,
"Master Plan"). However, as public goods
and a kind of infrastructure, those bids are
quite different from xMOOC advocates'
request for freedom from both government
support *and* accountability.

70. Part of my critique of xMOOCs is that
the concept(s) of freedom on which they're
built are seriously scattered and, in most cases,
seriously underthought. The primary idea of
freedom I cite in the remainder of this chapter
is drawn from Levinas, which isn't the one
xMOOC advocates have in mind when they
use the word "free." However, it does provide
a consistent position from which to hold to
account the less coherent notions of freedom
deployed to make the case for xMOOCs.

71. Chafkin, "Udacity's Sebastian Thrun."
Consult also Schuman, "King of MOOCs."

72. Chafkin, "Udacity's Sebastian Thrun."

73. Deresiewicz, "Miseducation of America."

74. For a narrative that clearly positions
xMOOC companies as heroes, and is related
to Thrun's anecdote about the Texas charter
school, see Ng, "Broadening Access."

75. "Massively Open Online Courses."

76. Ladson-Billings, "From the Achievement Gap"; Lozenski, "Beyond Mediocrity."

77. Koller's, Thrun's, and DiGiovanni's
arguments could actually be repurposed to
make an argument quite different from the
one they typically make: xMOOCs are well
suited to replace *elite* institutions. After all,
many of the students at such institutions
are what we might call "autodidacts" or
"independent learners"—*not* because they
were born with an innately high level of
autonomy, but because they've been thoroughly socialized (by well-funded primary
and secondary school systems, families
who could provide or afford supplemental
tutoring services, early access to cutting-
edge technologies, and/or other kinds of
networking) into the often tacit expectations
and demands of educational institutions. It is
not marginalized, at-risk student populations
who most stand to benefit from xMOOCs,
but those who already have the most support
(Koh, "Feminist Pedagogy," 123). How
might xMOOCs advocates, many of whom
are former or current Stanford professors,
respond to the argument that xMOOCs
give us excuse to take some of *Stanford*'s
funding—after all, its students are especially
well positioned to succeed without extensive
educational infrastructure—and redistribute
some of that funding to community colleges
and regional public institutions whose
students might especially deserve and benefit
from specialized, responsive feedback in well-
supported, well-funded networks if they are
to have equitable access to educational and
professional success?

78. Cottom, "Democratizing Ideologies."

79. Ibid.

Chapter 4

1. Morrissey, "Using Technology"; University of Phoenix, *We Can Do IT.*

2. Davis, *Inessential Solidarity*, 106.

3. Hegel, *Elements*, 68–69.

4. Ibid., 86.

5. Levinas, *Totality and Infinity*, 178.

6. To offer an admittedly simplistic
analogy, imagine you've spent your entire life
so far in a single room with no recognizable
entrance or exit. Analogically speaking, Hegel
might argue that you realize you're in a room

once you take it upon yourself to familiar-
ize yourself with its walls, dimensions, and
boundaries. For Levinas, you only realize
you're in a room when someone barrels
through the wall, revealing to you a broader
world beyond anything you've yet grasped,
which gives you the context to understand
that the room you've been occupying is
a finite, identifiable place rather than the
entirety of existence.

7. Levinas, *Totality and Infinity*, 43.

8. Ibid., 51.

9. Youngman, "Measuring the Impact," 52.

10. "Massively Open Online Courses."

11. Consult Levinas, *Totality and Infinity*, 43, 51, 81, 100.

12. *Inessential Solidarity*, 16.

13. Levinas, *Totality and Infinity*, 75.

14. Ibid., 81 (emphasis added).

15. Levinas, *Otherwise Than Being*, 117.

16. Davis, *Inessential Solidarity*, 50.

17. Levinas, "Trace of the Other," 351.

18. Davis, *Inessential Solidarity*, 51.

19. Levinas is far from the only theorist to theorize human relations as asymmetrical. Iris Marion Young, for instance, "insists that asymmetrical reciprocity offers a more accurate concept of communicative action than an imagined symmetry among positions" (Lyon, *Deliberative Acts*, 51). While I find much to agree with in Young's concept of "asymmetrical reciprocity," she focuses more on the asymmetries that arise because of structural power imbalances in political life. I dwell with Levinasian asymmetry because of the way he positions asymmetry as the inescapable condition of human relations rather than a subsequent condition that arises and displaces otherwise fundamentally symmetrical relations.

20. Levinas, *Otherwise Than Being*, 157 (emphasis added).

21. Davis, *Inessential Solidarity*, 120–21; see also Derrida, Ronell, and Holmes, "Number of Yes," 129–32.

22. Levinas, *Totality and Infinity*, 84 (emphasis added).

23. Davis, *Inessential Solidarity*, 112.

24. Consider also Cottom, "Audacity."

25. Lohr, "Remember the MOOCs?"

26. "Massively Open Online Courses."

27. Levinas, *Totality and Infinity*, 51. For compelling though distinct takes on the dangers of autonomy without responsibility, see A. Banks, *Race, Rhetoric, and Technology*, 84; Rooks, "Why the Online-Education Craze."

28. Davis, *Inessential Solidarity*, 113.

29. Derrida, "Mochlos," 83.

30. Lowe, "Introduction," xii.

31. "Massively Open Online Courses."

32. Gere, *Writing Groups*, 16.

33. Ching, "Peer Response," 311, 306.

34. I'll admit that, in this case, I find myself much more sympathetic to (2) than to (3) because of the humility and vulnerability that (2), unlike the self-satisfaction of (3), suggests (consider Ahmed, "Against Students"). As Barbara Biesecker notes, "having good taste" is not a given but is, rather, an "effect-structure," and I find myself less sensitive to students who've been effectively convinced of the unimpeachable quality of their own writerly tastes than those who've been exposed to judgments of inferiority ("Negotiating," 240).

35. Lundstrom and Baker, "To Give is Better."

36. Ching, "Peer Response," 305.

37. Ibid., 308, 307.

38. Ibid., 308.

39. Ibid., 313.

40. Ibid., 313.

41. Ibid., 305.

42. Ibid., 313.

43. Ibid., 315 (emphasis added).

44. On this point, consider also Oleksiak, "Queer Praxis," 311.

45. Davis, *Inessential Solidarity*, 113.

46. Blum, *Ungrading*; Stommel, "How to Ungrade." I will note, however, that some cases for ungrading rely on unqualified notions of "freedom" and individuality that are part of what I'm critiquing in this chapter (consider Gibbs, "Let's Talk," 95). While I frequently use ungrading in my courses, I do so to foreground the relational networks and attachments that inform any act of agentive decision-making and have led to the privileging of certain motives and concepts of agency and individuality, not to recover a foundational subject who was (purportedly) intrinsically curious and motivated to learn before grades gummed up the works.

47. On contract grading, consult Inoue, *Antiracist Writing Assessment*; Katopodis and Davidson, "Contract Grading." On portfolio-based assessment, consult Yancey, "Portfolios." One particularly important influence on my approach to assessing and responding to student writing is a model called the Learning Record (Barr and Syverson; "What Is the Learning Record?"; Syverson, "Social Justice").

48. "First Year Writing."

49. On literacy narratives, consult Comer and Harker, "Pedagogy of the Digital Archive"; Lindquist and Halbritter, "Documenting and Discovering Learning"; Young, *Minor Re/Visions*.

50. Warner, *Why They Can't Write*, 29.

51. For this particular course, students read five sample literacy narratives, ranging from an example by a past student who composed her narrative as a comic book to an excerpt from *The Autobiography of Malcolm X*. These examples, which students discussed and wrote about prior to turning in their first drafts, were meant to highlight the simultaneous flexibility and conventionality of literacy narratives as a genre.

52. Manning and Irvine, *DC Comics Encyclopedia*, 315.

53. This was the "Writing the Introduction" section of Roberts-Miller, "Advice on Writing."

54. Roberts-Miller, "Advice on Writing."

55. Oleksiak, "Queer Praxis," 320, 326.

56. Browning, "Digital Divide." The COVID-19 pandemic itself offers another harrowing case in point regarding this chapter's points about agency and responsibility, with individualistic attempts to curtail the virus via "personal responsibility"—emphasis on the "personal"—proving repeatedly and devastatingly insufficient in the face of our relentless exposure to one another. In epidemiology as in ethics, the fantasy of agency collapses in the face of such exposedness.

57. Borgman and McArdle, *Personal, Accessible, Responsive, Strategic*, 19.

58. Blanchot, *Writing*, 1.

59. In many ways, *Infinite Conversation* unfolds as a commentary on Levinas's *Totality and Infinity*.

60. Blanchot, *Infinite Conversation*, 81.

61. Ibid., 81.

62. Ibid., 82. For a take on entropy's possibilities for rhetoric, consult Brooke, "Entropics of Discourse."

63. Kerschbaum, *Toward a New Rhetoric*, 101.

64. Ching, "Peer Response," 306.

65. Fox, "Can MOOCs and SPOCs," 45.

66. Because my focus has been on peer networks, I have not spent much time addressing xMOOCs' "pedagogical instruments" in this chapter. As someone who grew up playing *Word Munchers, Math Blaster!*, and other educational video games, and who has inconsistently flirted with such apps as Duolingo, I see no reason to dismiss the reality that humans can and do learn from digital instruments and programs (consider Paul, "Why Students Prefer"). And yet, faced with the rise of machine learning and artificial intelligence (an important factor in the genesis of xMOOCs, as noted in chapter 3), those arguing for the preeminence of human teachers and humans more generally have often sought to pinpoint things humans can do that machines cannot, capacities that our would-be robotic counterparts supposedly lack (consider Aoun, *Robot-Proof*; Derrida, *Animal*, 84). I admit that this strikes me as a wild-goose chase, a sort of arms race for maximum agentive overdrive. While the history of technology is littered with devices that tried and failed to replace human teachers (Watters, *Teaching Machines*), and digital algorithms' well-documented tendency to scale up rather than overcome all-too-human biases throws their ascendancy into question (Noble, *Algorithms of Oppression*; O'Neil, *Weapons of Math Destruction*), bold claims about what capacities are distinctly human and beyond the scope of machines, robots, algorithms, and other mechanical wonders can prove obsolete as fast as a new smartphone. Given how quickly claims that "machines will never be able to do x!" become laughable in hindsight, my skepticism of xMOOCs' pedagogical instruments is not driven by an unshakable conviction that human teachers and students can exercise capacities that such instruments currently cannot or will not be able to exercise in the future. Rather, I think the more important question is this: Of the structural vulnerabilities that characterize relations between human teachers and students, which are increasingly removed from the equation as pedagogical instruments advance? And, as a corollary: What if these vulnerabilities are more indispensable to learning than the fleeting capacities that we take to be distinctly human? My concern, in short, is a matter of acknowledging vulnerabilities, not chasing the fantasy of ever-more agency. To invert a

key argument of Joseph Aoun's *Robot-Proof*, my question is not, "What can higher education do to make human teachers and students increasingly robot-proof?" but "What does higher education lose as teaching machines become increasingly human-proof?"

Chapter 5

1. Levinas, *Otherwise*, 184. Consider also Davis, *Inessential*, 126.

2. Levinas, *Otherwise*, 184.

3. Ibid.

4. Ibid.

5. In ancient Greek rhetorical theory, a *topos* is also a metaphorical "place" where rhetors can locate arguments (Aristotle, *On Rhetoric*).

6. Levinas, *Otherwise*, 184.

7. Ibid.

8. Let me note that I'm *not* claiming to be worn down by student writing because students these days can't write, can't think, can't pay attention, spend too much time tweeting and texting, or are otherwise deficient. It is just that the work of response, even (if not especially) when delimited by grades and other quantitative measures, is exhausting—perhaps more so for teachers who have a hard time being dismissive of the students to whom they're responding and for whom they're responsible. Response is exhausting because students are neither beatific beings nor absolutely awful but, like teachers, finite and complicated creatures.

9. Sullivan, *Experimental Writing*, 9; consult also Roberts-Miller, *Deliberate*, 216.

10. Rice, *Rhetoric of Cool*, 84.

11. Ibid.

12. Corbett, "Usefulness," 162, quoted in Rice, *Rhetoric of Cool*, 121–22.

13. Rice, *Rhetoric*, 124.

14. On broadening what counts as argument in pedagogical contexts, consult Knoblauch, "Textbook Argument."

15. Roberts-Miller, *Deliberate*, 215.

16. Ibid., 216.

17. Knoblauch, "Textbook Argument," 247.

18. Hacker and Sommers, *Pocket Style*, 105.

19. Hacker and Sommers, *Rules*, 18.

20. Ibid., 28.

21. Ibid., 26.

22. Ibid., *Rules*, 27. For more context on this point, consider Hyland, *Metadiscourse*, 133.

23. Roberts-Miller, *Deliberate*, 222.

24. Wardle, "You Can Learn to Write in General"; Yancey, Robertson, and Taczak, *Writing across Contexts*.

25. Roberts-Miller, *Deliberate*, 216.

26. Silver had engaged in similar analysis during the 2008 election cycle, at that time posting his predictions to his blog, FiveThirty Eight.com. His affiliation with the *New York Times* during the 2012 cycle was a testament to the popularity and success of his work in 2008 (he correctly predicted which presidential candidate forty-nine of the fifty states would vote for) and also raised his profile significantly (Clifford, "Finding Fame").

27. Byers, "Nate Silver."

28. Quoted in ibid.

29. Quoted in Coates, "Toward a Fraudulent Populism." Chambers's piece and *Examiner.com* itself are no longer readily accessible. For more context on Chambers and his rivalry with Silver, consult "Obscure Guy."

30. Coates, "Toward a Fraudulent Populism."

31. This isn't to say that hedging and certainty are pure opposites that can't ever work together. As Patricia Roberts-Miller observes, "assertions of certainty" can be "even more persuasive in the context of . . . hedging" (*Rhetoric and Demagoguery*, 82).

32. Silver, "Why FiveThirtyEight."

33. Flood, "Nate Silver Blew It."

34. Quoted in ibid.

35. Silver, "Why FiveThirtyEight."

36. Given the timing of this book's publication, readers might expect some consideration of Silver's and FiveThirtyEight's predictions about the 2020 presidential election and others' reactions to those predictions. However, critiques of Silver surrounding that election largely reiterated patterns from past cycles. Moreover, in the wake of that election, Silver attracted criticism less because of his analyses of political polls and more because

of his decision to tweet relentlessly about the coronavirus pandemic. In fact, in his pivot to epidemiology, Silver has leaned into the kinds of unhedged thetical claims critiqued in this chapter—and by much of Twitter (Cole, "Nate Silver"; Southpaw [@nycsouthpaw], "@NateSilver 538," Twitter, August 30, 2021, https://twitter.com/nycsouthpaw/status /1432340428221734915).

37. Fearman, "Postmodernism." Upvote and downvote totals are current as of January 2022.

38. For an article addressing related issues in the arena of climate change, consult Medimorec and Pennycook, "Language of Denial"; O'Grady, "Climate Scientists."

39. Žižek, "Slavoj Žižek," 254.

40. Ibid., 254. Consider also Nealon, "Cash Value."

41. Aspects of the op-ed are elaborated on in Pinker, Sense of Style. For another iteration of its line of argument, consider Clayton, "Needless Complexity."

42. Butler, "Values."

43. Consider Culler and Lamb, "Introduction," 1.

44. My very claim that "I don't want to browbeat Pinker," and really much of the paragraph that leads up to it, captures some of the issues at stake in this chapter. That is, when I say that I'm tempted to go after Pinker but won't, will that be read as (a) apophasis, a rhetorical omission that allows me to critique Pinker's claims while simultaneously distancing myself from that critique and thus maintaining—disingenuously, perhaps—the appearance of a charitable respondent, or is it possible that, (b) though I don't want to completely efface the line of thinking that led me not to pursue an extensive critique of Pinker's Chronicle piece, I have genuinely thought better of it and decided to pursue another path? In some ways, this was a central issue in the controversy around Nate Silver in 2012: is it really possible for a writer to hedge their claims in a manner that bespeaks genuine uncertainty and humility, or is it the case that, as soon as a writer records those hedges on the page or screen, they paradoxically contribute to an aura of authority and certainty? Like Kierkegaard's

Abraham, who only recovers his son Isaac after having genuinely relinquished him, does embracing uncertainty only allow the writer to recover a greater certitude, such as Nate Silver's correctly predicting the outcome of the 2012 presidential election? That is not what I'm after here, but something like what Kierkegaard describes as getting everything back "by virtue of the absurd" haunts this chapter (Kierkegaard, Fear and Trembling, 49). Is it possible to really resign oneself to uncertainty, to relinquish certainty, without expecting anything in return? The assumption I'm operating under, at least, is that the rhetorical atmosphere that both fosters and is fostered by an emphasis on thesis-driven arguments makes it harder for audiences to accept that a rhetor could ever espouse uncertainty in good faith.

45. Žižek, "Slavoj Žižek," 254.

46. Derrida, "Privilege," 3–4.

47. Fearman, "Postmodernism."

48. Coats, Garden Shrubs, 256. Blackthorn's Latin name is prunus spinosa, which seems like a fruitful pun for any Spinoza-influenced writers out there. The pun gains an extra layer given Spinoza's influence on Gilles Deleuze and, in turn, Deleuze and Félix Guattari's oft-cited thoughts on the "rhizome" (Thousand Plateaus, 6): blackthorn can grow rhizomatically.

49. Fisher, Mazes and Follies, 18.

50. Ibid., 18.

51. Derrida, "Privilege," 4.

52. Davis, Breaking Up, 103.

53. Walker, Rhetoric and Poetics, 60.

54. Ibid., 60.

55. Aphthonius, Preliminary Exercises, 120–21.

56. Walker, Rhetoric and Poetics, 60.

57. In his Exercises, for instance, the ancient rhetorician Aelius Theon writes, "Since some theses are theoretical—where the inquiry is for the sake of understanding and knowledge; for example, whether the gods provide for the world—and some are practical—having reference to some action such as whether one should marry—, it is clear that the practical are more political and have a rhetorical character, while the theoretical are more appropriate for philosophers. None the less,

it is possible for students of rhetoric to handle the latter by starting from topics for practical theses" (*Exercises*, 56).

58. Walker, *Rhetoric and Poetics*, 60.

59. Ronell, *Test Drive*, 23.

60. Ibid., 25. Consult Derrida, "Interpretations," 55.

61. Ronell, *Test Drive*, 24. Consult Derrida, "Interpretations," 70.

62. Derrida and Dufourmantelle, *Of Hospitality*, 77. For more on the relevance of Derrida's work on hospitality to rhetoric and writing, see Brown, *Ethical Programs*, 7; Davis, *Inessential Solidarity*, 129–35.

63. In addition to Telescopic Text—which, like many digital experiments, may well break or disappear from the internet—readers might also consider things like Twine, "an open-source tool for telling interactive, nonlinear stories" (*Twine*). While Twine is often used to create works of interactive fiction or small video games that may not have conventional rhetorical aims, it can and has been used to highlight the ethical complexities of institutional decision-making and to craft scholarly works (Helms, "Play Smarter Not Harder"; Kirby, *October 5th, 2020*; Salter and Moulthrop, *Twining*). These sorts of interactive textual tools have proliferated over the past decade, and they offer rich possibilities for expanding how writers engage with texts.

64. Erasmus, *Copia*, 300. Consider Brown, "Machine."

65. Fearman, "Postmodernism."

66. Examples drawn from MacDonald, *Professional Academic Writing*. Consider also Hyland, *Disciplinary Discourses*; Russell, *Writing in the Academic Disciplines*; Wilder and Wolfe, "Sharing the Tacit Rhetorical Knowledge."

67. For a similar tool, consider Omizo and Hart-Davidson, "Hedge-O-Matic."

68. LeMieux, "Machinic Invention."

69. Micciche, "Writing," 181; Foss and Griffin, "Beyond Persuasion," 16; Anzaldúa, *Borderlands / La Frontera*, 66–68; Goggin and Rose, *Women's Ways of Making*, 5.

70. Davis, *Breaking Up*, 262; consult also Vitanza, *Negation*, 57–58.

71. Recall the debate between Weaker Argument and Stronger Argument in Aristophanes's *Clouds*, discussed in chapter 1 of this book, which is a dramatized version of *dissoi logoi* (Aristophanes, *Clouds*, 1105–10). Consult also Kennedy, *New History*, 18; Laks and Most, *Early Greek Philosophy*, 164–65.

72. Sullivan, *Experimental Writing*, 159.

73. Levinas, *Otherwise*, 184.

74. Ibid., 185.

75. Gerdes, "Habit-Forming," 354.

Epilogue

1. Critchley, *Very Little*, 62.

2. Ibid., 62.

3. Ibid., 63.

4. Derrida and Dufourmantelle, *Of Hospitality*, 27.

5. Ibid., 27–28.

6. Butler, *Giving*, 50.

7. Davis, *Inessential Solidarity*, 16–17.

8. Derrida, "Mochlos," 83.

9. Warner, *Sustainable*, 37.

10. American Association of University Professors, "Contingent Faculty."

11. Warner, *Sustainable*, 38.

12. Ibid., 25.

13. For the sake of transparency regarding labor, during most of my career as a pre-tenure assistant professor, I have had a 3-3 teaching load, a reduction from my institution's typical 4-4 load for tenured and tenure-track faculty. It's a reduction I get because I am a member of the university's graduate faculty, doing the rewarding but morally complicated and time-intensive work of teaching, mentoring, and advising students in my department's master's and PhD programs. Given my base salary (I started at $49,500 in 2016 and am making a little over $54,000 as of 2021–22) and the cost of living in my region, I have also picked up an optional course for a little extra pay every summer since I started my current position. So far, given the somewhat idiosyncratic pedagogical focus of my scholarship, I have been unsuccessful in my attempts to secure external grants or internal sabbaticals and stipends that would have

given me a summer or full semester to focus solely or even primarily on the research and writing reflected in this book. To be honest, I did not have to write this book, given my institution's tenure requirements, but given the tenuous situation of liberal arts faculty and programs at many public institutions, I have felt—like a lot of faculty—pushed to overperform in case the worst should happen (massive budget cuts, program cancellations, etc.) and I need to go on the job market as a competitive mid-career candidate. For better and for worse, I like writing, care about the subject matter, and have a sharp and supportive core group of colleagues, which has provided indispensable motivation as I've worked on this book.

14. As rhetorician Leigh Gruwell succinctly put it in a tweet about the ethical fallout of university administrators' meager responses to the ongoing pandemic during the 2021–22 academic year, "Maybe the worst thing about in-person teaching during a pandemic (aside from the obvious health risks) is that instead of looking to my students with hope and compassion, I first see them through fear and suspicion." Gruwell's observation resonates with a number of other institutional factors that can pit teachers and students against each other rather than encouraging responsible relations. Leigh Gruwell (@leighthinks), Twitter, September 14, 2021, https://twitter .com/leighthinks/status/1437924837113085958.

15. Bechdel, *Fun Home*, 223.

Acuitus. "DARPA—Education Dominance: Training and Human Effectiveness." Accessed January 3, 2016. http://www.acuitus.com/web/education-dominance.html.

Ahmed, Sara. "Against Students." *New Inquiry*, July 29, 2015. https://thenewinquiry.com/against-students.

"The Alison Bechdel Interview." *Comics Journal* 282 (April 2007). http://www.tcj.com/the-alison-bechdel-interview.

Allen, Danielle S. *Talking to Strangers: Anxieties of Citizenship Since Brown v. Board of Education*. Chicago: University of Chicago Press, 2004.

Allen, Ira. *The Ethical Fantasy of Rhetorical Theory*. Pittsburgh: University of Pittsburgh Press, 2018.

American Association of University Professors. "Contingent Faculty and the Global Pandemic." August 11, 2020. https://www.aaup.org/news/contingent-faculty-and-global-pandemic.

———. "Data Snapshot: Contingent Faculty in US Higher Ed." October 11, 2018. https://www.aaup.org/news/data-snapshot-contingent-faculty-us-higher-ed.

Anzaldúa, Gloria. *Borderlands / La Frontera: The New Mestiza*. San Francisco: Aunt Lute, 1987.

Aoun, Joseph E. *Robot-Proof: Higher Education in the Age of Artificial Intelligence*. Cambridge, MA: MIT Press, 2017.

Aphthonius the Sophist. "The *Preliminary Exercises* of Aphthonius the Sophist." In *Progymnasmata: Greek Textbooks of Prose Composition and Rhetoric*, edited by George A. Kennedy, 89–128. Atlanta: Society of Biblical Literature, 2003.

Archibald, Robert B., and David H. Feldman. "Drivers of the Rising Price of a College Education." Midwestern Higher Education Compact. August 2018. https://www.mhec.org/sites/default/files/resources/mhec_affordability_series7_20180730.pdf.

Arendt, Hannah. "The Crisis in Education." In *Between Past and Future*, 170–93. New York: Penguin, 2006.

———. "Reflections on Little Rock." *Dissent* (Winter 1959): 45–56.

———. "What Is Authority?" In *Between Past and Future*, 91–141. New York: Penguin, 2006.

Aristophanes. *Clouds*. In *Clouds, Wasps, Peace*, translated by Jeffrey Henderson. Cambridge, MA: Harvard University Press, 1998.

Aristotle. *On Rhetoric: A Theory of Civic Discourse*. 2nd ed. Translated by George A. Kennedy. Oxford: Oxford University Press, 2007.

Arnett, Ronald C. *Levinas's Rhetorical Demand: The Unending Obligation of Communication Ethics*. Carbondale: Southern Illinois University Press, 2017.

Austern, Linda Phyllis. "'No Women Are Indeed': The Boy Actor as Vocal Seductress in Late Sixteenth- and Early Seventeenth-Century English Drama." In *Embodied Voices: Representing Female Vocality in Western Culture*, edited by Leslie C. Dunn and Nancy A. Jones, 83–102. Cambridge: Cambridge University Press, 1994.

Austin, J. L. *How to Do Things with Words*. 2nd ed. Cambridge, MA: Harvard University Press, 1975.

Baca, Damián, and Victor Villanueva. *Rhetorics of the America: 3114 BCE to 2012 CE*. New York: Palgrave Macmillan, 2010.

Bady, Aaron. "Against Students Stories." *New Inquiry*, August 25, 2015. https://thenewinquiry.com/blog/against-students-stories.

Baker-Bell, April. *Linguistic Justice: Black Language, Literacy, Identity, and Pedagogy*. New York: Routledge, 2020.

Baker-Bell, April, Bonnie J. Williams-Farrier, Davena Jackson, Lamar Johnson, Carmen Kynard, and Teaira McMurtry. "This Ain't Another Statement! This Is a DEMAND for Black Linguistic Justice!" Conference on College Composition and Communication, July 2020. https://cccc.ncte.org/cccc/demand-for-black-linguistic-justice.

Ballentine, Claire. "Freshmen Skipping 'Fun Home' for Moral Reasons." *Chronicle*, August 21, 2015. https://www.dukechronicle.com/article/2015/08/freshmen-skipping-fun-home-for-moral-reasons.

Banks, Adam J. *Race, Rhetoric, and Technology: Searching for Higher Ground*. Mahwah: Lawrence Erlbaum, 2005.

Banks, William M. *Black Intellectuals: Race and Responsibility in American Life*. New York: W. W. Norton, 1996.

Bariso, Justin. "Google Has Announced a Plan to Disrupt the College Degree." *Inc.Com*, August 2020. https://www.inc.com/justin-bariso/google-plan-disrupt-college-degree-university-higher-education-certificate-project-management-data-analyst.html.

Barr, Mary, and M. A. Syverson. "What Is the Learning Record?" Learning Record. Accessed August 11, 2021. http://www.learningrecord.org/intro.html.

Bechdel, Alison. *Fun Home: A Family Tragicomic*. Boston: Mariner, 2006.

Benjamin, Ruha. *Race after Technology: Abolitionist Tools for the New Jim Code*. Cambridge, UK: Polity, 2019.

Bernard-Donals, Michael, and Janice W. Fernheimer. *Jewish Rhetorics: History, Theory, Practice*. Waltham: Brandeis University Press, 2014.

Bey, Marquis. "How Ya Mama'n'em? Blackness, Nonbinariness, and Radical Subjectivity." *Peitho* 22, no. 4 (2020). https://cfshrc.org/article/how-ya-mamanem-blackness-nonbinariness-and-radical-subjectivity.

Biesecker, Barbara. "Negotiating with Our Tradition: Reflecting Again (without Apologies) on the Feminization of Rhetoric." *Philosophy and Rhetoric* 26, no. 3 (1993): 236–41.

———. "Rethinking the Rhetorical Situation from Within the Thematic of *Différance*." *Philosophy and Rhetoric* 22, no. 2 (1989): 110–30.

Blanchot, Maurice. *The Infinite Conversation*. Translated by Susan Hanson. Minneapolis: University of Minnesota Press, 1993.

———. *The Work of Fire*. Translated by Charlotte Mandell. Stanford: Stanford University Press, 1995.

———. *The Writing of the Disaster*. New ed. Translated by Ann Smock. Lincoln: University of Nebraska Press, 1995.

Blum, Susan D., ed. *Ungrading: Why Rating Students Undermines Learning (and What to Do Instead)*. Morgantown: West Virginia University Press, 2020.

Booth, Wayne. *A Rhetoric of Irony*. Chicago: University of Chicago Press, 1974.

Borges, Jorge Luis. "The Garden of Forking Paths." In *Labyrinths*, reprint ed., 19–29. New York: New Directions, 2007.

Borgman, Jessie, and Casey McArdle. *Personal, Accessible, Responsive, Strategic: Resources and Strategies for Online Writing Instructors*. Fort Collins: WAC Clearinghouse, 2020.

Boring, Anne. "Gender Biases in Student Evaluations of Teaching." *Journal of Public Economics* 145 (January 2017): 27–41. https://doi.org/10.1016/j.jpubeco.2016.11.006.

Boxall, Mike. "MOOCs: A Massive Opportunity for Higher Education, or Digital Hype?" *Guardian*, August 8, 2012. http://www.theguardian.com/higher-education-network/blog/2012/aug/08/mooc-coursera-higher-education-investment.

Britto, Brittany. "False Positive COVID Tests at Rice Prompted Return to Online Learning." *Houston Chronicle*, August 25, 2021. https://www.houston chronicle.com/news/houston-texas /education/article/Rice-officials-say -COVID-19-testing-provider-16408 580.php.

Brooke, Collin. "Entropics of Discourse: An Interview with Collin Brooke." *Zeugma*, n.d. https://zeugma.dwrl .utexas.edu/brooke.html.

Brown, James J., Jr. *Ethical Programs: Hospitality and the Rhetorics of Software*. Ann Arbor: University of Michigan Press, 2015.

———. "The Machine That Therefore I Am." *Philosophy and Rhetoric* 47, no. 4 (2014): 494–514.

Browning, Kellen. "The Digital Divide Starts with a Laptop Shortage." *New York Times*, October 12, 2020. https:// www.nytimes.com/2020/10/12 /technology/laptops-schools-digital -divide.html.

Bruch, Patrick, and Richard Marback, eds. *The Hope and the Legacy: The Past, Present, and Future of "Students' Right" to Their Own Language*. New York: Hampton Press, 2005.

Butler, Judith. *Giving an Account of Oneself*. New York: Fordham University Press, 2005.

———. "Values of Difficulty." In *Just Being Difficult? Academic Writing in the Public Arena*, edited by Jonathan Culler and Kevin Lamb, 119–216. Stanford: Stanford University Press, 2003.

Byers, Dylan. "Nate Silver: One-Term Celebrity?" *Politico*, October 29, 2012. https://www.politico.com/blogs /media/2012/10/nate-silver-one -term-celebrity-147618.

Campbell, Kermit. "Rhetoric from the Ruins of African Antiquity." *Rhetorica: A Journal of the History of Rhetoric* 24, no. 3 (2006): 255–74.

Carbado, Devon W., and Cheryl I. Harris. "Intersectionality at 30: Mapping the Margins of Anti-Essentialism, Intersectionality, and Dominance

Theory." *Harvard Law Review* 132, no. 8 (June 2019): 2193–239. https:// harvardlawreview.org/2019/06 /intersectionality-at-30-mapping -the-margins-of-anti-essentialism -intersectionality-and-dominance -theory.

Caulfield, Michael. "XMOOC Communities Should Learn from CMOOCs." *Educause*, July 11, 2013. https:// er.educause.edu/blogs/2013/7 /xmooc-communities-should -learn-from-cmoocs.

Chafkin, Max. "Udacity's Sebastian Thrun, Godfather of Free Online Education, Changes Course." *Fast Company*, November 14, 2013. https://www .fastcompany.com/3021473/udacity -sebastian-thrun-uphill-climb.

Chávez, Karma, R., and Cindy L. Griffin, eds. *Standing in the Intersection: Feminist Voices, Feminist Practices in Composition Studies*. Albany: SUNY Press, 2012.

Chávez, Kerry, and Kristina M. W. Mitchell. "Exploring Bias in Student Evaluations: Gender, Race, and Ethnicity." *PS: Political Science and Politics* 53, no. 2 (2020): 270–74. https://doi.org/10.1017/S1049096 519001744.

Ching, Kory Lawson. "Peer Response in the Composition Classroom: An Alternative Genealogy." *Rhetoric Review* 26, no. 3 (2007): 303–19.

Christakis, Erika. "Email from Erika Christakis: 'Dressing Yourselves,' Email to Silliman College (Yale) Students on Halloween Costumes." *FIRE*, October 30, 2015. https:// www.thefire.org/email-from-erika -christakis-dressing-yourselves-email -to-silliman-college-yale-students-on -halloween-costumes.

Christensen, Clayton M., and Michelle R. Weise. "MOOCs' Disruption Is Only the Beginning." *Boston Globe*, May 2014. https://www.bostonglobe.com /opinion/2014/05/09/moocs -disruption-only-beginning/S2Vls XpK6rzRx4DMrS4ADM/story.html.

Chute, Hillary. "An Interview with Alison Bechdel." *Modern Fiction Studies* 52, no. 4 (2006): 1004–13.

———. "The Texture of Retracing in Marjane Satrapi's Persepolis." *Women's Studies Quarterly* 36, nos. 1–2 (2008): 92–110.

Chute, Hillary L., and Marianne DeKoven. "Introduction: Graphic Narrative." *Modern Fiction Studies* 52, no. 4 (2006): 767–82.

Cixous, Hélène. "Sorties: Out and Out: Attacks / Ways Out / Forays." *Newly Born Woman*, by Hélène Cixous and Catherine Clément, translated by Betsy Wing, 63–134. Minneapolis: University of Minnesota Press, 1986.

Clayton, Victoria. "The Needless Complexity of Academic Writing." *Atlantic*, October 2015. https://www.the atlantic.com/education/archive /2015/10/complex-academic -writing/412255.

Clifford, Stephanie. "Finding Fame with a Prescient Call for Obama." *New York Times*, November 9, 2008. https://www.nytimes.com/2008 /11/10/business/media/10silver.html.

Coates, Ta-Nehisi. "Toward a Fraudulent Populism." *Atlantic*, November 1, 2012. https://www.theatlantic.com/sexes /archive/2012/11/toward-a-fraudulent -populism/264401.

Coats, Alice M. *Garden Shrubs and Their Histories*. Boston: E. P. Dutton, 1965.

Cole, Brendan. "Nate Silver Told to 'Shut Up' as Twitter COVID Musings Face Huge Backlash." *Newsweek*, September 9, 2021. https://www.newsweek.com /nate-silver-told-shut-twitter-covid -musings-face-huge-backlash-1627470.

Cole, Rachel, James J. Kemple, and Micha D. Segeritz. "Assessing the Early Impact of School of One: Evidence from Three School-Wide Pilots." Research Alliance for New York City Schools, June 2012. https://steinhardt.nyu .edu/sites/default/files/2021-01 /AssessingEarlyImpactSo1.pdf.

Colebrook, Claire. *Irony*. New York: Routledge, 2004.

Comer, Kathryn B., and Michael Harker. "The Pedagogy of the Digital Archive of Literacy Narratives: A Survey." *Computers and Composition* 35 (March 2015): 65–85.

Committee on CCCC Language Statement. "Students' Right to Their Own Language." *College Composition and Communication* 25, no. 3 (1974): 1–18.

Conn, Steven. "The Rise of the Helicopter Teacher." *Chronicle of Higher Education*, August 5, 2014. https://www.chronicle .com/blogs/conversation/2014/08/05 /the-rise-of-the-helicopter-teacher.

Cooper, Marilyn M. "Rhetorical Agency as Emergent and Enacted." *College Composition and Communication* 62, no. 3 (2011): 420–49.

Copeland, Rita, ed. *Criticism and Dissent in the Middle Ages*. Cambridge: Cambridge University Press, 1996.

Corbett, Edward P. J. "The Usefulness of Classical Rhetoric." *College Composition and Communication* 14, no. 3 (1963): 162–64.

Cormier, Dave. "Rhizomatic Learning and MOOCs—Assessment." *Dave's Education Blog*, August 6, 2012. http:// davecormier.com/edblog/2012/08 /16/rhizomatic-learning-and-moocs -assessment.

———. "Your Unguided Tour of Rhizo14." *Dave's Education Blog*, January 12, 2014. http://davecormier.com /edblog/2014/01/12/your-unguided -tour-of-rhizo14.

Cottom, Tressie McMillan. "The Audacity: Thrun Learns a Lesson and Students Pay." *Tressiemc*, November 19, 2013. https://tressiemc.com/uncategorized /the-audacity-thrun-learns-a-lesson -and-students-pay.

———. "Democratizing Ideologies and Inequality Regimes in Digital Domains." Berkman Klein Center for Internet and Society, July 29, 2014. https://cyber.harvard.edu/events /luncheon/2014/07/cottom.

———. *Lower Ed: The Troubling Rise of For-Profit Colleges in the New Economy*. New York: New Press, 2018.

Cox, Joshua, and Sharifa Love. "White Yalies in Blackface Reveal Racism on Campus." *Yale Daily News*, November 1, 2007. https://yaledailynews.com/blog/2007/11/01/white-yalies-in-blackface-reveal-racism-on-campus.

Cribiore, Raffaella. *Gymnastics of the Mind: Greek Education in Hellenistic and Roman Egypt*. Princeton: Princeton University Press, 2001.

———. *The School of Libanius in Late Antique Antioch*. Princeton: Princeton University Press, 2007.

Critchley, Simon. *Very Little . . . Almost Nothing: Death, Philosophy, Literature*. 2nd ed. London: Routledge, 2004.

Crowley, Sharon. *Composition in the University: Historical and Polemical Essays*. Pittsburgh: University of Pittsburgh Press, 1998.

———. "Composition Is Not Rhetoric." *enculturation* 5, no. 1 (2003). http://www.enculturation.net/5_1/crowley.html.

Culler, Jonathan, and Kevin Lamb. "Introduction: Dressing Up, Dressing Down." In *Just Being Difficult? Academic Writing in the Public Arena*, edited by Jonathan Culler and Kevin Lamb, 1–14. Stanford: Stanford University Press, 2003.

Cvetkovich, Ann. "Drawing the Archive in Alison Bechdel's Fun Home." *Women's Studies Quarterly* 36, nos. 1–2 (2008): 111–28.

Davis, Diane. "Autozoography: Notes Toward a Rhetoricity of the Living." *Philosophy and Rhetoric* 47, no. 4 (2014): 533–53.

———. *Breaking Up [at] Totality: A Rhetoric of Laughter*. Carbondale: Southern Illinois University Press, 2000.

———. *Inessential Solidarity: Rhetoric and Foreigner Relations*. Pittsburgh: University of Pittsburgh Press, 2010.

Deleuze, Gilles, and Félix Guattari. *A Thousand Plateaus: Capitalism and Schizophrenia*. Translated by Brian Massumi. Minneapolis: University of Minnesota Press, 1987.

de Man, Paul. *Allegories of Reading: Figural Language in Rousseau, Nietzsche, Rilke, and Proust*. New Haven: Yale University Press, 1979.

———. "The Concept of Irony." In *Aesthetic Ideology*, by Paul de Man, edited by Andrzej Warminski, 163–84. Minneapolis: University of Minnesota Press, 1996.

Deresiewicz, William. "The Miseducation of America." *Chronicle of Higher Education*, June 2014. https://www.chronicle.com/article/The-Miseducation-of-America/147227.

Derrida, Jacques. *The Animal That Therefore I Am*. Edited by Marie-Louise Mallet, translated by David Wills. New York: Fordham University Press, 2008.

———. *The Gift of Death; And, Literature in Secret*. Translated by Davis Wills. 2nd ed. Chicago: University of Chicago Press, 2007.

———. "Interpretations at War: Kant, the Jew, the German." *New Literary History* 22, no. 1 (1991): 39–95.

———. *Limited Inc*. Evanston: Northwestern University Press, 1988.

———. "Mochlos, or The Conflict of the Faculties." In *Eyes of the University: Right to Philosophy 2*, by Jacques Derrida, translated by Richard Rand and Amy Wygant, 83–112. Stanford: Stanford University Press, 2004.

———. *On Cosmopolitanism and Forgiveness*. London: Routledge, 2001.

———. "Privilege: Justificatory Title and Introductory Remarks." In *Who's Afraid of Philosophy? Right to Philosophy 1*, by Jacques Derrida, translated by Jan Plug, 1–66. Stanford: Stanford University Press, 2002.

———. "Remarks on Deconstruction and Pragmatism." In *Deconstruction and Pragmatism*, edited by Chantal Mouffe, translated by Simon Critchley, 79–90. London: Routledge, 1996.

Derrida, Jacques, and Anne Dufourmantelle. *Of Hospitality: Anne Dufourmantelle Invites Jacques Derrida to Respond*. Translated by Rachel Bowlby. Stanford: Stanford University Press, 2000.

Derrida, Jacques, Avital Ronell, and Brian Holmes. "A Number of Yes (Nombre de Oui)." *Qui Parle* 2, no. 2 (1988): 118–33.

Detweiler, Eric. "Sounding Out the *Progymnasmata.*" *Rhetoric Review* 38, no. 2 (2018): 205-218.

———. "Toward Pedagogical Turnings." *ADE Bulletin* 155 (2018): 52–60.

Dobrin, Sidney I. *Postcomposition.* Carbondale: Southern Illinois University Press, 2011.

Downes, Stephen. "An Introduction to Connective Knowledge." *Stephen's Web*, December 22, 2005. https://www.downes.ca/cgi-bin/page.cgi?post=33034.

———. "What Connectivism Is." *Half an Hour*, February 3, 2007. https://halfanhour.blogspot.com/2007/02/what-connectivism-is.html.

Driscoll, Molly. "Alison Bechdel's Memoir 'Fun Home' Runs into Trouble with the South Carolina House of Representatives." *Christian Science Monitor*, February 28, 2014. https://www.csmonitor.com/Books/chapter-and-verse/2014/0228/Alison-Bechdel-s-memoir-Fun-Home-runs-into-trouble-with-the-South-Carolina-House-of-Representatives.

Driskill, Qwo-Li. "Decolonial Skillshares: Indigenous Rhetorics as Radical Practice." In *Survivance, Sovereignty, and Story: Teaching American Indian Rhetorics*, edited by Joyce Rain Anderson, Rose Gubele, and Lisa King, 57–78. Boulder: Utah State University Press, 2015.

Duffy, John, and Lois Agnew, eds. *After Plato: Rhetoric, Ethics, and the Teaching of Writing.* Louisville: Utah State University Press, 2020.

Eberly, Rosa A. "From Writers, Audiences, and Communities to Publics: Writing Classrooms as Protopublic Spaces." *Rhetoric Review* 18, no. 1 (1999): 165–78.

Edwards, Jessica, Meg McGuire, and Rachel Sanchez, eds. *Speaking Up, Speaking Out: Lived Experiences of Non-Tenure-Track Faculty in Writing Studies.* Louisville: Utah State University Press, 2021.

El-Alayli, Amani, Ashley A. Hansen-Brown, and Michelle Ceynar. "Dancing Backwards in High Heels: Female Professors Experience More Work Demands and Special Favor Requests, Particularly from Academically Entitled Students." *Sex Roles* 79 (2018): 136–50.

Ellison, Ralph. "Leadership from the Periphery." In *Who Speaks for the Negro?* by Robert Penn Warren, 268–354. New Haven: Yale University Press, 2014.

Enders, Jody. "Rhetoric, Coercion, and the Memory of Violence." In *Criticism and Dissent in the Middle Ages*, edited by Rita Copeland, 24–55. Cambridge: Cambridge University Press, 1996.

Enterline, Lynn. *Shakespeare's Schoolroom: Rhetoric, Discipline, Emotion.* Philadelphia: University of Pennsylvania Press, 2012.

Erasmus, Desiderius. *Collected Works of Erasmus: Literary and Educational Writings, 1 and 2.* Edited by Craig R. Thompson. Toronto: University of Toronto Press, 1978.

Esarey, Justin, and Natalie Valdes. "Unbiased, Reliable, and Valid Student Evaluations Can Still Be Unfair." *Assessment and Evaluation in Higher Education* 45, no. 8 (February 2020): 1106–20. http://www.tandfonline.com/doi/abs/10.1080/02602938.2020.1724875.

Fain, Paul. "Paying for Proof." *Inside Higher Ed*, January 9, 2013. https://www.insidehighered.com/news/2013/01/09/courseras-fee-based-course-option.

Fares, Melissa, and Angela Moon. "U.S. Campuses Hold Race Protests After Missouri Resignations." *Reuters*, November 11, 2015. https://www.reuters.com/article/us-missouri-boycott-protests-idUSKCN0SZ2QD20151111.

Fearman. "Postmodernism." Urban Dictionary, June 18, 2007. https://www.urbandictionary.com/define.php?term=postmodernism.

Feathers, Todd, and Janus Rose. "Students Are Rebelling Against Eye-Tracking Exam Surveillance Tools." *Motherboard*, September 2020. https://www.vice.com/en/article/n7wxvd/students-are-rebelling-against-eye-tracking-exam-surveillance-tools.

Fedewa, Kate, Jeffrey T. Grabill, Kristen Heine, Julie Lindquist, and Jennifer Royston. "Thinking about Thinking Like a Writer: Learning at Scale in a Writing MOOC." *Journal of Global Literacies, Technologies, and Emerging Pedagogies* 2, no. 3 (2014): 163–84.

Felman, Shoshana. "Psychoanalysis and Education: Teaching Terminable and Interminable." *Yale French Studies* 63 (1982): 21–44.

"First Year Writing at MTSU." Middle Tennessee State University. Accessed October 12, 2020. https://www.mtsu.edu/genedenglish/GEEfirstyearwriting.php.

Fisher, Adrian. *Mazes and Follies*. Norwich, UK: Jarrold, 2004.

Flaherty, Colleen. "Harassment and Power." *Inside Higher Ed*, August 20, 2018. https://www.insidehighered.com/news/2018/08/20/some-say-particulars-ronell-harassment-case-are-moot-it-all-comes-down-power.

———. "Next-Level Precarity: Non-Tenure-Track Professors and COVID-19." *Inside Higher Ed*, April 10, 2020. https://www.insidehighered.com/news/2020/04/10/next-level-precarity-non-tenure-track-professors-and-covid-19.

Fleming, J. David. "The Very Idea of a *Progymnasmata*." *Rhetoric Review* 22, no. 2 (2003): 105–20.

Flood, Brian. "Nate Silver Blew It Bigly on the Election—Can His Brand Recover?" *Wrap*, November 9, 2016. https://www.thewrap.com/nate-silver-blew-it-bigly-on-the-election-can-his-brand-recover.

Foss, Sonja K., and Cindy L. Griffin. "Beyond Persuasion: A Proposal for an Invitational Rhetoric." *Communication Monographs* 62, no. 1 (1995): 2–18. https://doi.org/10.1080/03637759509376345.

Foucault, Michel. "The Discourse on Language." In *The Archaeology of Knowledge*, translated by Rupert Swyer, 215–38. New York: Vintage, 1982.

Fox, Armando. "Can MOOCs and SPOCs Help Scale Residential Education While Maintaining High Quality?" In *MOOCs and Their Afterlives: Experiments in Scale and Access in Higher Education*, edited by Elizabeth Losh, 37–50. University of Chicago Press, 2017.

Framework for Success in Postsecondary Writing. CWPA, NCTE, and NWP, 2011. http://wpacouncil.org/aws/CWPA/asset_manager/get_file/350201?ver=2324.

Fredal, James. "Why Shouldn't the Sophists Charge Fees?" *Rhetoric Society Quarterly* 38, no. 2 (2008): 148–70.

Freire, Paulo. *Pedagogy of the Oppressed*. 30th anniversary ed. Translated by Myra Bergman Ramos. London: Bloomsbury, 2000.

Friedersdorf, Conor. "Campus Activists Weaponize 'Safe Space.'" *Atlantic*, November 10, 2015. https://www.theatlantic.com/politics/archive/2015/11/how-campus-activists-are-weaponizing-the-safe-space/415080.

———. "The New Intolerance of Student Activism." *Atlantic*, November 9, 2015. https://www.theatlantic.com/politics/archive/2015/11/the-new-intolerance-of-student-activism-at-yale/414810.

Friedner, Michele, Rebecca Sanchez, and Mara Mills. "How to Teach with Text: Platforming Down as Disability Pedagogy." *Avidly*, August 2, 2020. http://avidly.lareviewofbooks.org/2020/08/02/how-to-teach-with-text-platforming-down-as-disability-pedagogy.

Galer, Susan. "How MOOCs Are Disrupting Education." *Forbes*, May 19, 2014.

https://www.forbes.com/sites/sap
/2014/05/19/how-moocs-are-disrupting
-education.

Geisler, Cheryl. "How Ought We to
Understand the Concept of
Rhetorical Agency? Report from
the ARS." *Rhetoric Society Quarterly*
34, no. 3 (2004): 9–17.

———. "Teaching the Post-Modern Rhetor:
Continuing the Conversation on
Rhetorical Agency." *Rhetoric Society
Quarterly* 35, no. 4 (2005): 107–13.

Gerdes, Kendall. "Habit-Forming: Humility
and the Rhetoric of Drugs."
Philosophy and Rhetoric 8, no. 3
(2015): 337–58.

———. "Trauma, Trigger Warnings, and the
Rhetoric of Sensitivity." *Rhetoric
Society Quarterly* 48, no. 5 (2018): 1–22.

Gere, Anne Ruggles. *Writing Groups: History,
Theory, and Implications.* Carbondale:
Southern Illinois University Press,
1987.

Gibbs, Laura. "Let's Talk About Ungrading."
In *Ungrading: Why Rating Students
Undermines Learning (and What to
Do Instead)*, edited by Susan D.
Blum, 91–104. Morgantown: West
Virginia University Press, 2020.

Goggin, Maureen Daly, and Shirley K. Rose,
eds. *Women's Ways of Making.*
Louisville: Utah State University
Press, 2021.

Gomes, Mathew, and Wenjuan Ma. "Engaging
Expectations: Measuring Helpfulness
as an Alternative to Student
Evaluations of Teaching." *Assessing
Writing* 45 (July 2020). https://doi
.org/10.1016/j.asw.2020.100464.

Gorgias. "Encomium of Helen." In *On
Rhetoric: A Theory of Civic Discourse*,
by Aristotle, 2nd ed., translated by
George A. Kennedy. Oxford: Oxford
University Press, 2007.

Graff, Gerald. "The Pedagogical Turn." *Journal
of the Midwest Modern Language
Association* 27, no. 1 (1994): 65–69.

Hacker, Diana, and Nancy Sommers. *A Pocket
Style Guide.* 7th ed. Boston: Bedford/
St. Martin's, 2014.

———. *Rules for Writers.* 7th ed. Boston:
Bedford/St. Martin's, 2011.

Halberstam, Jack. "You Are Triggering Me!
The Neo-Liberal Rhetoric of Harm,
Danger and Trauma." *Bully Bloggers*,
July 5, 2014. https://bullybloggers
.wordpress.com/2014/07/05/you
-are-triggering-me-the-neo-liberal
-rhetoric-of-harm-danger-and-trauma.

Hamacher, Werner, Neil Hertz, and Tom
Keenan, eds. *Responses: On Paul de
Man's Wartime Journalism.* University
of Nebraska Press, 1988.

Hannah-Jones, Nikole. "The Idea of America."
New York Times, August 14, 2019.
https://www.nytimes.com/interactive
/2019/08/14/magazine/black-history
-american-democracy.html.

Harris, Cheryl I. "Whiteness as Property."
Harvard Law Review 106, no. 8 (1993):
1707–91.

Hauser, Gerard. "Teaching Rhetoric: Or Why
Rhetoric Isn't Just Another Kind of
Philosophy or Literary Criticism."
Rhetoric Society Quarterly 34, no. 3
(2004): 39–53.

Hawhee, Debra, and Christa J. Olson.
"Pan-Historiography: The Challenges
of Writing History across Time and
Space." In *Theorizing Histories of
Rhetoric*, edited by Michelle Ballif,
90–105. Carbondale: Southern
Illinois University Press, 2013.

Hawisher, Gail E., and Cynthia L. Selfe, eds.
*Passions, Pedagogies, and 21st Century
Technologies.* Boulder: Utah State
University Press, 1999.

Haynes, Cynthia Ann, and Jan Rune
Holmevik, eds. *High Wired: On the
Design, Use, and Theory of Educational
MOOs.* Ann Arbor: University of
Michigan Press, 1998.

Hegel, Georg Wilhelm Friedrich. *Elements
of the Philosophy of Right.* Edited by
Allen W. Wood, translated by H. B.
Nisbet. Cambridge: Cambridge
University Press, 1991.

Helms, Jason. 2019. "Play Smarter Not Harder:
Developing Your Scholarly Meta."
Scholarly and Research Communication
10, no. 3 (2019). https://doi.org/10
.22230/src.2019v10n3a333.

Henderson, Jeffrey. "Introductory Note." In
Aristophanes, *Clouds, Wasps, Peace,*

edited and translated by Jeffrey Henderson, 3–7. Cambridge, MA: Harvard University Press, 1998.

Hewett, Beth L., and Kevin Eric DePew, eds. *Foundational Practices of Online Writing Instruction*. Fort Collins: WAC Clearinghouse, 2015.

Hewett, Beth L., and Christa Ehmann. *Preparing Educators for Online Writing Instruction: Principles and Processes*. Urbana: National Council of Teachers of English, 2004.

Hibbard, Lee. "Out in the Classroom: A Transgender Pedagogical Narrative." *Peitho* 22, no. 4 (2020). https://cfshrc .org/article/out-in-the-classroom -a-transgender-pedagogical-narrative.

Hitt, Allison Harper. *Rhetorics of Overcoming: Rewriting Narratives of Disability and Accessibility in Writing Studies*. Champaign: National Council of Teachers of English, 2021.

hooks, bell. *Teaching Community: A Pedagogy of Hope*. New York: Routledge, 2003.

———. *Teaching to Transgress: Education as the Practice of Freedom*. New York: Routledge, 1994.

Hyland, Ken. *Disciplinary Discourses: Social Interactions in Academic Writing*. Michigan Classics. Ann Arbor: University of Michigan Press, 2004.

———. *Metadiscourse: Exploring Interaction in Writing*. London: Continuum, 2005.

Inoue, Asao B. *Antiracist Writing Assessment Ecologies: Teaching and Assessing Writing for a Socially Just Future*. Fort Collins: WAC Clearinghouse, 2015.

Intercultural Affairs Committee. "Email_ From_Intercultural_Affairs." *FIRE*, November 6, 2015. https://www.the fire.org/presentation/wp-content /uploads/2015/11/06103238/Email _From_Intercultural_Affairs.pdf.

Isocrates. "Against the Sophists." In *Isocrates I*, by David C. Mirhady and Yun Lee Too, 61–66. Austin: University of Texas Press, 2000.

———. "Antidosis." In *Isocrates I*, by David C. Mirhady and Yun Lee Too, 205–64. Austin: University of Texas Press, 2000.

———. *Isocrates I*. Translated by David C. Mirhady and Yun Lee Too. Austin: University of Texas Press, 2000.

Jackson, Abby. "Obama Rips into 'Coddled' College Students at Town Hall in Iowa." *Business Insider*, September 15, 2015. https://www.businessinsider .com/obama-on-coddled-college -students-2015-9.

Jarratt, Susan C. *Rereading the Sophists: Classical Rhetoric Refigured*. Carbondale: Southern Illinois University Press, 1998.

Kahn, Seth, William B. Lalicker, and Amy Lynch-Biniek, eds. *Contingency, Exploitation, and Solidarity: Labor and Action in English Composition*. Fort Collins: WAC Clearinghouse, 2017.

Kaiser Health News. "COVID Crisis Endangers Adjunct Professors." *US News and World Report*, July 2020. https://www.usnews.com/news /healthiest-communities/articles /2020-07-21/adjunct-professors-face -high-coronavirus-risk-with-jobs-low -on-pay-health-benefits.

Kaster, Robert A. *Guardians of Language: The Grammarian and Society in Late Antiquity*. Berkeley: University of California Press, 1988.

Katopodis, Christina, and Cathy N. Davidson. "Contract Grading and Peer Review." In *Ungrading: Why Rating Students Undermines Learning (and What to Do Instead)*, edited by Susan D. Blum, 105–22. Morgantown: West Virginia University Press, 2020.

Keith, William, and Roxanne Mountford. "The Mt. Oread Manifesto on Rhetorical Education." *Rhetoric Society Quarterly* 44, no. 1 (2014): 1–5.

Kennedy, George A. *A New History of Classical Rhetoric*. Princeton: Princeton University Press, 1994.

———, ed. *Progymnasmata: Greek Textbooks of Prose Composition and Rhetoric*. Atlanta: Society of Biblical Literature, 2003.

Kerschbaum, Stephanie L. *Toward a New Rhetoric of Difference*. Urbana: CCCC/ NCTE, 2014.

Kierkegaard, Søren. *The Concept of Irony with Continual Reference to Socrates.* Edited by Howard V. Hong and Edna H. Hong. Princeton: Princeton University Press, 1989.

———. *Fear and Trembling / Repetition.* Edited by Howard V. Hong and Edna H. Hong. Princeton: Princeton University Press, 1983.

King, Alison. "From Sage on the Stage to Guide on the Side." *College Teaching* 41, no. 1 (1993): 30–35.

Kirby, Cait S. *October 5th, 2020.* Cait S. Kirby, PhD. https://caitkirby.com/down loads/October5th2020.html. Accessed January 30, 2022.

Knoblauch, A. Abby. "A Textbook Argument: Definitions of Argument in Leading Composition Textbooks." *College Composition and Communication* 63, no. 2 (2011): 244–68.

Koh, Adeline. "Feminist Pedagogy in the Digital Age: Experimenting between MOOCs and DOCCs." In *MOOCs and Their Afterlives: Experiments in Scale and Access in Higher Education,* edited by Elizabeth Losh, 123–34. Chicago: University of Chicago Press, 2017.

Kolowich, Steve. "MIT Will Offer MOOC Curricula, Not Just Single Courses, on EdX." *Chronicle of Higher Education,* September 18, 2013. https://www .chronicle.com/blogs/wiredcampus /mit-will-offer-mooc-curricula-not -just-single-courses-on-edx/46715.

Kop, Rita. "The Challenges to Connectivist Learning in Open Online Networks: Learning Experiences during a Massive Open Online Course." *International Review of Research in Open and Distance Learning* 12, no. 3 (2011): 19–38.

Kop, Rita, and Adrian Hill. "Connectivism: Learning Theory of the Future or Vestige of the Past?" *International Review of Research in Open and Distance Learning* 9, no. 3 (2008). http://www.irrodl.org/index.php /irrodl/article/view/9.3.4.

Kopelson, Karen. "Rhetoric on the Edge of Cunning: Or, The Performance of Neutrality (Re)Considered as a Composition Pedagogy for Student Resistance." *College Composition and Communication* 55, no. 1 (2003): 115–46.

Kraus, Manfred. "Rehearsing the Other Sex: Impersonation of Women in Ancient Classroom Ethopoeia." In *Escuela y Literatura En Grecia Antigua,* edited by José Antonio Fernández Delgado, Francisca Pordomingo, and Antonio Stramaglia, 455–68. Cassino: Università degli Studio di Cassino, 2007.

Krause, Steven D. *More Than a Moment: Contextualizing the Past, Present, and Future of MOOCs.* Louisville: Utah State University Press, 2019.

Kreitzer, Rebecca J., and Jennie Sweet-Cushman. "Evaluating Student Evaluations of Teaching: A Review of Measurement and Equity Bias in SETs and Recommendations for Ethical Reform." *Journal of Academic Ethics* (February 2021). https:// doi.org/10.1007/s10805-021 -09400-w.

Kruesi, Kimberlee. "Tennessee Bans Teaching Critical Race Theory in Schools." *AP News,* May 25, 2021. https://apnews .com/article/tennessee-racial -injustice-race-and-ethnicity-religion -education-9366bceabf309557811eab 645c8dad13.

LaBarre, Suzanne. "Zoom Is Failing Teachers. Here's How They Would Redesign It." *Fast Company,* September 2020. https://www .fastcompany.com/90542917 /zoom-is-failing-teachers-heres -how-they-would-redesign-it.

Ladson-Billings, Gloria. "From the Achievement Gap to the Education Debt: Understanding Achievement in U.S. Schools." *Educational Researcher* 35, no. 7 (2006): 3–12.

Laks, André, and Glenn W. Most, trans. *Early Greek Philosophy.* Vol. 9, *Sophists.* Part 2. Cambridge, MA: Harvard University Press, 2016.

Latour, Bruno. "Socrates' and Callicles' Settlement—Or, The Invention of the

Impossible Body Politic." *Configurations* 5, no. 2 (1997): 187–240.

Lebeau, Vicky. "The Unwelcome Child: Elizabeth Eckford and Hannah Arendt." *Journal of Visual Culture* 3, no. 1 (2004): 51–62.

Leckart, Steven. "The Stanford Education Experiment Could Change Higher Learning Forever." *Wired*, March 20, 2012. https://www.wired.com/2012/03/ff_aiclass.

Lederman, Doug. "2U, EdX to Combine to Create Online Learning Behemoth." *Inside Higher Ed*, June 29, 2021. https://www.insidehighered.com/news/2021/06/29/2u-edx-combine-create-online-learning-behemoth.

Leff, Michael, and Andrea A. Lunsford. "Afterwords: A Dialogue." *Rhetoric Society Quarterly* 34, no. 3 (2004): 55–67.

LeMieux, Steven. "Machinic Invention in Media Res." Presentation at the Computers and Writing Conference, Pullman, WA, June 5–8, 2014.

Levinas, Emmanuel. *Otherwise Than Being, or Beyond Essence*. Translated by Alphonso Lingis. Pittsburgh: Duquesne University Press, 1974.

———. *Totality and Infinity*. Translated by Alphonso Lingis. Pittsburgh: Duquesne University Press, 1969.

———. "The Trace of the Other." In *Deconstruction in Context: Literature and Philosophy*, edited by Mark C. Taylor, 345–59. Chicago: University of Chicago Press, 1986.

Lewin, Tamar. "Instruction for Masses Knocks Down Campus Walls." *New York Times*, March 4, 2012. https://www.nytimes.com/2012/03/05/education/moocs-large-courses-open-to-all-topple-campus-walls.html.

Libanius. *Libanius's "Progymnasmata": Model Exercises in Greek Prose Composition and Rhetoric*. Translated by Craig A. Gibson. Atlanta: Society of Biblical Literature, 2008.

Lindquist, Julie, and Bump Halbritter. "Documenting and Discovering Learning: Reimagining the Work of

the Literacy Narrative." *College Composition and Communication* 70, no. 3 (2019): 413–45.

Lohr, Steve. "Remember the MOOCs? After Near-Death, They're Booming." *New York Times*, May 26, 2020. https://www.nytimes.com/2020/05/26/technology/moocs-online-learning.html.

Long, Heather, and Danielle Douglas-Gabriel. "The Latest Crisis: Low-Income Students Are Dropping Out of College This Fall in Alarming Numbers." *Washington Post*, September 16, 2020. https://www.washingtonpost.com/business/2020/09/16/college-enrollment-down.

Losh, Elizabeth, ed. *MOOCs and Their Afterlives: Experiments in Scale and Access in Higher Education*. Chicago: University of Chicago Press, 2017.

Lowe, Charles. "Introduction: Building on the Tradition of CCK08." In *Invasion of the MOOCs: The Promises and Perils of Massive Open Online Courses*, edited by Steven D. Krause and Charles Lowe, ix–xiv. Anderson, SC: Parlor Press, 2014.

Lozenski, Brian D. "Beyond Mediocrity: The Dialectics of Crisis in the Continuing Miseducation of Black Youth." *Harvard Educational Review* 87, no. 2 (2017): 161–85. https://doi.org/10.17763/1943-5045-87.2.161.

Lu, Min-Zhan. "Professing Multiculturalism: The Politics of Style in the Contact Zone." In *Cross-Talk in Comp Theory*, 3rd ed., edited by Victor Villanueva and Kristin L. Arola, 467–84. Urbana: National Council of Teachers of English, 2011.

Lucian. *A Professor of Public Speaking*. In *Lucian: Volume IV*, translated by A. M. Harmon. Cambridge: William Heinemann, 1925.

Lukianoff, Greg, and Jonathan Haidt. "The Coddling of the American Mind." *Atlantic*, September 2015. https://www.theatlantic.com/magazine/archive/2015/09/the-coddling-of-the-american-mind/399356.

———. *The Coddling of the American Mind: How Good Intentions and Bad Ideas*

Are Setting Up a Generation for Failure.
New York: Penguin Press, 2018.

Lundberg, Christian, and Joshua Gunn.
"'Ouija Board, Are There Any
Communications?' Agency,
Ontotheology, and the Death of the
Humanist Subject, or, Continuing
the ARS Conversation." *Rhetoric
Society Quarterly* 35, no. 4 (2005):
83–105.

Lundstrom, Kristi, and Wendy Baker. "To
Give Is Better Than to Receive:
The Benefits of Peer Review to the
Reviewer's Own Writing." *Journal of
Second Language Writing* 18, no. 1
(2009): 30–43.

Lynch, Paul. *After Pedagogy: The Experience
of Teaching.* Urbana: CCCC/NCTE,
2014.

Lyon, Arabella. *Deliberative Acts: Democracy,
Rhetoric, and Rights.* University Park:
Penn State University Press, 2013.

MacDonald, Susan Peck. *Professional Academic
Writing in the Humanities and Social
Sciences.* Carbondale: Southern Illinois
University Press, 2010.

Maleficent. Burbank: Walt Disney Pictures,
2014.

Manning, Matthew K., and Alex Irvine. *DC
Comics Encyclopedia: The Definitive
Guide to the Characters of the DC
Universe.* All new ed. New York:
DK, 2016.

Maraj, Louis M. *Black or Right: Anti/Racist
Campus Rhetorics.* Boulder: Utah
State University Press, 2020.

Marcus, Jon. "All Hail MOOCs! Just Don't
Ask If They Actually Work." *Time,*
September 12, 2013. http://nation
.time.com/2013/09/12/all-hail-moocs
-just-dont-ask-if-they-actually-work.
———. "Most Americans Don't Realize
State Funding for Higher Ed Fell by
Billions." *PBS NewsHour,* February 26,
2019. https://www.pbs.org/newshour
/education/most-americans-dont
-realize-state-funding-for-higher-ed
-fell-by-billions.

Marrou, Henri I. *A History of Education in
Antiquity.* Translated by George

Lamb. Madison: University of
Wisconsin Press, 1948.

Martinez, Aja Y. *Counterstory: The Rhetoric
and Writing of Critical Race Theory.*
Champaign: CCCC/NCTE, 2020.

"Massively Open Online Courses and STEM
Education." President's Council of
Advisors on Science and Technology,
November 30, 2012. http://www
.tvworldwide.com/events/pcast
/121130/default.cfm?id=15034&type
=flv&test=0&live=0.

McCammon, Sarah. "Books with Gay Themes
Put S.C. Colleges' Funding at Risk."
NPR, May 9, 2014. https://www.npr
.org/2014/05/09/310726247/gay
-friendly-book-selections-put-college
-funding-at-risk.

Medimorec, Srdan, and Gordon Pennycook.
"The Language of Denial: Text
Analysis Reveals Differences in
Language Use Between Climate
Change Proponents and Skeptics."
Climatic Change (2015): 1–9.

Meyerhoff, Eli. *Beyond Education: Radical
Studying for Another World.*
Minneapolis: University of
Minnesota Press, 2019.

Micciche, Laura R. "Writing as Feminist
Rhetorical Theory." In *Rhetorica in
Motion: Feminist Rhetorical Methods
and Methodologies,* edited by Eileen E.
Schell and K. J. Rawson, 173–88.
Pittsburgh: University of Pittsburgh
Press, 2010.

Morissette, Alanis. "Ironic." *Jagged Little Pill.*
Los Angeles: Maverick, 1995.

Morris, Sean Michael, and Jesse Stommel.
"Open Education as Resistance:
MOOCs and Critical Digital
Pedagogy." In *MOOCs and Their
Afterlives: Experiments in Scale
and Access in Higher Education,*
edited by Elizabeth Losh, 177–97.
Chicago: University of Chicago
Press, 2017.

Morrison, Debbie. "The Ultimate Student
Guide to XMOOCs and CMOOCs."
MOOC News and Reviews, April 22,
2013. http://moocnewsandreviews

.com/ultimate-guide-to-xmoocs
-and-cmoocso.

Morrissey, Janet. "Using Technology to Tailor Lessons to Each Student." *New York Times*, September 29, 2020. https://www.nytimes.com/2020/09/29/education/schools-technology-future-pandemic.html.

Muckelbauer, John. "Implicit Paradigms of Rhetoric: Aristotelian, Cultural, and Heliotropic." In *Rhetoric, Through Everyday Things*, edited by Scot Barnett and Casey Boyle, 30–41. Tuscaloosa: University of Alabama Press, 2016.

National Center for Education Statistics. "Characteristics of Postsecondary Faculty." National Center for Education Statistics, May 2020. https://nces.ed.gov/programs/coe/indicator/csc.

National Communication Association. "The National Communication Association's Guidelines for Undergraduate Communication Classrooms." National Communication Association, April 2011. https://www.natcom.org/sites/default/files/pages/Chairs_Corner_Guidelines_for_Undergraduate_Communication_Programs.pdf.

National Council of Teachers of English. "Why Class Size Matters Today." National Council of Teachers of English, April 2014. http://www2.ncte.org/statement/why-class-size-matters.

Nealon, Jeffrey T. "The Cash Value of Paradox: Žižek's Rhetoric." *JAC* 21, no. 3 (2001): 599–605.

Nehamas, Alexander. *The Art of Living: Socratic Reflections from Plato to Foucault.* Berkeley: University of California Press, 2000.

Ng, Kristy. "Broadening Access to Higher Education: A Story from a Texas Charter School Pilot." *Udacity Blog*, November 29, 2012. https://blog.udacity.com/2012/11/broadening-access-to-higher-education.html.

Noble, Safiya Umoja. *Algorithms of Oppression: How Search Engines Reinforce Racism.* New York: New York University Press, 2018.

"Obscure Guy Gets Famous Overnight." *Roanoke Times*, June 6, 2019. https://roanoke.com/news/local/obscure-guy-gets-famous-overnight/article_f1ebfb2f-4a47-5e1f-b258-3ecd6cf9be93.html.

O'Grady, Cathleen. "Climate Scientists Write Tentatively; Their Opponents Are Certain They're Wrong." *Ars Technica*, October 9, 2015. https://arstechnica.com/science/2015/10/climate-scientists-are-tentative-their-opponents-are-certain-theyre-wrong.

Oleksiak, Timothy. "A Queer Praxis for Peer Review." *College Composition and Communication* 72, no. 2 (2020): 306–32.

Omizo, Ryan, and Bill Hart-Davidson. "Hedge-O-Matic." *enculturation* 22 (2016). http://enculturation.net/hedge-o-matic.

O'Neil, Cathy. *Weapons of Math Destruction: How Big Data Increases Inequality and Threatens Democracy.* New York: Crown, 2016.

Ore, Ersula J. "Black Feelings, Rhetorical Education, and Public Memory." *Rhetoric Society Quarterly* 51, no. 4 (2021): 1–8. https://doi.org/10.1080/02773945.2021.1957333.

Orem, Sarah, and Neil Simpkins. "Weepy Rhetoric, Trigger Warnings, and the Work of Making Mental Illness Visible in the Writing Classroom." *enculturation* 20 (2015). http://enculturation.net/weepy-rhetoric.

Panopto. "Panopto for Education—Product Overview." Accessed September 19, 2021. https://demo.hosted.panopto.com/Panopto/Pages/Viewer.aspx?id=4a1f66f0-5194-4139-a790-8b26f74dffc4.

paperson, la. *A Third University Is Possible.* Minneapolis: University of Minnesota Press, 2017.

Pappano, Laura. "The Year of the MOOC." *New York Times*, November 2, 2012. https://www.nytimes.com/2012/11

/04/education/edlife/massive-open
-online-courses-are-multiplying-at-a
-rapid-pace.html.

Pareles, Jon. "The Solipsisters Sing Out Once
Again." *New York Times*, May 16, 2004.
https://www.nytimes.com/2004/05
/16/arts/music-the-solipsisters-sing
-out-once-again.html.

Patil, Anushka, and Jonah Engel Bromwich.
"How It Feels When Software
Watches You Take Tests." *New York
Times*, September 29, 2020. https://
www.nytimes.com/2020/09/29
/style/testing-schools-proctorio.html.

Paul, Annie Murphy. "Why Students Prefer to
Learn from a Machine." *Slate*, August
13, 2014. https://slate.com/technology
/2014/08/robo-readers-robo-graders
-why-students-prefer-to-learn-from-a
-machine.html.

Perryman-Clark, Staci, David E. Kirkland,
and Austin Jackson, eds. *Students'
Right to Their Own Language: A
Critical Sourcebook*. Boston: Bedford/
St Martin's, 2015.

Petronius, Gauis. *The Satyricon*. Translated by
P. G. Walsh. Oxford: Oxford
University Press, 1997.

Pinker, Steven. *The Sense of Style: The Thinking
Person's Guide to Writing in the 21st
Century*. New York: Penguin, 2015.

———. "Why Academics Stink at Writing."
Chronicle of Higher Education,
September 26, 2014. https://www
.chronicle.com/article/Why
-Academics-Writing-Stinks/148989.

Pitkin, Hanna Fenichel. *The Attack of the Blob:
Hannah Arendt's Concept of the Social*.
Chicago: University of Chicago Press,
2000.

Plato. *Gorgias*. Translated by Robin Waterfield.
Oxford: Oxford University Press, 1994.

———. *Gorgias*. Translated by Donald J.
Zeyl. Indianapolis: Hackett, 1987.

———. *Lysis*. In *Lysis, Symposium, Gorgias*,
translated by W. R. M. Lamb.
Cambridge, MA: Harvard University
Press, 1925.

———. *Phaedrus*. Translated by Alexander
Nehamas and Paul Woodruff.
Indianapolis: Hackett, 1995.

———. *Seventh Letter*. In *Phaedrus and
Letters VII and VIII*, edited by Walter
Hamilton, 111–50. New York:
Penguin, 1973.

———. *Sophist: The Professor of Wisdom*.
Translated by Eva Brann, Peter
Kalkavage, and Eric Salem.
Newburyport: Focus Philosophical
Library, 1996.

Plug, Jan. "Translator's Note." In *Who's
Afraid of Philosophy? Right to
Philosophy 1*, by Jacques Derrida.
Stanford: Stanford University Press,
2002.

Porter, Eduardo. "A Smart Way to Skip
College in Pursuit of a Job." *New York
Times*, June 17, 2014. https://www
.nytimes.com/2014/06/18/business
/economy/udacity-att-nanodegree
-offers-an-entry-level-approach-to
-college.html.

Porter, James E. "Framing Questions About
MOOCs and Writing Courses." In
*Invasion of the MOOCs: The Promises
and Perils of Massive Open Online
Courses*, edited by Steven D. Krause
and Charles Lowe, 14–28. Anderson,
SC: Parlor Press, 2014.

Pratt, Mary Louise. "Arts of the Contact
Zone." *Profession* (1991): 33–40.

Quintilian. *The Orator's Education*. Translated
by Donald A. Russell. Loeb.
Cambridge, MA: Harvard University
Press, 2002.

Ramsey, Paul. "Plato and the Modern
American 'Right': Agendas,
Assumptions, and the Culture of
Fear." *Educational Studies* 45, no. 6
(2009): 572–88.

Randle, Aaron. "Racial Slurs, and the 15
Days That Shook Syracuse." *New
York Times*, November 27, 2019.
https://www.nytimes.com/2019/11
/27/nyregion/syracuse-university
-racism.html.

Rault, Jasmine, and T. L. Cowan. "Haven't
You Ever Heard of Tumblr?
FemTechNet's Distributed Open
Collaborative Course (DOCC),
Pedagogical Publics, and Classroom
Incivility." In *MOOCs and Their*

Afterlives: Experiments in Scale and Access in Higher Education, edited by Elizabeth Losh, 161–76. Chicago: University of Chicago Press, 2017.

Ray, Brian. "A *Progymnasmata* for Our Time: Adapting Classical Exercises to Teach Translingual Style." *Rhetoric Review* 32, no. 2 (2013): 191–209.

Restaino, Jessica. *First Semester: Graduate Students, Teaching Writing, and the Challenge of Middle Ground.* Carbondale: Southern Illinois University Press, 2012.

Reynolds, Nedra. "Interrupting Our Way to Agency: Feminist Cultural Studies and Composition." In *The Norton Book of Composition Studies*, edited by Susan Miller, 897–910. New York: Norton, 2009.

Rice, Jeff. "MOOCversations: Commonplaces as Argument." In *Invasion of the MOOCs: The Promises and Perils of Massive Open Online Courses*, edited by Steven D. Krause and Charles Lowe, 86–97. Anderson, SC: Parlor Press. 2014.

———. *The Rhetoric of Cool: Composition Studies and New Media.* Carbondale: Southern Illinois University Press, 2007.

Roberts-Miller, Patricia. "Advice on Writing." *Patricia Roberts-Miller.* Accessed October 12, 2020. https://www.patriciarobertsmiller.com/advice-on-writing.

———. *Deliberate Conflict: Argument, Political Theory, and Composition Classes.* Carbondale: Southern Illinois University Press, 2004.

———. "Fighting without Hatred: Hannah Arendt's Agonistic Rhetoric." *JAC* 22, no. 3 (2002): 585–601.

———. *Rhetoric and Demagoguery.* Carbondale: Southern Illinois University Press, 2019.

Ronell, Avital. *Loser Sons: Politics and Authority.* Urbana: University of Illinois Press, 2012.

———. *Stupidity.* Urbana: University of Illinois Press, 2002.

———. *The Test Drive.* Urbana: University of Illinois Press, 2007.

Rooks, Noliwe M. "Why the Online-Education Craze Will Leave Many Students Behind." *Time*, July 30, 2012. http://ideas.time.com/2012/07/30/why-online-education-will-leave-many-students-behind.

Russell, David R. *Writing in the Academic Disciplines: A Curricular History.* 2nd ed. Carbondale: Southern Illinois University Press, 2002.

Ryan, Cynthia. "Rhetoric(s) of Becoming: Possibilities for Composing Intersectional Identities of Difference." *JAC* 27, no. 3/4 (2007): 686–92.

Salter, Anastasia, and Stuart Moulthrop. *Twining: Critical and Creative Approaches to Hypertext Narratives.* Amherst: Amherst College Press, 2021.

Sánchez, Raúl. *The Function of Theory in Composition Studies.* Albany: SUNY Press, 2005.

San José Philosophy Department. "The Open Letter to Michael Sandel and Some Thoughts About Outsourced Online Teaching." In *MOOCs and Their Afterlives: Experiments in Scale and Access in Higher Education*, edited by Elizabeth Losh, 255–70. Chicago: University of Chicago Press, 2017.

Saul, Stephanie, and Sophie Kasakove. "Rice University Turns to Online Classes." *New York Times*, August 20, 2021. https://www.nytimes.com/2021/08/20/us/rice-university-online-classes-delta-variant.html.

SB 0623. Tennessee General Assembly, June 1, 2021. https://wapp.capitol.tn.gov/apps/BillInfo/Default.aspx?Bill Number=SB0623&GA=112.

Schlosser, Edward. "I'm a Liberal Professor, and My Liberal Students Terrify Me." *Vox*, June 3, 2015. https://www.vox.com/2015/6/3/8706323/college-professor-afraid.

Schuman, Rebecca. "The King of MOOCs Abdicates the Throne." *Slate*, November 19, 2013. https://slate.com/human-interest/2013/11

/sebastian-thrun-and-udacity -distance-learning-is-unsuccessful -for-most-students.html.

Seltzer, Rick. "Missouri 3 Years Later: Lessons Learned, Protests Still Resonate," September 12, 2018. https://www .insidehighered.com/news/2018/09 /12/administrators-students-and -activists-take-stock-three-years-after -2015-missouri.

Siemens, George. "MOOCs Are Really a Platform." Elearnspace, July 25, 2012.

Silver, Nate. "How FiveThirtyEight's 2020 Forecasts Did and What We'll Be Thinking About for 2022." Five ThirtyEight, June 8, 2021. https:// fivethirtyeight.com/features/how -fivethirtyeights-2020-forecasts-did -and-what-well-be-thinking-about -for-2022.

———. "Why FiveThirtyEight Gave Trump a Better Chance Than Almost Anyone Else." FiveThirtyEight, November 11, 2016. https://fivethirtyeight.com /features/why-fivethirtyeight-gave -trump-a-better-chance-than-almost -anyone-else.

Skinnell, Ryan. "A Master Plan: A History of Higher Education and the Rhetorical Redefinition of Tenure." Presentation at the Rhetoric Society of America Conference, San Antonio, TX, May 22–26, 2014.

Sleeping Beauty. Los Angeles: Walt Disney, 1959.

Smith, Martin. "What Universities Have in Common with Record Labels." *Quartz*, July 6, 2014. https://qz.com /223771/universities-are-the-record -labels-of-education.

Smitherman, Geneva. *Talkin and Testifyin: The Language of Black America*. Detroit: Wayne State University Press, 1986.

Smitherman, Geneva, and Victor Villanueva, eds. *Language Diversity in the Classroom: From Intention to Practice*. Carbondale: Southern Illinois University Press, 2003.

Spivak, Gayatri Chakravorty. "Can the Subaltern Speak?" In *Can the Sub- altern Speak? Reflections on the Histsory of an Idea*, by Rosalind C. Morris, 21–78. New York: Columbia University Press, 2021.

———. "Translating into English." In *An Aesthetic Education in the Era of Globalization*, by Gayatri Chakravorty Spivak, 256–74. Cambridge, MA: Harvard University Press, 2012.

———. "Translation as Culture." In *An Aesthetic Education in the Era of Globalization*, by Gayatri Chakravorty Spivak, 241–55. Cambridge, MA: Harvard University Press, 2012.

Sprague, Rosamond Kent, ed. *The Older Sophists*. Indianapolis: Hackett, 2001.

Srnicek, Nick. *Platform Capitalism*. Cambridge: Polity, 2016.

Steele, Meili. "Arendt Versus Ellison on Little Rock: The Role of Language in Political Judgment." *Constellations* 9, no. 2 (2002): 184–206.

Stommel, Jesse. "How to Ungrade." Jesse Stommel, March 11, 2018. https:// www.jessestommel.com/how-to -ungrade.

Storey, Ian C. "Clouds: Introduction." In *Aristophanes 1: Clouds, Wasps, Birds*, 2–7. Indianapolis: Hackett, 1998.

———. "General Introduction." In *Aristophanes 1: Clouds, Wasps, Birds*, vii–xxxv. Indianapolis: Hackett, 1998.

Straus, Joe. "83rd Legislature Interim Committee Charges." Texas House of Representatives, January 2014. https://house.texas.gov/_media /pdf/interim-charges-83rd.pdf.

Sullivan, Patricia Suzanne. *Experimental Writing in Composition: Aesthetics and Pedagogies*. Pittsburgh: University of Pittsburgh Press, 2012.

Swauger, Shea. "Our Bodies Encoded: Algorithmic Test Proctoring in Higher Education." *Hybrid Pedagogy*, April 2020. https://hybridpedagogy .org/our-bodies-encoded-algorithmic -test-proctoring-in-higher-education.

Syverson, Margaret A. "Social Justice and Evidence-Based Assessment with the Learning Record." *Forum on Public Policy Online* 2009, no. 1 (2009): 1–27.

Theon, Aelius. "The *Exercises* of Aelius Theon." In *Progymnasmata: Greek Textbooks of Prose Composition and Rhetoric*, edited by George A. Kennedy, 1–72. Atlanta: Society of Biblical Literature, 2003.

Tlostanova, Madina V., and Walter D. Mignolo. *Learning to Unlearn: Decolonial Reflections from Eurasia and the Americas*. Columbus: Ohio State University Press, 2012.

Too, Yun Lee. *The Pedagogical Contract: The Economies of Teaching and Learning in the Ancient World*. Ann Arbor: University of Michigan Press, 2000.

Turnitin. Accessed September 20, 2021. https://www.turnitin.com.

Twine. Accessed September 12, 2021. https://twinery.org.

University of Phoenix. *We Can Do IT (:60)— University of Phoenix*. YouTube, 2017. https://www.youtube.com/watch?v=2TTd2FmYrog.

Vasiliou, Iakovos. "Socrates' Reverse Irony." *Classical Quarterly* 52, no. 1 (2002): 220–30.

Vitanza, Victor J. *Negation, Subjectivity, and the History of Rhetoric*. Albany: SUNY Press, 1996.

———. "Three Countertheses: Or, A Critical In(ter)vention into Composition Theories and Pedagogies." In *Contending with Words: Composition and Rhetoric in a Postmodern Age*, edited by Patricia Harkin and John Schilb, 139–72. New York: Modern Language Association, 1991.

Vought, Russell. "Memorandum for the Heads of Executive Departments and Agencies." White House Executive Office of the President, September 4, 2020. https://www.whitehouse.gov/wp-content/uploads/2020/09/M-20-34.pdf.

Walker, Jeffrey. *The Genuine Teachers of This Art: Rhetorical Education in Antiquity*. Columbia: University of South Carolina Press, 2011.

———. *Rhetoric and Poetics in Antiquity*. Oxford: Oxford University Press, 2000.

———. "What Difference a Definition Makes, or, William Dean Howells and the Sophist's Shoes." *Rhetoric Society Quarterly* 36, no. 2 (2006): 143–53.

Wardle, Elizabeth. "You Can Learn to Write in General." In *Bad Ideas About Writing*, edited by Cheryl E. Ball and Drew M. Loewe, 30–33. Morgantown: West Virginia University Libraries, 2017. https://textbooks.lib.wvu.edu/badideas.

Warner, John. *Sustainable. Resilient. Free. The Future of Higher Education*. Cleveland: Belt, 2020.

———. *Why They Can't Write: Killing the Five-Paragraph Essay and Other Necessities*. Baltimore: Johns Hopkins University Press, 2018.

Warren, Kenneth W. "Ralph Ellison and the Problem of Cultural Authority." *Boundary* 30, no. 2 (2003): 157–74.

Watters, Audrey. 2014. "The History of 'Personalization' and Teaching Machines." *Hack Education*, July 2, 2014. http://hackeducation.com/2014/07/02/personalization-teaching-machines.

———. *Teaching Machines: The History of Personalized Learning*. Cambridge, MA: MIT Press, 2021.

Webley, Kayla. "MOOC Brigade: Will Massive, Open Online Courses Revolutionize Higher Education?" *Time*, September 4, 2012. http://nation.time.com/2012/09/04/mooc-brigade-will-massive-open-online-courses-revolutionize-higher-education.

Weinberg, Adam. "Google Just Changed the Higher Education Game. Colleges and Universities Should Be Paying Attention." *Business Insider*, September 13, 2020. https://www.businessinsider.com/google-careers-certificate-program-changed-game-universities-should-pay-attention-2020-9.

Welch, Kathleen E. *Electric Rhetoric: Classical Rhetoric, Oralism, and a New Literacy*. Cambridge, MA: MIT Press, 1999.

Welch, Nancy, and Tony Scott, eds. *Composition in the Age of Austerity*. Boulder: Utah State University Press, 2016.

Weller, Martin. "The Dangerous Appeal of the Silicon Valley Narrative." *Ed Techie*, January 23, 2014. http:// nogoodreason.typepad.co.uk/no _good_reason/2014/01/the-dangers -of-the-silicon-valley-narrative.html.

Wilder, Craig Steven. *Ebony and Ivy*. New York: Bloomsbury, 2013.

Wilder, Laura, and Joanna Wolfe. "Sharing the Tacit Rhetorical Knowledge of the Literary Scholar: The Effects of Making Disciplinary Conventions Explicit in Undergraduate Writing About Literature Courses." *Research in the Teaching of English* 44, no. 2 (2009): 170–209.

Wilson, Ryan. "Open Letter to Associate Master Christakis." *Down Magazine*, October 31, 2015. https://downatyale .com/post.php?id=430.

Wolfsdorf, David. "The Irony of Socrates." *Journal of Aesthetics and Art Criticism* 65, no. 2 (2007): 175–87.

Woods, Marjorie Curry. "Boys Will Be Women: Musings on Classroom Nostalgia and the Chaucerian Audience(s)." In *Speaking Images: Essays in Honor of V. A. Kolve*, edited by Robert F. Yeager, Charlotte C. Morse, and Verdel A. Kolve, 143–66. Asheville: Pegasus, 2001.

———. "Weeping for Dido: Epilogue on a Premodern Rhetorical Exercise in the Postmodern Classroom." In *Latin Grammar and Rhetoric: From Classical Theory to Medieval Practice*, edited by Carol Dana Lanham, 284–94. New York: Continuum, 2003.

Woolston, Chris. "Signs of Depression and Anxiety Soar Among US Graduate Students During Pandemic." *Nature* 585 (August 18, 2020): 147–148. https://doi.org/10.1038/d41586-020 -02439-6.

Worsham, Lynn. "Writing Against Writing: The Predicament of Écriture Féminine in Composition Studies." In *Contending with Words: Composition and Rhetoric in a Postmodern Age*, edited by Patricia Harkin and John Schilb, 82–104. New York: Modern Language Association, 1991.

Wu, Hui, trans. *Guiguzi, China's First Treatise on Rhetoric: A Critical Translation and Commentary*. Carbondale: Southern Illinois University Press, 2016.

Yancey, Kathleen Blake. "Portfolios, Learning, and Agency: Promises, Perceptions, Possibilities." *JAC* 31, no. 3/4 (2011): 717–36.

———. "Writing Agency, Writing Practices, Writing Pasts and Futures." *College Composition and Communication* 62, no. 3 (2011): 416–19.

Yancey, Kathleen, Liane Robertson, and Kara Taczak. *Writing across Contexts: Transfer, Composition, and Sites of Writing*. Boulder: Utah State University Press, 2014.

Yergeau, M. Remi, Elizabeth Brewer, Stephanie Kerschbaum, Sushil K. Oswal, Margaret Price, Cynthia L. Selfe, Michael J. Salvo, and Franny Howes. "Multimodality in Motion: Disability and Kairotic Spaces." *Kairos: A Journal of Rhetoric, Technology, and Pedagogy* 18, no. 1 (2013). http://kairos .technorhetoric.net/18.1/coverweb /yergeau-et-al/index.html.

Young, Morris. *Minor Re/Visions: Asian American Literacy Narratives as a Rhetoric of Citizenship*. Carbondale: Southern Illinois University Press, 2004.

Young, Vershawn Ashanti, Rusty Barrett, Y'Shanda Young-Rivera, and Brian Kim Lovejoy. *Other People's English: Code-Meshing, Code-Switching, and African American Literacy*. Anderson, SC: Parlor Press, 2018.

Youngman, Owen R. "Measuring the Impact of a MOOC Experience." In *MOOCs and Their Afterlives: Experiments in Scale and Access in Higher Education*, edited by Elizabeth Losh, 51–65. Chicago: University of Chicago Press, 2017.

Zahneis, Megan. "The Covid-19 Crisis Is Widening the Gap Between Secure and Insecure Instructors." *Chronicle of Higher Education*, March 18, 2020. https://www.chronicle.com/article /the-covid-19-crisis-is-widening-the -gap-between-secure-and-insecure -instructors.

Zamora, Mia. "Reimagining Learning in CLMOOC." In *MOOCs and Their Afterlives: Experiments in Scale and Access in Higher Education*, edited by Elizabeth Losh, 104–20. Chicago: University of Chicago Press, 2017.

Zeyl Donald J. "Introduction." In *Gorgias*, by Plato. Indianapolis: Hackett, 1987.

Žižek, Slavoj. "Slavoj Žižek: Philosopher, Cultural Critic, and Cyber-Communist." *JAC* 21, no. 2 (2001): 251–86.

Printed in the United States
by Baker & Taylor Publisher Services